THE REFORMATION

A HANDBOOK

THE REFORMATION

A HANDBOOK

T. M. LINDSAY

THE BANNER OF TRUTH TRUST

THE BANNER OF TRUTH TRUST
3 Murrayfield Road, Edinburgh EH12 6EL, UK
P.O. Box 621, Carlisle, PA 17013, USA

*

First published 1882
First Banner of Truth edition, 2006

© The Banner of Truth Trust 2006

ISBN-10: 0 85151 932 6
ISBN-13: 978 0 85151 932 6

*

Typeset in 11 /14 pt Adobe Caslon at
the Banner of Truth Trust, Edinburgh
Printed in the U.S.A. by
Versa Press, Inc.,
Peoria, IL

CONTENTS

PART THREE:

THE ANGLICAN REFORMATION

PREFACE

*T*he first three parts of this little book are simply a compilation from the best and most easily accessible histories of the Reformation, and make no pretence to original treatment of the vast and complicated religious movement which they describe. I have adopted Dr Merle d'Aubigné's view, that the Reformation was a revival of religion, and cannot be described successfully unless this, its essential character, is kept distinctly in view. The Reformers were men who, under the impulse of a great religious movement arising in the midst of peculiar intellectual, social, and political conditions, desired to be allowed to worship God in their own fashion, and according to the directions of Scripture and the dictates of reason and conscience. But this apparently simple desire involved such a change in the social and political conditions not merely of single provinces and countries, but also of Europe as a whole, that the story of the religious revival cannot be written without introducing a great deal of the political and social history of the times.

Dr Leopold von Ranke has made the political history of the period so peculiarly his own, that the writer of even the humblest of manuals must place himself almost exclusively under his directions. I have done so, and in almost every page am indebted to his masterly descriptions of the political and social movements of the times.

It would be needless to mention the very long list of writers consulted in the writing of this little manual; but as no references have been made to the authorities quoted, I ought to say that besides d'Aubigné and Ranke, those acquainted with the subject will notice continual use made of Hagenbach's and Henke's *Church Histories*, Häusser's *Period of the*

Reformation, Baird's *Huguenots*, and two volumes of Longman's *Epochs of Modern History*, Mr Seebohm's *Era of the Protestant Revolution*, and Mr Creighton's *Age of Elizabeth*. I have commonly referred to Dr Schaff's *History of the Creeds of Christendom* for the Confessions, and to Richter's invaluable collection of *Books of Discipline* for the ecclesiastical organization of the various Reformed Churches.

The fourth part, which discusses briefly the fundamental principles of the Reformation movement, ought perhaps to have been put first as an introduction, but I preferred to place it at the end; partly because such an introduction might have frightened young readers,[1] and partly because the principles of the movement can best be judged after the reader has known something about its history. The fourth part is the only portion of this small manual which has any claim to belong exclusively to the writer, and to represent views of the subject treated for which he is alone responsible.

The chronological summary has been taken almost entirely from Weingarten's admirable tables.

T. M. LINDSAY
Free Church College, Glasgow
October 1882

---

[1] The work was originally published in a series entitled 'Hand-Books for Bible Classes' and published in Edinburgh by T. and T. Clark in 1882. For the present edition, only minor editorial changes have been made.

PART ONE

THE GERMAN REFORMATION

LEADING TO THE LUTHERAN CHURCHES

I

THE REFORMATION IN GERMANY

THE BEGINNING OF THE REFORMATION

*T*he Reformation began, if such a movement, having its impulses far back in the past, can be said to have a beginning at all, when Martin Luther nailed his ninety-five theses against indulgences on the door of the Castle-Church in the small town of Wittenberg in Saxony. John Tetzel, a Dominican monk, had been sent into Germany by Pope Leo X, to collect money for the use of the Church – to help to pay for a war against the Turks, it was said, but really to provide funds for the Pope to spend on paintings and other works of art in the great Church

3

of St Peter's in Rome. The money was to be got by the sale of pieces of stamped paper or tickets, declaring that the purchaser had received pardon for the commission of sins which had been named, valued, and paid for.

The indulgence seller travelled under the protection of the Archbishop of Mainz, one of the seven Electors of Germany. In the autumn of 1517 he had passed through Middle Germany, and in October he reached Leipzig in Saxony. His presence had not been very welcome either to the princes, to the more earnest-minded of the parish clergy, or to the better disposed among the people. The princes did not like him, because he got so much money from the people and sent it all to Rome: he made the country poorer; and some princes would not allow him to enter their territories until he had promised to give them a share.

The better class of the parish clergy did not like him, because wherever he went the people became more wicked; he sold the right of murdering an enemy for seven ducats; those who wished to rob a church were pardoned if they paid nine ducats; while the murder of father, mother, sister, or brother, cost only four ducats. The men and women who bought these indulgences naturally liked to get value for their money, and so crime abounded where the pardon-seller went.

Quiet people also objected to him, because his presence caused such a tumult and so many scandals. He sent men before him strangely dressed, who stuck up notices, and who went through the streets and along the country roads telling that he was coming, and boasting the excellence of the pardon tickets he had for sale. Here are some of these proclamations: 'The pardon makes those who buy it cleaner than baptism, purer even than Adam in a state of innocence in Paradise.' 'As soon as the money chinks in the bottom of the strong box, the buyer is pardoned and is free from sin.' After these mountebanks came the pardon-seller with his assistant in a strong wagon, which was drawn up in the middle of the market place. Then Tetzel appeared – on his one side an iron cage, in which were the pardon tickets hanging from the bars; on the other, a strong box, into which the money was thrown; and he puffed his wares like a quack doctor at a country fair.

Luther had long been watching Tetzel, and his righteous soul had been vexed that the princes and bishops, in spite of letters and remonstrances, had allowed him to go from one diocese to another. He had preached against Tetzel and the indulgences, and still the pardon-seller came nearer. At last Tetzel got to Jüterbogk, near Wittenberg, and Luther, who was already famous as a great preacher and a wise professor in the University of the town, could stand it no longer. He wrote out ninety-five theses against the indulgences and nailed them to the church door: these sentences declared that if there was room for Tetzel and his pardon tickets in the Church, then there was no room for Luther and his belief in what sin was and how God pardoned it. The whole of Germany was smouldering with indignation against Rome and the indulgences. A spark would set it all ablaze; the theses kindled the fire, and so the Reformation began.

THE INDULGENCES, AND LUTHER'S THESES AGAINST THEM

The indulgences which Luther denounced were not a new thing in the Church, and, although Luther did not think so, they really were so connected with the whole round of the external life of the Church in these times that it was difficult to find fault with them without objecting to a great deal more. The Church of the Middle Ages thought a great deal of the external expression of spiritual facts and forces, and it became quite a common thing to pay so very much attention to the external expression as to lose sight of the spiritual meaning expressed, and in this way many good evangelical truths became crusted over with a hard casing of barren forms which crushed out the old evangelical life.

It is an evangelical truth that if a man is sorry for his sins he will show sorrow in some way or other – true repentance will make itself seen. The Church of the Middle Ages took this truth and crusted it over with the idea that repentance must always show itself in certain definite ways which the Church prescribed; and these outward ways of showing repentance, by saying so many prayers, fasting on certain days, or practising other enjoined mortifications, came to be looked at as, and actually called repentance – for penance just means repentance.

In course of time, when the Church got more corrupt, it was held that on payment of certain fixed sums of money the outward signs of repentance might be dispensed with, provided the repentant sinner did feel sorry in his heart for his sins. When the Church got still worse, it was asserted that the payment of money could actually win pardon – God's pardon – for sins done and to be done. Hence arose the shameless traffic in indulgences. The Popes and their dependants at Rome found this doctrine a very profitable one, and, as was openly said, tried to make as much money as possible out of the 'sins of the Germans'. This indulgence, against which Luther protested, had been the fifth within the last seventeen years.

Luther's ninety-five theses make one continuous speech against the doctrine and the practice of the indulgence; and he makes plain these three things: (1) There may be some good in the indulgence if it only means one of the many ways of proclaiming *God's* forgiveness of sin; but this proclamation should never be made for money. (2) The external signs of repentance are not the real inward sorrow for sin which makes true repentance, and no permission to do without them can mean that God actually pardons. (3) Every Christian who feels true repentance for sin has perfect pardon, and is a partaker in all the riches of Christ by the direct gift of God without any letter of indulgence or other intervention of man. And, in a sermon which he published to further explain his theses, he declares that repentance consists in contrition, confession, and absolution, and that contrition is the most important of the three. If the sorrow or contrition be true and heartfelt, the confession and the absolution will follow naturally. And so Luther makes the inward spiritual fact of sorrow for sin the great matter: the outward expression of sorrow is a good thing; but what God looks to is the spiritual state, not its outward expression.

LUTHER'S THESES ATTACKED MORE THAN INDULGENCES

Luther, in his theses and in his sermon, had declared that the inward spiritual facts of man's experience were of infinite value compared with the outward expression of these in stereotyped forms recognized by the Church; and he had also made it clear that in such a solemn thing as forgiveness of sin man could go to God directly without any human mediation. When he said this, he did much more than attack indulgences; he protested against the most cherished ideas of the Mediæval Church.

Pious Christians since the day of Pentecost had thought the same, and all through the times of superstition men and women had humbly gone to God for pardon, trusting in Christ. They had found the pardon they sought; and their simple Christian experience had been sung in the grand old hymns of the Mediæval Church; it had found expression in the prayers of the Church; it had formed the heart of the evangelical preaching of the Church, and had stirred the masses of the people in the many revivals of the Middle Ages. But somehow or other those pious preachers and hymn writers had not seen how utterly opposed all this precious experience of theirs was to the common ecclesiastical machinery of their days. The Church set such store on external things that the inward spiritual life lay buried under them, and the common speech of the times had changed the very meaning of the words 'spiritual' and 'holy'. A man was 'spiritual' if he had been ordained to office in the Church; money was 'spiritual' if it had been given to the Church; an estate, with its roads, woodland, and fields, was called 'spiritual' or 'holy' if it belonged to a bishop or abbot.

And then the Church, which, by its thoughts, actions, and speech, had so degraded spiritual things, and been so blind to them, had thrust itself in between God and man, and had proclaimed that no man could approach God unless by the Church, and that God could never speak to man's heart save through the Church. Confession of sin was to the priest, and pardon was given in absolution. Luther had spoken out against all this in those theses of his, and he scarcely knew it himself. His pious nature was shocked at the profanity of supposing and saying that God's pardon for sin could be got by buying a ticket, that sin and guilt and God's wrath at sin could all be got rid of by paying a few shillings. When he spoke out his indignation, he thought only of the profanity of the thing before him; nevertheless he had attacked not merely the worst part of a bad system, but the whole system itself. The Reformation had begun.

Luther's Early History

The man who opposed Tetzel had, after a long and troubled experience, come to know what God's pardon of sin really meant. He had gone the whole round of the means which the Church had appointed to help troubled minds, and had not been comforted; and in the end he had gone straight to God himself, and found the peace he sought. He knew from personal experience that God's pardon was not to be had by buying a ticket stamped with the Papal arms, and so he made his protest in the name of all those who in all ages of the Church had felt bowed down under the weight of sin, and had at last found peace in God. His own spiritual history makes this plain.

Luther was born on 10 November 1483, at Eisleben. 'I am a peasant, and the son of a peasant', he used to say. His father was a miner, his mother a stern peasant matron. His child life was a sad one, and, in spite of the joyousness of his later years, there was in Luther always a vein of sadness which he himself traced back to the sorrows of his childhood. His father had determined to make a man of him. He had the worker's contempt for the lazy monk, and his son was to be a lawyer; to learn law, to master that dreadful tyrant of the German peasant – Roman law, which always treated him as a serf, almost an outlaw. Luther was accordingly sent to school, to Mansfeld, to Magdeburg, to Eisenach.

The life of the poor scholar in these days was a very hard one. He was starved, beaten, bullied, from day to day. His daily bread was got by singing in the streets for alms. It was at Eisenach that the first gleam of human kindness reached him, when Frau Cotta, attracted by his lonely sadness and sweet voice, took him to her house and made much of him there. From Eisenach he went to Erfurt, to the University, and soon made rapid progress. He learned more than law. He read Cicero, Plautus, Terence, and Livy. He read the great theological books of the Mediæval Church; and, above all, he read and re-read till he had got them by heart the writings of the brave English Franciscan William of Occam [or Ockham], who had stoutly withstood the Popes in the fourteenth century, and had taught both Wycliffe and Huss to do so too. 'Occam, my dear master', Luther fondly called him. He took his Bachelor's degree in 1503, and his Master's in 1505. He became noted for his keen wit and ready eloquence. He was on the road to becoming what his father wished to see him – a great lawyer.

All the while, however, conscience had been at work: his sins had troubled him; the wrath of God had lain heavy upon him. He could not see the love of God. His own father had been stern and hard, and he could think of 'our Father in heaven' only as a taskmaster. On 17 July 1505, when twenty-two years of age, his religious feelings overpowered him; he entered the Augustinian convent at Erfurt, and cut himself off from the society of his family and friends, and from all hope of worldly preferment. His Plautus and Virgil, which he took with him, were the only memorials of his old life.

In the convent he set to work to find the way of salvation. He read books on theology, he fasted and prayed, he submitted to all manner of privations, yet he did not find peace. Soon he found a *whole* Bible, the first he had met with, and studied it diligently; but the terror of sin was upon him, and he could not see the Gospel. He went to the Vicar-General of his order, Staupitz, a pious man, who sent him to Augustine, and to the German Mystics, and both these helped him greatly. The one taught him what sin meant, and what sovereign grace meant; and the other made him see that true religion must be heart religion. Still he had not peace.

In the midst of this conflict he was called to new work. Frederick the Magnanimous, the Elector of Saxony, and the most eminent of the German princes, had founded a new University at Wittenberg, and Staupitz was invited to find the professors. In 1508 Luther was made professor of philosophy, and began lecturing. In 1512 he became doctor of Biblical Theology, and lectured on the Psalms and on the Epistles of St Paul to the Romans and to the Galatians. In his study he read the Mystics, Tauler's *Sermons,* and 'that noble little book', *The German Theology.* At length the crisis of his life came. In 1511 he was sent on business to Rome. He went there a mediæval theologian; he came back a Protestant: he went believing in Justification by Works; he came back believing in Justification by Faith.

Luther found Rome what it had been for centuries, a mass of moral corruption. He had gone there as a Jew might have gone to Jerusalem. He tells us himself that when he came in sight of the city he knelt and cried, 'I greet thee, Holy Rome, thrice holy from the blood of the martyrs which has been shed in thee.' He found the monks and priests bad men, scoffing at the religious services they took part in. He found the people treacherous and greedy, the Pope himself little better than a pagan.

Luther had come to Rome to find in the Holy City, as he had called it when far away in Germany, some sure way of working out his salvation; and strange to say, he did find Christ. For it was in Rome, in the midst of the corruption and blasphemy, that it suddenly came to him that the way of salvation was just to go to Christ and leave all to him; that pardon comes freely from God and begins the Christian life, and is not painfully won at the end of it.

He went back to Wittenberg a changed man. He had already won some fame as a preacher; but after his visit to Rome he preached as no other man then could preach. He became the foremost man in the University, and the friend of Staupitz, his general, and of Frederick, his prince. Then came the indulgences.

LUTHER'S SUPPORTERS AND HIS OPPONENTS

At first it seemed as if all Germany was going to support Luther. The traffic in indulgences had been so shameless that all good people and all patriotic Germans had been scandalized. But Luther had struck a blow at more than the indulgences, and opponents soon came. Conrad Wimpina at Frankfurt, Hogstraten at Cologne, Sylvester Prierias at Rome, and, above all, John Eck, an old fellow-student at Ingolstadt – all attacked his theses, and discovered heresy in them.

The result was that Luther was summoned to appear before the Pope at Rome; but the Elector of Saxony got this altered, and Luther was ordered to go to Augsburg to be examined by Cardinal Cajetan, the Pope's Legate to the German Diet. The Pope did not wish to quarrel with the Elector of Saxony, and Cajetan was told to be conciliatory. Luther went, but the interview was not very successful. The Cardinal began by scolding Luther, and ended by being somewhat afraid of him. 'I can dispute no longer with this beast', said he; 'It has two wicked eyes, and marvellous thoughts in its head'; while Luther said roundly that the Legate was as fit to judge in spiritual things 'as a donkey was to play on the harp'.

He left Augsburg condemned, but appealing 'from the Pope ill informed to the Pope to be better informed'. The Pope was unwilling to break with Germany, for Luther appeared to have the best part of Germany at his back, and Cardinal Miltitz was sent to bring about peace. He did not summon the young monk before him, but met him in a friendly manner at the house of Spalatin, the Elector's chaplain. Before the interview Luther had appealed from the Pope to a General Council. Cardinal Miltitz at once gave up Tetzel, said that indulgences were wrong, agreed with most of Luther's statements; but pointed out that he had not been respectful enough to the Pope, and that he was weakening the power and authority of the Church. In short, his argument was, 'You may be right; but why be rude? Write to the Pope and apologize.' Luther promised to do so, and made an agreement with Miltitz, which, as he afterwards told the Elector, had two clauses:

1.   Both parties were to cease from preaching or writing on the matters in controversy.
2.   Miltitz was to inform the Pope about the exact state of affairs, and the Pope was to commission a body of learned theologians to investigate.

Meanwhile, Luther wrote to the Pope, telling him that he 'freely confessed that the authority of the Church was superior to everything; and that nothing in heaven or earth can be preferred before it, save only Jesus Christ, who is Lord over all.' This was in March 1519.

THE DISPUTATION AT LEIPZIG

Luther had promised to keep quiet if his opponents kept quiet – that was his bargain with Cardinal Miltitz; but his enemies did not keep quiet, and Luther judged himself free to attack them. The injudicious friend of the Church was John Eck. He had challenged Carlstadt, a friend of Luther's, to a public disputation, and meanwhile published thirteen theses attacking Luther's ninety-five. Luther instantly replied, and the public disputation between Carlstadt and Eck was followed by one between Eck and Luther. In this disputation at Leipzig the controversy reaches a higher stage. It is no longer a theological dispute; it is the opposition of two conflicting sets of principles, affecting the whole round of Church life. Here, for the first time, German Christendom breaks away from Roman Christendom by insisting upon the priesthood of all believers, and the right of each Christian to judge in all things according to his conscience, enlightened by the Word of God and his Holy Spirit.

Luther and Eck began about indulgences and penance, but the debate soon turned upon the authority of the Roman Church and of the Pope. Eck maintained the supreme authority of the Bishop of Rome as the successor of St Peter and the Vicar-General of Christ. Luther denied the superiority of the Roman Church to other Churches, and supported his denial by the testimony of the history of eleven centuries, of the Decrees of Nicea, the most holy of Councils, and of Holy Scripture. This occasioned great debate. 'No Pope, no Church', said Eck. 'The Greek Church has existed without a Pope, and you are the first to call it no Church', said Luther. 'Were Athanasius, Basil, and the two Gregories outside the Church? The Pope has more need of the Church than the Church has of the Pope.' 'You are as bad as Wycliffe and Huss', said Eck, 'and they were condemned at Constance.' 'Well,' said Luther, 'every opinion of Huss was not wrong.' 'Oh, if you refuse to abide by the decisions of Councils, I refuse to dispute', said Eck, and so the affair ended.

But Luther immediately afterwards published and completed his argument. He, for the first time, tells what he thinks the church is. He says that he will not deny the primacy of the Pope, if the Pope does not turn his back upon the church. Let the Pope keep his place as servant of the church, as 'servant of the servants of God', as the Bulls say, and Luther will give him all honour.

But the church is the communion of the faithful – it consists of true believers, of the elect. The church never lacks the Holy Spirit, although Popes and Councils often do. This church, which always has the Holy Spirit, is invisible; and therefore a layman, who has the Scripture and holds by it, is more to be believed than Pope and Council who have not.

This Leipzig Disputation had the most important consequences. On the one hand, Eck and other opponents felt that Luther must now be put down by force, and pressed for a Papal Bull condemning him; and, on the other, Luther himself, for the first time, felt what lay in his opposition to the indulgences. He now saw that his Augustinian theology, with its knowledge of the moral heinousness of sin, and of the need of the sovereign grace of God, struck at the whole round of mediæval ceremonial life; made it impossible that any man should live a perfectly pure and holy life, and so made saints and saint-worship impossible; made relics and pilgrimages, and monastic life with its vigils and fasts and scourgings, useless. All these things were not helps, but hindrances, to the true religious life. It followed, too, that as there could be no mediator between God and man save Jesus Christ, the mediation of the Pope was useless.

If the Leipzig Disputation made Luther see that he had now broken with Rome, it made Germany see it too, and raised their enthusiasm to a white heat. The people of the towns declared their sympathy with the bold monk. Ulrich von Hutten and the literary men from this time recognized Luther as their leader. Franz von Sickingen and the free knights looked to him as a useful ally. The poor burdened peasants hoped that he might help them to free themselves from the intolerable miseries of their position. Luther became the leader of the German people. This took place in 1519.

THE POPE'S BULL AND ITS BURNING

Eck and the other opponents of Luther felt that something must be done to silence the bold monk, and urged the Pope to issue a Bull condemning his opinions. Luther, too, was not idle. He knew that he had broken with Rome, and with his usual speed and courage he made the fact known, and asked the German people to help him. Germany was a poor country, and yet every year it sent a great quantity of money to Rome.

In these days the Church was a great ecclesiastical empire, and Rome was its capital. All Europe was divided into bishoprics, and the clergy were very wealthy. They had large estates, and drew the rents; they also had a right to a tenth part (the tithes) of all other property; they got money for baptisms, for marriages, for absolution, for attending deathbeds and burials, and for saying masses. The various orders of monks had also become very rich. They had large estates in land given them during the lifetime or at the death of devout people. Almost every country in Europe had passed laws trying to prevent or limit these bequests; but these laws had been so unsuccessful, that at the time of the Reformation the monks owned almost one-third of the land in Europe. And, although rich, they begged daily from the people. Part of this wealth went every year to Rome. The Pope levied taxes called Annates.

When a bishopric was vacant, the revenues went to the Pope, and the Pope delayed nomination. The Pope often tried to make Italians bishops or heads of abbeys; and these Italians lived in Rome, and their monies were sent to them there. When a new bishop was appointed, he had to send to the Pope his first year's income. All this money went out of the country to Rome, and made the countries poorer; and in Luther's time the Popes got still more money by the indulgences. Luther, in his tract, *To the Nobility of the German Nation*, pointed all this out, and asked how long they were going to endure it. He told them that the Romanist doctrine of two separate estates – the one spiritual, including the Pope, and bishops, priests, monks, and nuns; and the other temporal, and including every one else – was a wall raised by Romanists to defend the oppressions of the Church. He told them that all Christians are spiritual, and that all should be obedient to the secular power. And he asked why the Germans allowed 300,000 florins to be sent every year out of their poor country to Rome?

He also wrote another tract, *The Babylonish Captivity of the Church of Christ*, to show that he did not wish to destroy but to purify the true church of Christ. The title explains the book. Luther thought that the Pope and the Romanists had carried the Church away into captivity, as the Jews had been carried away to Babylon. He gives instances of this taking captive. Our Lord said at the Last Supper, when he gave the cup to his disciples, 'Drink ye all of it'; but the Romanists say, 'Drink ye not of it unless ye are priests.' And he believed that it was the duty of every true Christian to bring back the church from her bondage. He concluded in a characteristic way, 'I hear that Bulls and other papistical things have been prepared, in which I am urged to recant or be proclaimed a heretic. If that be true, I wish this little book to be part of my future recantation.'

The printing-press sent thousands of these books through Germany, and the people awaited the Bull. It came. It was published in Rome on 15 July 1520. It accused Luther of holding the opinions of Huss, and condemned him. Eck brought it to Leipzig in October. It was posted up in various German towns, and generally the citizens and students pulled it down.

At last it reached Luther. He answered its accusations in a pamphlet, in which he called it the execrable Bull of Antichrist, and at last he proclaimed in Wittenberg that he would burn it. On 10 December, at the head of a procession of professors and students, Luther passed out of the University to the market place. One of the professors kindled the bonfire, and Luther threw the bull into the flames. He had utterly defied the Pope. A copy of the Canon Law was also burned; for

Germany was to be ruled henceforth by the law of the land, not by the law of Rome. The news flashed all over Germany, awakening stern joy. Rome had shot its last bolt; if Luther was to be crushed, the Emperor only could do it.

THE EMPEROR AND THE REFORMATION

The Emperor at this time was Charles V. He had been elected in 1519, and had not yet been in Germany, nor was he so powerful as his title implied. In those days the old mediæval ideas of government still lingered, and Charles V had resolved to restore the old imperial rule in its full strength.

In the early Middle Ages men took their ideas of government from the old Roman Empire – not the pagan Empire of Augustus Caesar and his successors, but the Christian Empire of Constantine and those who came after him. Although that old Empire had been destroyed by the invasions of the wild Teutonic tribes, yet, when the times of conquest had passed, the new peoples who inhabited Europe adopted the government and laws of the state they had overthrown.

According to mediæval thinkers, who always thought in pictures, civil government and social order were impossible unless all power was gathered into one focus and united under one person – the world-King; and all Church government and religious fellowship were in the same way represented in the rule of one person – the world-priest. The world-King was the Emperor, and he ruled *circa civilia*[1] as God's vicar or representative; while the world-priest was the Pope, who ruled *circa sacra*[2] as God's vicar or representative. The one ruled over men's bodies, and the other over men's souls; and the dominion of both was worldwide. The one had the power of the sword, and the other had the power of the keys. This mediæval dream had scarcely ever come true; but the dream was there, and the Emperor and Pope were both in Europe in Reformation times.

In the end of the fifteenth century, Ferdinand the Wise, King of Aragon, by an elaborate system of marriages, conceived the plan of restoring the Empire to its earlier grandeur. He had three daughters. The eldest married the King of Portugal, which united Spain and

---

[1] *circa civilia:* concerning civil matters   [2] *circa sacra:* concerning sacred matters

Portugal under one sovereign. The second married Philip of Austria, the head of the house of Habsburg, and in right of his mother the ruler of Burgundy and the Netherlands. The third married Henry VIII of England. From the first marriage came Isabella, heiress of Spain and Portugal. From the second came Charles of Austria and Burgundy. From the third came Mary, Queen of England. Then Charles married his cousin Isabella, and thus became ruler over Spain and Portugal, Austria, Burgundy, and the Netherlands. He afterwards became Emperor and King of Italy.

Charles V was therefore a more powerful Emperor than there had been for centuries; and he longed to rule with the same authority as did Charles the Great or Otto I. His eyes were always fixed on the past; his policy was to restore that political unity to Europe which had been lost after the birth of modern European nations. But that old unity required an unbroken Church as well as a united Empire, and this dream of Charles made him intolerant of any such disturber of the Church's peace as he thought Luther was. Although he had been elected Emperor, his empire was not very stable. He was powerful, not because he was Emperor, but because he was lord of Spain and Burgundy and Austria – his imperial honours lessened his power, because Germany was so disunited, and there were so many burning questions requiring settlement.

THE POLITICAL STATE OF GERMANY

Germany, in the times of the Reformation, had no political unity. It was nominally united under the Empire, and ruled by the Diet; but the power both of Emperor and Diet was practically extremely small. The Empire was elective, and since the year 1356 the election had been in the hands of seven prince-electors, three on the Elbe and four on the Rhine.

On the Elbe were the King of Bohemia, the Elector of Saxony, the Elector of Brandenburg; on the Rhine, the Count Palatine of the Rhine, and the Archbishops of Mainz, Trier, and Cologne[3]. At almost every election fresh concessions to the princes had lessened the imperial power.

[1] Cologne = Köln

Between the Emperor and his people was the Diet, which was the great council of the Empire, and contained three chambers or colleges: 1. Six electoral princes, three lay and three clerical (the King of Bohemia was left out); 2. The princes or great barons, lay and ecclesiastical; 3. Representatives from the free imperial cities – from those cities which had charters directly from the Emperor. As there were almost as many clerical as lay princes, the power of the Church was very strong in the Diet, and it could easily be used as an instrument to put down all religious reform. The Diet, however, had very little power over the country. Germany was so divided that each independent prince could do very much as he pleased. The towns and the smaller barons were able, by forming leagues among themselves, to resist to a certain extent the tyranny of the great princes; but the peasants, incapable of such combination, were ground down on all sides by the Church, the great princes, and the small barons alike.

The lot of the German peasants was hard indeed. They had once been cottar[1] farmers, and had been pretty well off; but the lords of the soil had been encroaching more and more upon their rights, enclosing commons, taking away rights of fuel, fishing, and so on; and there seemed to be no remedy. They were friendless, hopeless, and outside the law. Their only hope lay in revolution, and their one passionate longing was to do what the Swiss had done – free themselves, have no lords, and become peasant proprietors. When the young Emperor came into Germany for the first time, he found various grave matters waiting for settlement – the people were longing for some central government, the towns wished private war between barons put down, there were several disputes between the civil and ecclesiastical powers that required settlement, and then there was the affair of Luther.

LUTHER AT THE DIET OF WORMS
The Diet was opened by Charles in January 1521, and the Papal Nuncio urged the assembled princes to put an end to the heresies of Luther at once, and without hearing him. But the princes had their own quarrels with Rome, and urged, besides, that it would be both unjust and undignified to condemn a man unheard and untried.

---

[1] Cottar: a peasant occupying a cot or a cottage, for which he has to give labour.

At length the Emperor consented to summon Luther before him, and give him a safe-conduct. A herald was sent to demand his presence, and in April Luther set off for Worms. He went resolved not to retract, but in his heart believing that he would not return from the Diet alive. He wrote to Spalatin: 'I have no intention of fleeing, nor of leaving the Word in danger; but I mean to confess it unto death, so far as Christ's grace sustains me. But I am certain that the bloodhounds will not rest till they have put me to death.' And to Melanchthon: 'If I do not come back, and my enemies murder me, I implore you, dear brother, that you will go on teaching, and stand fast in the truth.'

Before leaving Wittenberg he had devised, along with Lucas Cranach, a 'good book for the laity', a series of woodcuts depicting contrasts between Christ and the Pope, with explanations in pithy German: Christ washing the disciples' feet on the one page – the Pope holding out his toe to be kissed on the other; Christ bearing his cross – the Pope carried in state through Rome on men's shoulders; Christ driving the money-changers out of the temple – the Pope selling indulgences, with piles of money before him; and so on.

His friends thought he was going to his death. Duke George of Saxony was reported to be lying in wait for him. 'I'll go if it rains Duke Georges', said Luther. They told him the devil would catch him in some way. 'I would go', he said, 'if there were as many devils in Worms as tiles on the house-tops.' His progress was almost a triumphal march: the people came out in crowds to meet him, blessing him as he went; and at last he reached Worms. Next day he was brought before the Diet. Beside the Emperor sat his brother Ferdinand, Archduke of Austria, the six Electors, twenty-eight dukes, thirty prelates, and a number of the lesser nobility – two hundred princes in all. Luther had to confess Christ before this great crowd of princes. When he entered, a pile of books was placed before him, and he was asked if the books were his, and if he would retract what he had written. He begged for time. He was allowed till the next day, and so went back to his lodging.

When he returned to the Diet, he passed through great crowds of people, most of them encouraging him to stand firm; and as he entered the chamber, old General Frundsberg clapped him on the shoulders, saying, 'Fear not, little monk!' On the first day he had been confused, almost timid; but on this second day he had recovered his courage.

The Chancellor of the Archbishop of Trier questioned him in the name of the Emperor. 'Do you acknowledge these books to be yours, and will you retract what you have written?'

Luther answered, that some of his books contained writing which had been praised by his opponents, and that he could not be expected to retract it; others were directed against manifest abuses, and that he would be false and a coward if he retracted what he and most right-hearted men knew to be true; a third set contained many hasty judgments upon his opponents, and these, he said, he would retract if he could be shown to be wrong. 'The Emperor demands a plain answer, and not argument', said Eck. 'Do you retract what you have said against the Church, and especially what you have said against the Council of Constance? 'If you will have a plain answer', said Luther, 'I will give you one without horns or teeth. I can retract nothing unless I be convinced either from Scripture or by clear argument. It is as clear as day that both Pope and Councils have often erred. My conscience must submit to the Word of God: to act against conscience is unholy and dangerous; and therefore I cannot and will not retract. So help me God. Amen.' The lawyer could scarcely believe his ears. 'Do you actually say that a Council can have erred?' 'Yes', answered Luther finally. 'Here stand I. I can do nought else. God help me. Amen.'

His firmness only made the Spaniards and Italians angry; they wished the Emperor to cancel the safe-conduct and put him to death without further ado. The Germans felt that he was fighting for Germany as well as for conscience' sake, and resolved to stand by him. They persuaded the Emperor at least to delay sentence; and one or two days were spent in vain attempts to argue Luther into retracting.

At last the Emperor made up his mind. He was too eager to stand well with the Pope to take the side of Luther and Germany, and yet he did not wish to break his word by taking away the safe-conduct. So he dismissed Luther, but issued an Edict in which the Reformer's writings were condemned, and he himself was put under the ban of the Empire and made an outlaw.

To be put under the ban of the Empire was a dreadful thing. It meant that no one could give Luther food or drink or shelter; that any one who met him was bound to seize him and hand him over to the guards of the Emperor; and that when secured he was to be put to death. All this was to happen when the term of days mentioned in the safe-conduct had expired.

LUTHER IN THE WARTBURG

Luther's friends were afraid that his life would not be safe even in Wittenberg after the Edict of Worms; and the Elector of Saxony ordered a band of soldiers to seize him on his way home and carry him off to the Wartburg, a strong castle near Eisenach, where he could remain concealed and secure. None of his friends at first knew where he was. He lived in the Wartburg in retirement, was ordered to let his beard grow, wore a knight's dress, and went by the name of Junker George. Luther remained ten months in his hiding-place.

It was there that he began his greatest work, the translation of the Bible from the original Greek and Hebrew texts into German. He had found means to let his friends know where he was, and Melanchthon sent him what books he needed from Wittenberg. He began by translating the New Testament, and finished it almost without assistance. To help him with the Old Testament he had what one of his biographers calls 'a private sanhedrin of learned men', of whom some were Jewish rabbis. They met once a week in Luther's house, and compared notes and helped each other with difficult passages.

Luther was anxious to make his translation of the Bible a book for the people of Germany. He would not allow in it any fine courtly phrases; he wished to make it a book to be understood by 'plain men', women, and children, and he took incredible pains with it. Some of his manuscript has been preserved, and we can still see how he went over the sentences again and again, in some cases as often as fifteen times. 'We are working very hard', he wrote once, 'to bring out the prophets in the mother-tongue. What a great and difficult work it is to make the Hebrew writers speak the mother-tongue! They resist it so. They are not willing to give up their Hebrew existence and imitate German barbarism.' The task was the more difficult because the German language could scarcely be said to exist. German before Luther's time was like English before Chaucer's – there were many dialects but not a language; and in fact, it was Luther's Bible that made the German language, for it has formed a standard from then till now, and Germans have tried to write in the same style; and so gradually all

German prose writing came to be very much the same; the dialects faded into the background, and the language was formed, and remained a unity when everything else in Germany fell asunder.

LUTHER BACK AT WITTENBERG – THE DISORDERS THERE

While Luther was in the Wartburg, his friends were preaching the gospel in security all over Germany, and his books were everywhere read. It seemed that all Germany was becoming Protestant in spite of the Edict of the Emperor. There was a great movement spreading out on all sides in favour of gospel teaching, and against superstition and idolatry. It often happens in such a time of religious revival as this was, that some people lose their heads and wish to move too fast or too far; and this happened in Germany.

There stands on the borders of Saxony and Bohemia, among the range of hills called the Erzgebirge, or Iron Mountains, the small town of Zwickau. The people of Zwickau accepted the Reformation. Among them was a weaver, Claus Storch, an excitable man, who embraced it with more zeal than wisdom, and gathered round him some foolish followers. They thought that they did not require priests or clergymen, for they were all taught of God; that the Bible was useless, for they were all inspired. They insisted on purging their village of all signs of the old religion – church decoration, crosses, altars, clergy, etc. – and caused some riots, till their fellow-townsmen rose against them and banished them.

Driven from Zwickau, they went to Wittenberg, and expounded their views to the impetuous Carlstadt and the pliable Melanchthon, who in Luther's absence were the religious leaders there. Carlstadt became a convert, Melanchthon was persuaded to some extent, the mass of the people was stirred. The images were torn down from the churches; even Carlstadt preached against learning, study, and universities; the Reformation was in danger of speedy destruction.

Luther heard the news in his solitude at the Wartburg, and felt that he could not remain any longer in retirement. He hurried to Wittenberg, and the people soon heard his familiar voice thundering from the pulpit against violence, fanaticism, and want of charity. He struggled against the fanatics for eight days, and at length triumphed. The authority of Scripture was re-established, and the Lutheran movement was separated from the excesses of Storch and his companion Munzer. This short reign of the fanatics in Wittenberg had one good result. It led to a reform in worship. The old Roman Catholic service was done away with, and a more scriptural worship begun.

THE DIET OF NÜRNBERG

The ban of the Empire still hung over Luther, for the Edict of Worms was still in force; but no one thought of executing it. Luther was preaching, writing, and publishing in Wittenberg, and no one in Germany considered him an outlaw. Moreover, some of the German princes felt that the Edict of Worms ought to be reversed. The Emperor had gone back to Spain: a council of regency ruled in his stead, made up of those who knew Germany and the feelings of its people, and were not prejudiced in favour of the Pope.

Accordingly, when the Diet met at Nürnberg in 1522 and 1524, the Pope's Nuncio found that the German princes would not listen to his demand for Luther's death. They rather pressed on him demands of their own, and had drawn up a long list of grievances for the Pope to redress; and some of these grievances related to the very matters for which Luther had been condemned.

In the end, after much disputing between the German princes and the Papal Nuncio, the Diet declared that a General Council of the Church was needed to abolish abuses and to settle doubtful questions which had arisen in doctrine; that the Edict of Worms was annulled; and that the whole question of religious differences was to be settled at another Diet to be held at Speyer. In short, almost all Germany seemed to be on Luther's side; and some states – for example, Brandenburg – stated openly what reforms in religion were necessary. They demanded the abolition of the five false sacraments, of the abuses of the Mass, of saint-worship, and of the Papal supremacy. The Reformation, too, had spread beyond Germany, and followers of Luther were to be found in France, in Denmark, and in the Low Countries as early as 1524.

THE REVOLT OF THE NOBLES

The Revolt of the Nobles gave the Reformation movement its first great check. Up to 1524, Luther's doctrines had been spreading without much hindrance through all Germany and in countries beyond. Such abuses of the Church as the five pretended sacraments, indulgences, auricular confession, saint and relic worship, the celibacy of the clergy, the denial of the cup to the laity, the sacrifice in the Mass, episcopal usurpation, and the Pope's supremacy, were protested against. Men also looked forward to a simpler and more scriptural form of worship, and such a form of government as would make manifest the spiritual priesthood of all believers. The Diet had repeatedly, in its list of grievances, called the attention of the Pope to the abuses in the Church, and at last had demanded that a General Council should be called to introduce reforms.

But Germany had need of other reforms besides ecclesiastical reorganization. The position of the imperial knights was getting more and more desperate; they saw themselves overshadowed and crushed by the more powerful princes. The peasants were for the most part in cruel bondage, and were secretly preparing for revolution. Both parties felt that the movement of the Reformation might help them. The times were out of joint; old arrangements were being found useless, men were openly declaring the necessity of changes; might they not take advantage of this general state of dissatisfaction? Accordingly, both discontented parties broke out into open revolt.

The revolt of the nobles was soon put down; it never had any chance of success. The men who engaged in it were really fighting against time and against the current of history. They saw all German land becoming absorbed in the hands of a few princely families, and all the townspeople becoming wealthy by trade and able to protect themselves against attack. They foresaw Germany parcelled out among princes whom they hated and townspeople whom they despised, and they wished to bring back the old days when each German noble acknowledged no rule but that of the Emperor. At their head was Franz von Sickingen, a very remarkable man, a great soldier, and a German patriot after a fashion. Their revolt failed, and the princes seized the opportunity to reduce still further the power of the nobles, and compel them to acknowledge the authority of the nearest princely family.

This revolt had no real connection with the Reformation, but many people thought it had, and began to dislike the Reformation because they hated the nobles who had revolted. Sickingen had in many ways tried to make it appear that the cause he headed was the cause of religious liberty. When Luther's life was in danger at Worms, Sickingen had gathered soldiers and threatened to attack the city and the Diet. When some of the followers of Luther were threatened with persecution after the Diet of Worms, Sickingen had offered to protect all who came to him; and when he raised the standard of revolt against the princes, he declared that he meant to fight for the Reformation, and to establish the new doctrines. So, when he failed, some of the princes were not slow to accuse Luther and the preachers of aiding and abetting this civil war.

Out of all this came what was called the Convention of Ratisbon or Regensburg, which was a confederation or league of Roman Catholic princes against the Reformation; and thus Germany, which had hitherto been united for reforms, became divided into two parties, and this of course made the work much more difficult. The confederates at Regensburg tried to come to terms with the Papal party at Rome. The Pope promised that there should be no more indulgences, that the great drain of money out of Germany to Rome should cease, and that better men should be made bishops and abbots; and the confederates pledged themselves to disavow the German demand for reform, and especially to oppose any demands for change in worship and doctrine. Bavaria, Austria, and the great ecclesiastical provinces of South Germany were henceforth to side with Rome in the struggle that was approaching. The Convention of Regensburg meant a divided Germany, and foretold the horrors of the Thirty Years' War.

THE REVOLT OF THE PEASANTS

The Revolt of the Peasants had much more serious consequences. It not only made some of the princes afraid of reform; it made Luther hesitate, and in the end change many of his opinions. The peasant revolt was not caused by the Reformation; it was due to the hopeless misery in which the peasants lived. Their lot was so bad that it could not be worse, and life was so painful that death had little terror. The peasants had been in revolt in various places over Europe from the middle of the fifteenth century, and although the revolts had been quelled, no reforms had been given, so the causes of rebellion were still unchanged. They were cottar farmers paying rent for their holdings, and as the cultivation of the soil was their one way of living, rents were asked and paid far beyond the real value of the ground.

Besides rent they also paid certain customary services to their proprietors without receiving wages in return; these services varied in various parts of the land, but the common result of them was that the landlord got all the work on his farm and on the estate done free of cost.

The peasants, burdened in this way were oppressed by severe game laws, which forbade them, under severe penalties, to kill wild animals or fish. They were not allowed to cut fuel in the woods, the old village commons had in most cases been taken from them by the landlords, and their industry was hampered in many irritating ways. When a peasant died, the landlord claimed the best chattel, whether cow or sheep or bedstead, and took it from the widow and orphans.

The Church imposed fresh burdens. It claimed tithes; a tenth portion of the crop, which was called the great tithe; and a tenth of the produce of animals, which was the little tithe. These had to be paid after the landlord was satisfied; and when rent and services were paid, when the Church had taken a tenth part of the corn grown, and every tenth lamb or pig or egg, there was very little over for the poor peasant and his family.

But this was not all. The hardest life can be lived and the worst lot endured if only the people are sure that they know the worst, that the conditions of their life will not be changed, and that they will get justice done them if those above them try to take advantage of their poverty and helplessness. The German peasant had no such security. The old Roman law had gradually driven out the common law of Germany, and in the old Roman Empire there had been no free wage-earning peasants. The Roman proprietors had employed slaves or serfs to till their lands and work their estates, and when the Roman law was applied to German matters it spoke of the German peasants as it had done of the Roman serfs.

These poor peasants therefore found themselves outside of the law, and dared not appeal to it. They could be punished at the landlord's pleasure. The law did not secure any rights to them; the landlord could increase forced services and payments, and every kind of exaction.

In the times just before the Reformation, a great deal of wealth had come into Europe. America, with its gold and silver, had been discovered, and trade had wonderfully increased. This wealth had been gained by adventurous traders and merchants, and the merchant classes became richer and able to live more luxuriously than before. The landed proprietors could not bear to live less finely than the merchants, and felt in need of money to enable them to keep up their position; and they could only get money by grinding the poor unprotected peasants, whose lot became more miserable while the condition of the towns-people was improving. Rents were raised, forced services increased, and the taxes were unreasonably multiplied.

Those oppressions caused very violent outbreaks long before Luther's day. In the Netherlands, in Franconia, on the Main, in the Rhineland, peasants had risen against their tyrants, and secret associations formed during those insurrections had lived on after their repression. The most formidable of these secret societies in Germany was the Bundschuh, i.e. tied shoe, as opposed to buckled shoe, peasant's shoe, not burgher's or ruler's, so called from its symbol. The Bundschuh League had arisen as early as 1423, and had scarcely ever died out; and during the excitement of Luther's appearance at Worms, while the Germans were afraid that their Reformer's life was to be sacrificed, the dreaded word Bundschuh was found chalked on the walls.

The peasants' revolt in 1524 came in direct succession from these older insurrections and secret societies, not without the hope that the gospel preached by Luther would at last come to their assistance. Thomas Munzer, the disciple of Claus Storch, banished from Wittenberg as well as from Zwickau, had betaken himself to preach to the peasantry in Thuringia and Saxony, and his wild eloquence had warmed them for a new struggle. The Bundschuh had reappeared in Wurtemberg owing to the cruel oppression of Duke Ulrich. In 1524 the peasantry in the Rhineland raised the standard of open revolt, and the flame spread all around.

These insurrections did not at first involve an appeal to arms. Had they broken out into open violence at the beginning, the peasants might have been more successful in the end. They meant only to hold large meetings to state their grievances, and they expected that such demonstrations would be enough. More than one of these lists of demanded reforms have been preserved. The most important was the Twelve Articles. The peasants began by saying that they asked only what the principles of the gospel warranted them in demanding, that they had no desire to fight, because the gospel required them to live in peace and in love. They asked all Christians to read the following articles, and judge them according to the Word of God:

1. The whole congregation shall have power to elect their minister, and to dismiss him if he does not conduct himself properly; and the minister must preach the pure gospel, without human addition.

2. They promise to pay the great tithe of corn for the support of the ministry, provided that after the stipend is paid the rest goes to support the poor; but they refuse to pay the lesser tithe, the tenth pig, egg, etc., for, they say, God created beasts for man's free use.

3. Serfdom must be abolished. Scripture teaches that men are free.

4. Game, fowl, and fish shall be free as God created them, and for man's use.

5. Whatever woods have not been bought by the proprietors shall be restored to the commune, and every inhabitant shall be at liberty to take what he needs for fuel or carpenter's work, an officer appointed by the commune taking care that there be no wanton destruction.

6. The forced services shall be restricted to what was allowed by the old customs.

7. Anything done over and above this shall be done for reasonable pay.

8. The rents are too high; lands should be revalued and fair rents adjudged.

9. Punishments for crimes shall be fixed by law, and all wanton punishments and arbitrary infliction shall cease.

10. The grass lands and other fields taken by the proprietors from the commons shall be restored.

11. The death right shall be abolished.

12. All these propositions shall be tested by Scripture, and if they can be refuted they shall be withdrawn.

Most of the articles were reasonable enough, and almost all of them are now law within Germany. Had the peasants been treated as they had a just right to expect, some compromise might have been come to. Their opponents pretended to treat with them, only to gain time, however; and the peasants, betrayed, rose in arms.

They appealed to Luther. He had been a peasant's son; he had known what poverty was. And Luther at first answered their appeal by interceding for them. He said to the proprietors: 'I might now make common cause with the peasants against you, who impute this insurrection to the gospel and to my teaching; whereas I have never ceased to enjoin obedience to authority, even to authority so tyrannical and intolerable as yours. But I will not envenom the wound; therefore, my lords, whether friendly or hostile to me, do not despise either the advice of a poor man, or this sedition; not that you ought to fear the insurgents, but fear God the Lord, who is incensed against you. He may punish you and turn every stone into a peasant, and then neither your cuirasses[1] nor your strength would save you. Put then bounds to your exactions, pause in your hard tyranny, consider them as intoxicated, and treat them with kindness, that God may not kindle a fire throughout Germany which none will be able to extinguish. What you may perhaps lose will be made good to you a hundredfold by peace.

'Some of the twelve articles of the peasants are so equitable that they dishonour you before God and the world; they cover the princes with shame, as the 109th Psalm says. I should have yet graver things to tell you respecting the government of Germany, and I have addressed you in this cause in my book to the German nobility. But you have considered my words as wind, and therefore all these demands come now upon you. You must not refuse their demand as to choosing pastors who may preach to them the gospel; the government has only to see that insurrection and rebellion be not preached; but there must be perfect liberty to preach the true gospel as well as the false. The remaining articles, which regard the social state of the peasant, are equally just. Government is not established for its own interest, nor to make the people subservient to caprice and evil passions, but for the interest of the people. Your exactions are intolerable; you take away from the peasant the fruit of his labour, in order to spend his money upon your finery and luxury. So much for you.

'Now, as regards you, my dear friends, the peasants. You want the free preaching of the gospel to be secured to you. God will assist your just cause if you follow up your work with conscience and justice. In

---

[1] Cuirasses: a defensive breastplate and backplate fastened together.

that case you are sure to triumph in the end. Those of you who may fall in the struggle will be saved. But if you act otherwise you are lost, soul and body, even if you have success, and defeat the princes and lords. Do not believe the false prophets who have come among you, even if they invoke the holy name of the gospel. They will call me a hypocrite, but I do not mind that. I wish to save the pious and honest men among you. I fear God and none else. Do you fear him also, and use not his name in vain, that he may not punish you. Does not the Word of God say: "He who takes up the sword, shall perish by the sword"; and, "Let every soul be subject to the higher powers"? You must not take justice into your own hands; that is also the prescription of the natural law. Do you not see that you put yourself in the wrong by rebellion? The government takes away part of what is yours, but you take away all in destroying fixed principles. Fix your eye on Christ in Gethsemane rebuking St Peter for using the sword although in the defence of his Master; and on Christ on the cross praying for his persecutors. And has not his kingdom triumphed? Why have Pope and Emperor not been able to put me down? Why has the gospel spread the more, the greater the effort they made to hinder and destroy it? Because I have never had recourse to force, but preached obedience even towards those who persecuted me, depending exclusively on God. But whatever you do, do not try to cover your enterprise by the cloak of the gospel and the name of Christ. If war there must be, it will be a war of pagans, for Christians use other weapons: their General suffered the cross, and their triumph is humility: that is their chivalry. Pray, my dear friends, stop and consider before you proceed further. Your quotations from the Bible do not prove your case.'

He concluded: 'You see you are both in the wrong, and are drawing the divine punishments upon you and upon your common country, Germany. My advice would be that arbitrators should be chosen, some from the nobility, and some from the towns. You both have to give up something: let the matter be settled equitably by human law.'

His advice was not followed. War broke out, and then mediation was impossible. Luther himself, after violence had begun, showed no mercy to the rebels. The princes leagued together, and the peasants were everywhere routed. Fifty thousand of them were butchered, it is said, slain in one way or another.

This frightful catastrophe had a most disastrous effect on the Reformation. Many of the nobles laid the whole blame of what occurred at
Luther's door, and did all in their power afterwards to stay his work.
The Reformation lost to a large extent its hold over the poorer classes,
who thought that Luther and the middle classes had deserted them;
and they were the more easily led away into Anabaptist excesses, which
proved so hurtful to religion in those days. Luther himself lost a great
deal of his firm quiet courage, and shrank back from many opinions he
had formerly held. All these things hindered the Reformation. Indeed,
some have thought that the effect of the Peasants' War, and of Luther's
lack of courage then and afterwards, really was to take the future of
the work out of the hands of Luther and Germany, and to give it to
Zwingli and Switzerland.

While the Peasants' War was still going on, Luther lost his protector,
and Germany the greatest of her princes. Frederick the Wise, Elector
of Saxony, died. He had asked his brother, who was to succeed him,
and who was away with the army, to deal gently with the peasants; and
his last thoughts were with the poor down-trodden serfs. 'We princes
do many things to the poor we ought not to do', he said, and soon
after received the sacrament and died.

THE DIETS OF SPEYER, 1526 AND 1529

The Emperor had not returned to Germany since he left it after the
Diet of Worms. He was in Spain, ceaselessly occupied with his policy
of humbling the power of France. Before the end of 1525 it seemed as
if he had succeeded. The battle of Pavia had been fought, and Francis
I of France lost his army, and remained a prisoner in the hands of the
Emperor, his rival. The league of Madrid, which followed, bound
Francis to aid Charles to put down the revolt against the Church in
Germany; and its terms show how anxiously Charles had been
watching the Reformation, and how eager he was to crush it. He sent
word that the provisions of the Diet of Worms must be carried out,
plainly intimating that Luther's doctrines were not to be tolerated
within the Empire, and he proposed to enforce his wishes by a decree
of a Diet to be held at Speyer.

Political intrigues once more prevented him returning to Germany.
The Pope who ruled at Rome was Clement VII, a Medici, and he acted

throughout this period more in the interest of his Italian principality than for the sake of the Church of which he was head. The Pope did not wish to see Francis and Charles reconciled. He was afraid that if the two great monarchs came to terms the smaller Italian states would suffer, and he plotted to bring on another European war. The Emperor had not yet gained the repose he needed ere he could go in person to settle the affairs of Germany. Thus the Pope himself saved the Reformation for this time.

When the German princes met at Speyer, it was soon very manifest that a large number had no wish to see Luther and his doctrines banished from Germany; and the Diet which was to have put down the Reformation really issued a decree tolerating it. This famous edict, which was believed at the time to have secured toleration for the evangelical religion, declared that in the matter of religion and the Edict of Worms *every state shall live, rule, and believe so that it shall be ready to answer for itself before God and his Imperial Majesty.* Thus it was really left with each state to declare what religion should be professed within its borders, and this edict foreshadowed the famous Peace of Augsburg, which has practically determined the legal religion of Germany down to the present time. The states which had embraced the evangelical doctrines felt themselves free, in accordance with German imperial law, to reorganize the Church within their dominions, and to carry out the necessary reforms.

The edict left it to each state to decide for itself, and so there was no united attempt to introduce into the evangelical provinces one uniform system of church government and worship: each state made its own regulations. The first ruler who tried to do so, in accordance with the true principles of the Reformation, was Philip, Landgrave of Hesse. He asked Martin Lambert to draw up articles of church government for the church within his dominions. And these articles are interesting, because they recognize to some extent the power of the Christian people within the church; and they also entrust the discipline of the congregations to grave men, whose duties were not unlike those of Presbyterian elders.

Luther in earlier days would have welcomed all such indications of the recognition of the rights of the Christian people, and of the spiritual priesthood of all believers, but the Peasants' War had made him jealous of the power of the people. He thought that the people were not fit to govern the church, and actually wrote to Philip warning him against the dangers of his scheme of church order. Luther preferred to give the rule of the church into the hands of the secular power – of the princes within the principalities, of the town councils in the free imperial cities. This idea of his gave rise to what is called the *Consistorial* system of church government – a system which is peculiar to the Lutheran Church, and which, although it did not come into working order until later, may be briefly explained here.

In all Christian Churches it has always been regarded as a very important thing to preserve what is called *discipline* in the church. God requires his people to live good and decent lives, and it is the duty of the church to see that all its members behave themselves in a way becoming their profession of religion. When members of the church do not behave themselves seemly, then they ought to be rebuked and punished in the various ways lawful within the church, by debarring from church privileges, and so on.

In Germany, in mediæval times, the bishops of the Church were responsible for the discipline of the members of the Church living within their dioceses; and as their dioceses were usually large, and the bishops were unable themselves to look after all the duties involved in this supervision, they appointed courts or committees, composed of clergymen and lawyers, to look after them. Those courts were called consistories, and they took under their care the whole discipline of the dioceses, and many other things besides, such as the making of wills and bequests, cases of slander and evil-speaking, which were left to them by the ordinary law courts.

When the bishops were driven away, as they were in the evangelical states, their courts remained, and could still carry on the government of the Church. Luther, who liked to make as few changes as possible, proposed to the Elector of Saxony to use these old bishops' courts, and this was done. They became the Lutheran consistories, only for the future they were appointed, not by the bishops, but by the supreme civil authority, either prince or town council, and governed in their name. Some changes were found necessary, and were from time to time introduced; but still it may be said with much more truth than error, that the government of the Lutheran Church is now the same as that of the mediæval German Church, with this difference, that the civil government takes the place of the mediæval bishops. These changes went on all over Germany after the Diet of 1526, in the states which had embraced the Reformation.

Luther had also written some hymns, and had published a collection to be sung in church; he had written a catechism for the instruction of the young; and so all over Germany, wherever evangelical doctrines prevailed, Churches were organized, with simple evangelical worship, and provision for teaching and catechizing the young. There was not as yet any confession of faith or common creed, but the people knew well enough what to believe from the tracts of Luther and Melanchthon and others which were read and passed from hand to hand.

While these things were going on in Germany, the Emperor found himself again confronted by an alliance between France and the Papacy. He had not expected that the Pope would desert him, still less that the Pope would fail him at the very time when he was preparing to reduce Germany to submission to the Papal government from which it had revolted, and he resolved to punish him for his treachery. A numerous army was got together, reinforced by a large number of German Lutheran soldiers, under the command of that General Frundsberg who had encouraged Luther at Worms, and, led by Constable Bourbon, it poured down into Italy, devastating the country wherever it went.

On 6 May 1527, Bourbon led his troops against the city of Rome. It was taken by assault. The Pope and the cardinals escaped to Fort St Angelo, and the fearful sack of the city began. The inhabitants were maltreated and slain, the churches were plundered of their treasures, and the rude scoffing Germans proclaimed Luther Pope. The French were not able to do much to help their allies, and in 1529 a peace was proclaimed between the Emperor, the King, and the Pope, and Charles was again free, he thought, to crush heresy in Germany.

In Germany also it seemed as if things were going badly for the Reformation. The Edict of Speyer had given toleration to the Lutherans, but it had also made clear the separation between the two parties in a way unknown before.

This became clear when the Diet met again at Speyer in 1529. The Emperor was not present, but his commissioner told the princes that his master refused to acknowledge the decree of 1526, and held that the decree of Worms was still law, and ought to be enforced. For the first time it appeared as if a majority of the Diet was ready to obey the Emperor's command and enforce the edict against Luther. The final decree enjoined that whoever had enforced the edict should continue to do so and that in the districts where it had not been enforced, no further innovations were to be made, and no one was to be prevented from celebrating Mass.

However mild this seemed to be, it meant that the Edict of Speyer was abandoned, and the evangelical minority resolved to protest against the decision. They did so on the ground that religious matters could only be decided by the conscience, and could not be submitted to the Diet to be ruled by a majority. 'In matters which concern the glory of God and the salvation of the soul of each one of us, it is their bounden duty, according to God's command, and for the sake of their own consciences, before all things to have respect to the Lord our God.' 'In matters which relate to the glory of God and to the salvation of our souls, we must all stand before God and give account of ourselves to him.' The protest which embodied this great witness for freedom of conscience was signed by John of Saxony, George of Brandenburg, Ernest of Lüneburg, Philip of Hesse, Wolfgang of Anhalt, and by the representatives of the imperial cities of Nürnberg, Ulm, Constance, Lindau, Memmingen, Kempten, Nördlingen, Heilbronn, Reutlingen, Isny, St Gall, Weissenburg, and Windsheim.

From this protest came the name of Protestant.

THE EMPEROR MEANS TO CRUSH THE REFORMATION

This protest made the line of separation between the Protestant princes and their neighbours still sharper and more definite. It marked out those whom the Emperor had to crush before he could restore the mediæval Empire; and he now seemed to be at leisure to do it. Indeed, only this handful of princes stood between him and the fulfilment of his policy. He had thoroughly humbled France, the Pope had submitted to him, the Turks had been driven back, the Reformation only seemed to stand between him and a restored mediæval Empire. The Protestant princes felt the danger of their position. Were they to resist the Emperor, and if so, would they stand together firmly? Luther, who had hitherto been the leader of the movement, was now a hindrance to united action. He did not wish resistance at all at first. He did not even wish a league of princes. He actually dissuaded the Elector of Saxony from sending delegates to the meeting at Schmalkald, and when the delegates went and returned with the news that nothing had been done, he was pleased beyond measure. Had not Philip of Hesse stood forth and laboured ceaselessly for union and united effort, it had fared ill with the Reformation.

What made Luther act in this manner? He had a sound and loyal dread of rebellion in any form, and he did not believe in fighting with earthly weapons the battles of the kingdom of heaven. Then he had a large fund of quietism or fatalism in him, partly physical and constitutional, partly due to his devotion to Tauler and the German Mystics. But doubtless Philip of Hesse was right when he traced a good deal of this obstinacy of Luther's to a theological dispute. It was proposed to include all the Protestants in an offensive and defensive league, and there were Protestants who did not own Luther for their religious leader. There was a Swiss Reformation as well as a German Reformation, with its peculiar type of doctrine – a type which Luther did not like, and which, much to his displeasure, was spreading in South Germany. Philip saw this, and in his usual hearty fashion tried to get rid of the difficulty by going to the root of it. He proposed a conference. He thought if he only got the people together they would like each other better, and the differences would vanish. Accordingly he arranged for a conference between the leading theologians of Germany and Switzerland at Marburg in 1529.

THE CONFERENCE AT MARBURG

One can fancy the scene in those anxious October days. Zwingli and Œcolampadius had come, at the risk of their lives, from Switzerland; Bucer was there from Strasbourg; Luther and Melanchthon, from Wittenberg. They went over the great articles of the Christian faith, and the Germans found that the views of the Swiss were clear, scriptural, and evangelical. Fourteen articles stating all the principal points of evangelical truth were written out and agreed upon, and then the theologians proceeded to argue about the fifteenth and last, which declared the doctrine of the Lord's Supper. This was the article about which those who wished a union of all Protestants were most anxious.

In earlier days, before the Peasants' War had made Luther jealous of avoiding changes, it is possible that he might have been able to have come to some statement of the doctrine which the Swiss could have accepted; and many have supposed, on very good grounds, that had Calvin been present, and Calvin's view of the matter been before Luther, the union might have been brought about. But Luther distrusted the Swiss; he thought that they were rash and irreverent theologians, and, in spite of the anxieties of the German princes, he went to the conference determined to make no surrender.

THE POINT IN DEBATE BETWEEN LUTHER AND THE SWISS

The point in debate was this. All the Reformers, both German and Swiss, had rejected the Roman Catholic doctrine of the Sacrament of the Lord's Supper. Roman Catholic theologians divide this sacrament into two distinct things – the Eucharist and the Mass. The Mass is not so much a sacrament as a sacrifice. It is the prolongation through time of the sacrifice of Christ upon the cross; the bread and wine are, it is said, the true body and blood of Christ, and when these are tasted in the act of eating and drinking done by the priest, Christ suffers in that act what he suffered on the cross. In this way Roman Catholics teach that Christians see Christ actually crucified in their midst – see him enduring the pains of the cross for them in their very presence. Thus, on this theory, there is not the distance of long centuries between the believer and the sufferings of Christ for him. The suffering Christ and the worshipping believer are face to face in the one moment of time in the Mass.

Protestants of all kinds rejected this doctrine of the Mass as idolatrous and superstitious, and taught Christians to go back in faith to the one real sacrifice of Christ on the cross on Calvary for them and for their sins. The whole debate between Protestants is about what the Roman Catholics call the Eucharist, or sacrament of the altar.

The Roman Catholic doctrine of the Mass and their doctrine of the Eucharist have one point in common; both imply that Christ's real body and real blood are there present in the bread and wine, so that these elements are no longer what they seem to be, but are the very body and blood of Christ. They teach that the priest, because he is a priest, and has been consecrated by a bishop, is able by prayer and ceremony to perform the miracle of changing bread and wine into the very body and blood of Christ, with his reasonable soul and divine nature; that he is able to work the miracle of bringing Christ down from heaven and showing him to the people to be worshipped and partaken of. They also teach, although this part of their teaching is not always very clear, that Christ's benefits are imparted to his people when they eat the bread, which is no longer bread but Christ. Grace, they say, is given to all who partake, whether they have faith or not.

All the Protestants, whether Swiss or Lutheran, refused to accept at least two, and the two chief, points in this Roman Catholic doctrine. They would not believe that a priest was able to work the miracle which the Roman Catholics said was wrought; and they also all declared that something more was needed than the partaking to get good from the sacrament. When they described the connection between the sacrament and him that administers, they denied that a miracle was wrought; when they described the effect on partakers, they asserted that faith was needed.

They took away the miracle from the one part, and they inserted faith in the other part of the description of the sacrament and its effect. In this they were all agreed. They all held that, however Christ was present in the sacrament, he was not brought there by a miracle wrought by a priest; and however Christ helped his people, he aided them in a spiritual way through their faith, and not through their mere partaking.

But while Zwingli and Luther had these very important views in common, and so were able to write down the first half of the fifteenth article in such a way that both could thoroughly accept the statement, they differed in the way in which they described how Christ came to be in the sacrament, and how the believer felt his presence and got good from it. Zwingli said that Christ was not really in the sacrament at all in a bodily fashion. The bread and wine, he said, were only signs of his presence, in somewhat the same way that a letter is the sign of the absent writer; and when Christians partook of the sacrament they got good because the signs bread and wine refreshed their memory and made them think about Christ and all that he had done and suffered for them on the cross.

Luther thought that there was more in the sacrament than this. He had in earlier days taught that the bread and wine were promises or seals as well as signs, and this thought might have led him, as it led Calvin afterwards, to a clearer and simpler view upon the whole matter. He thought that the bread and wine must be in some real fashion the very body and blood of Christ, for had not our Lord said of the bread and wine, 'This is my body', 'This is my blood'? And as he was not very fond of making changes in doctrine, he went back to an old theory held in the Middle Ages and revived it.

The mediæval philosophers, who were fond of making very fine and subtle distinctions between the meanings of words, taught that the word *presence* meant two different things; a body was present in a portion of space when it so occupied that portion of space that no other body could be there at the same time, and a body might also be present when it occupied the very same space at the very same time with something else. The soul of man was, they said, in the very same space in which the body was, and at the very same time. One of these Schoolmen, as they were called, used this second kind of presence to describe the presence of Christ's body in the elements. It was present in the same place at the same time. The bread was not changed into Christ's body; the two things, the bread and Christ's body could be, and were in the same space at the same time, or, as the phrase ran, Christ's body was in, with, and under the bread in the Lord's Supper. But this did not explain the presence of Christ's body, nor how it was brought from God's right hand into the elements.

To explain this, Luther took another idea from these mediæval theologians. They had said that because Christ was God and man, two natures in one person, all the qualities of Christ's divine nature also became properties of his human nature. One of the attributes of God is that he is everywhere. Christ's human nature got this attribute from the divine, and is able to be everywhere too. If Christ's body is everywhere, it will be in the elements on the Lord's Table without any miracle, for it is everywhere. Luther took this *ubiquity* of Christ's body to explain how it was in, with, and under the elements of bread and wine without any miracle. When he was asked how it was that there was any special virtue in the one case of Christ's presence – his presence in the Sacrament – when he was present everywhere in his theory, he replied that God in the Bible had promised to bless his people by the presence of Christ's body and blood in the elements in the sacrament.

Thus Luther wove a most complicated doctrine of Christ's presence in the bread and wine; he certainly got rid of transubstantiation and of priestly miracle, but he put obscure and improbable scholastic ideas in their place. He was able, however, in this way to say that Christ's body was really present in true bodily fashion in the bread and in the wine, and that contented him greatly. So, when he met Zwingli to discuss the doctrine of the Lord's Supper, it is said that he took a piece of chalk, and wrote on the table which was in the middle of the room the words *HOC EST CORPUS MEUM*, 'This is my body.'

He would accept no explanation of these words which affirmed that the body and blood of our Lord were not present in bodily form in the elements, and he accused his opponents of explaining away Scripture when they spoke of metaphor and sign. It was in vain that Zwingli said that the word 'is' does not always mean substantial sameness; that when our Lord said, 'I am the true vine', 'I am the door', he could not mean that he was an actual bodily vine or door. Luther was immovable, and the conference ended without that unity of heart and purpose which the pious and warm-hearted Landgrave had hoped would be the result.

THE DIET OF AUGSBURG

The Diet approached. The Emperor had been victorious everywhere out of Germany, and was about to come to put down the Reformation, while the Protestants were, owing to Luther's obstinacy, divided and disheartened. The Landgrave Philip did all in his power to keep the evangelical party together, and succeeded in some measure.

The Emperor entered Augsburg with great pomp, and at first received the Protestant princes with great cordiality. Luther was not in the city. It was thought that his presence would be needlessly irritating, and he remained at Coburg, near enough at hand for consultation. Melanchthon took his place as theological adviser.

The leaders of the Protestants were: John, Elector of Saxony, called John the Constant, from his faithfulness to evangelical principles; Philip the Magnanimous, Landgrave of Hesse; and the aged Margrave of Brandenburg, the ancestor of the present Emperor of Germany.[1] These

---

[1] When this was written (1882), the Emperor was Wilhelm I.

princes were received by the Emperor with great show of cordiality. All was to be peace and concord in Germany.

Behind the scenes, however, were Ferdinand of Austria, the Emperor's brother, the head of the fanatical Romish party, with his theological advisers, protesting against encouragement to heresy. The Emperor wrote to calm him: 'I shall go on negotiating without concluding anything: fear nothing, even if I shall conclude: there will never be pretexts wanting to you to chastise the rebels, and you will find people happy enough to offer you their power as a means of vengeance.' His real intentions were soon declared.

The chaplains conducted public worship in the evangelical fashion in the hotels of the Protestant princes: the Emperor ordered that this should cease. The Elector declared, 'If the Emperor means to stop the preaching of the gospel, I shall at once go home.' When Charles in private conference asked the princes to silence their chaplains, the old Margrave of Brandenburg stepping forward, put his hands on his neck, and bowing, said, 'I would rather have my head roll at your Majesty's feet, than allow myself to be deprived of the Word of God, and deny my Lord.' Charles seemed startled; 'No heads off, dear Margrave', he said. Yet so little did he understand his Protestant subjects, that he was wrathful when they refused to join in the procession of the host at the festival of *Corpus Christi*. It would have been to acknowledge the idolatrous Mass, to have worshipped a wafer, said to be changed into God at the miracle-working prayer of a Romish priest, and they could not. 'Why not please the Emperor? why not show respect to the Cardinal?' said Ferdinand. 'We can and will worship none but God', they declared. And so the days passed.

Meanwhile the Protestant preachers spoke daily to great crowds in the Church of the Franciscans, and expounded eloquently the doctrines of the gospel. Charles resolved to stop this, and did so by a compromise which gave the Roman Catholics the advantage. Melanchthon, always timid and too fond of peace, urged concessions. The Protestant preachers left the town in dismay, and Luther, watching events at a distance, felt that Melanchthon's good intentions were betraying the cause.

When the Diet opened, the Emperor required the Protestants to state their opinions. The request had been expected, and Melanchthon with Luther's help had drawn up a Confession of Faith, stating in clear sentences the chief articles of their faith. This is the famous *Augsburg Confession* – the one creed acknowledged by all Lutherans, however they may differ otherwise. It is also called the *Confessio Augustana*, because it was prepared to be presented to *Augustus*, i.e. to the Emperor. Charles wished it read in Latin. 'No', said John the Constant; 'we are Germans and on German soil. I hope your Majesty will allow us to speak German.' And in German the Confession was read, not by a theologian, but by a spokesman for the princes.

THE AUGSBURG CONFESSION

The first part of this noble Confession expounds one by one the evangelical principles of the Reformation, and in particular the great principle of Justification by Faith. It is said that when the Elector's Chancellor, Von Bruck, read out, 'Faith which is not the mere knowledge of an historical fact, but that which believes not only the history but the effect of that history upon the mind', the whole assembly was visibly moved. 'Christ', said Justus Jonas, 'is in the Diet, and he does not keep silence: the Word of God is not bound.'

Then came the second part of the Confession, which denounced the abuses of the Church of Rome. It began: 'Inasmuch as the Churches among us dissent in no article of faith from the Holy Scriptures or the Church Catholic, and only omit a few of certain abuses which are novelties, and in part have crept in, in part have been introduced by violence, and contrary to the purport of the Canons have been received by the fault of the times, we beg that your Imperial Majesty would clemently hear both what ought to be changed, and what are the reasons that people ought not to be forced against their consciences to observe those abuses.' It goes on to declare that the withholding of the cup from the laity is a custom not only against Scripture, but 'also against the ancient Canons and example of the Church; that the celibacy of the clergy has 'taken away the commandment of God and his ordinance'; that the Mass is a 'profaning' of the sacrament of the Lord's Supper; that 'the distinction of meats and traditions' 'obscure the doctrines of grace', and lead people to believe that 'all Christianity is an observance of certain holidays, rites, fasts, and attire'; that monastic life and vows do much evil, and mislead men and women, for 'God is to be served in those commandments which he hath himself devised, not in the commandments which are devised by men'; and that the ecclesiastical power is not lordly but ministerial.

The Confession did contain a short clause giving the Lutheran view of the doctrine of the Lord's Supper, and this compelled the Swiss and certain South German theologians to present separate Confessions; but the reading of the Augsburg Confession by the princes in the Diet had a wonderfully heartening effect all over Germany, and the Protestants felt that they were a united band.

The Emperor saw that nothing but war would destroy the Reformation, and he was not ready for that. He tried to entangle the Protestants in conferences. Melanchthon's yielding character was well known. In these conferences he proposed to them, for the sake of peace, to surrender one point after another. Luther chafed at the news which came to him at Coburg. He wrote 'To Master Philip Kleinmuth' (Smallheart): 'I understand that you have begun a marvellous work, to make Luther and the Pope agree. . . . Now mind, if you mean to shut up that glorious eagle the gospel in a sack, as sure as Christ lives, Luther will come and deliver that eagle with might.' The princes and people were indignant when they found how Melanchthon was acting. 'Rather die with Jesus Christ', they said, 'than conquer the favour of the whole world without him.' The Roman Catholics in the end asked more than even Melanchthon could grant, and, to the great joy of the Protestants, these conferences came to an end.

THE SCHMALKALD LEAGUE OF PROTESTANTS

The princes knew that the Emperor meant to crush them. He announced his resolution to the Pope, and asked him to stir up all Catholic princes to aid in the work. A Catholic league was formed. The Protestant answer was to refuse all subsidies so long as German affairs remained unsettled.

The princes met at Schmalkald, and formed a Protestant league, of which Philip of Hesse was the most active member. The Roman Catholic States had no wish to engage in a civil war against their Protestant neighbours, and the Emperor found himself beset by the French and the Turks, and unable to crush the revolt.

The final decree of the Diet had stated that the Protestants would have till next spring to submit voluntarily and went on to say that if they did not submit, they should be exterminated. But when the spring came, the Emperor found that the Protestants were not to be exterminated. The League of Schmalkald was the most powerful confederacy within Germany. So in 1532, after long negotiations, a peace was concluded between the Protestant princes and Charles. This Peace of Nürnberg, as it was called, permitted the adherents of the Augsburg Confession to hold their doctrines, and granted other privileges. In return, the Protestant princes, and among them Philip of Hesse, cordially assisted the Emperor in all his national enterprises against the French, the Turks, and the Barbary pirates.

The Schmalkald League was still maintained, and other states, notably Würtemberg, gave in their adherence. The Emperor could not put it down, and yet was anxious to restore religious uniformity to Germany. His secret correspondence reveals his perplexity. At one time he thought of extermination, at another of conciliation. One of his schemes was to hold a General Council of the Church in Germany without sanction either of the Pope or of the King of France.

In 1538 his vice-chancellor Held formed a Catholic League of Nürnberg, with the express design of putting down Protestantism by force of arms. In 1540–1 the Emperor tried, through conferences at Hagenau, Worms, and Regensburg, to come to some understanding with the Protestants in matters of religion, and it was actually proposed at Rome to reform the Church. Finally a decree of the Diet was published in 1541 in which it was ordained 'that if any one wished to adopt the Protestant religion, he was not to be prevented'.

These successes of the Schmalkald League led to the rapid spread of Protestantism. Besides Würtemberg, Pomerania, Anhalt, Mecklenburg, and a great many cities became Protestant; the bishoprics of Magdeburg, Halberstadt, and Naumberg had disowned the Roman supremacy; and two electoral countries, Brandenburg and Albertine Saxony, had joined the league. The only states left in Germany able to withstand the league were Austria, Bavaria, the Palatinate, and the ecclesiastical provinces on the Rhine. Even these states were beginning to be influenced. The evangelical religion took large hold on the landowners, peasantry, and cities of Austria. The people of Bavaria were rapidly becoming leavened with the new views. It appeared to be only a question of time when the Palatinate would join the Schmalkald League.

The Emperor could not regard this rapid increase of Protestantism with indifference; he could not afford to allow his dominions in the Netherlands to be separated from him by a belt of Protestant states; he could not contemplate the possibility of a Protestant majority in the Electoral College, and a Protestant successor to the Empire. The action of the Elector-Archbishop of Cologne taught him that there was no time to lose. Hermann von Wied had long been convinced of the necessity of reforms in the Church, and after the Peace of Nürnberg, encouraged by many of his clergy and by the evident wishes of a large number of the people, he encouraged Protestant teaching in his vast diocese, and seemed about to convert his archiepiscopal province into a Protestant secular state.

The position of the archbishops and bishops in Germany in the days of the Reformation was somewhat peculiar. They were not merely bishops, they were also barons, and, like other great barons under the Emperor in Germany, they were sovereign princes. The Archbishops of Cologne, Trier, and Metz ruled over territories in the same fashion that John the Constant ruled Electoral Saxony and Philip the Magnanimous ruled Hesse. They were the supreme civic rulers, with their courts, and troops, and judges, and tax-gatherers. The decree of 1526 was as applicable to them as to the secular princes. They might become Protestants, and rule as secular princes over their territories, and declare they were 'living and ruling and believing, as they were ready to answer for themselves before God and his Imperial Majesty'.

Some bishops in North Germany had done so already: the opportunity was tempting: they could, by taking advantage of this decree of 1526, throw off allegiance to Rome, become free to marry, and bequeath their territory to their children. Charles saw how tempting the opportunity was, and yet for long he was not in a position to strike a blow. Whenever his plans had been laid, either the Pope or the French king or the Turks had done something to thwart him. When the news of the threatened conversion of Hermann von Wied came, he was not prepared, and the Schmalkald League seemed too strong for him in Germany. At length in 1544 he inflicted a crushing defeat on the French, and then offered favourable terms of peace, on condition that joint action was to be taken against the Protestants. At the Diet of Speyer in the same year he temporized, and spoke of a truce till the calling of a General Council; while he did all he could to detach princes from the Protestant league.

THE DEATH OF LUTHER, AND THE SCHMALKALD WAR

Meanwhile Luther, for long sick at heart and broken in health, died at Wittenberg on 18 February 1546, and with him perished the strong reluctance of the Protestants to try the fortunes of war. But the Protestants were no longer so well prepared for war as they had been. The early success of their league had made them feel too secure; jealousies arose between the cities and the states, and between the princes. Philip of Hesse was the only competent leader, and he was a prince of inferior rank. One great source of weakness, also, was the accession of Maurice to the principality of Duke George of Saxony who had been such an opponent of Luther and of the Reformation. Maurice was Duke George's nephew, and had been educated as a Lutheran: he had married the eldest daughter of Philip of Hesse. On his accession, Albertine Saxony, as it was called, had become confirmed in its Lutheranism, which had secretly spread even in Duke George's lifetime, and had become the recognized religion of the country, when Duke Henry, Maurice's father, had succeeded his brother.

All these things made it impossible for the Protestant princes to act apart from Maurice, and yet they felt the young man was not one of themselves. In fact, Maurice was the first of those German Protestant princes who looked at the Reformation simply as a political force to be used for their own advantage. They became common enough later, in the time of the Thirty Years' War, thanks to the endless disputes of the theologians, who almost seemed indifferent to the amount of blood shed and families ruined, if only their pet doctrines about *ubiquity* and *the real presence* were rightly defined. But in the early days of the Reformation the Protestant princes were men of earnest piety and disinterested motives; and yet they could not shake themselves clear of Maurice.

The Emperor saw his opportunity. He made overtures to Maurice. Maurice refused to join the league. He was a good Protestant, he said, and would defend his religion, but he would not join in a league against his sovereign. The Emperor acted on the hint. His preparations were at last made. He proclaimed that he did not make war on religion, but that he must crush a political conspiracy against the unity of the Empire.

It is needless to relate the short, sad story. The end was that, through the treachery of Maurice, the hesitation of others, and the want of mutual confidence among the leaders of the league, the Emperor gained an easy and apparently decisive victory. The battle of Mühlberg was fought on 24 April 1547, and John Frederick, Elector of Saxony, was wounded and taken, while Philip of Hesse shortly afterwards was treacherously imprisoned.

All Germany lay prostrate before the Emperor, who at once declared his intention of enforcing religious uniformity. He drew up a document called the *Augsburg Interim,* a Confession of Faith which he tried to force on the Germans. It provided for the re-establishment of the Roman hierarchy and worship, with the old feasts, fasts, and ceremonies, only it declared that the marriage of the clergy and the giving of the cup to the laity in the Lord's Supper were to be tolerated.

This Interim was Charles' scheme of reformation, and contained what concessions he thought should be made to the Protestants. It was nowhere heartily accepted. It was not enforced in the Roman Catholic districts, and the Protestants everywhere passively resisted. Even Maurice hesitated to proclaim it in Saxony, and instead, published the *Leipzig Interim,* which declared for popish ceremonies with Protestant doctrines.

It was soon found that this Emperor's creed could only be enforced where the presence of Spanish troops extorted an unwilling submission from the people. The Emperor had triumphed, his arms had been victorious, he seemed to be stronger in Germany than any ruler had been for centuries, and yet he was baffled and felt helpless. The unseen force of conscience – a power the Emperor had not reckoned on – was everywhere arrayed against him, and in the end was destined to overthrow his elaborate policy.

THE EMPEROR AND A GENERAL COUNCIL

While the Emperor had been planning and carrying out his schemes for the conquest of Protestant Germany, the Roman Court had been forced against its will to submit to the calling of a General Council. The Council had met at Trent in the Tyrol, and was sitting and deliberating upon the state of the Church at the time when the Emperor was subduing the Protestants.

In the earlier stages of the Reformation controversy, the Reformers had all appealed to a free Council, and a Council had been the favourite instrument of the Emperor for the settlement of disputes. The Popes had not wished a Council. In the fifteenth century the General Councils of Basle, Pisa, and Constance had been the means whereby ecclesiastics and princes had tried to curb the power of the Roman Court. A General Council also secured to a great many people a rallying-point for all who were opposed to Papal Christianity; and to a politician like Charles V it appeared a good way of exalting the Emperor and of humbling the Pope. Before the times of the Reformation, General Councils had been looked up to with great veneration. It was supposed that God's Holy Spirit spoke through these Councils, and many mediæval theologians who denied the infallibility of the Pope had asserted that Councils could not err.

In the early centuries of the Christian Church, a General or Ecumenical Council had simply meant such an assembly as might fairly be held to represent the *whole* church, so that its decisions could be called the opinions of all Christians. In these early days the bishops were elected by the clergy, and people, and were therefore representatives of the districts from which they came, and therefore a Council at which all the Christian bishops were present was really able to speak for all Christian people. Even in the purer times of the early church, no Council was ever held that contained all the bishops, and was therefore really ecumenical and representative of all Christians. During the Middle Ages the Church had entirely lost its old popular or democratic character, and the bishops could not be called in any strict sense the representatives of the people; they were often merely the nominees of the Pope, and could be sent to a Council to vote at his dictation.

These and other considerations had made the Protestants feel less respect for a Council, and had shown the Emperor that a Council, to be of use, must be as far away from the Pope's influence as possible.

The Germans had asked for a free Council to be held in Germany, and the Emperor had latterly asked this also: the Pope, on the other hand, wished the Council to be held in Italy, where he could better control its deliberations and decisions. After a great deal of bargaining between Pope and Emperor, the Council was at last arranged for – not in Italy, where the Pope might have too much power over it; nor in Germany, where the Emperor and the princes might overawe it; but at Trent, in the Tyrol, half-way between Germany and Italy.

The Emperor hoped great things from this Council. He knew that there were many able men within the Roman Church who were prepared to grant reforms, and that the Pope himself, Paul III, was not indifferent; but he had not calculated on the influence of a new and powerful organization which was destined to win its first great victory in the Council that he had laboured to bring together.

LOYOLA AND THE JESUITS

Ignatius Loyola, a young Spanish noble, trained amidst the chivalry of Spain, where long wars with the Moors had made devotion to the Papacy a great part of patriotism, had his leg shattered at the siege of Pamplona. Two painful operations at last convinced him that his career as a soldier had ended, and his thoughts turned towards a new service. He vowed that he would be a soldier of the Church.

In the fits of fever which his wound had caused, he had fantastic visions of the Virgin; and on his recovery he vowed his life, with all the ceremonial of mediæval chivalry, to God, the Virgin, and the Church. He had no share in the new learning. He knew nothing of theology. His religion was mediæval, and his dream was to be, in the sixteenth century, another Francis of Assisi.

It is strange to find this enthusiastic Spanish noble fired with the same thought which dictated the cool policy of Charles V. Both wished to bring back centuries that had for ever fled; and while the one was planning the restoration of the Empire of the earlier Middle Ages, the other was feasting his thoughts on a new order of monks whose missionary deeds might vie with those of the earlier Franciscans. The Emperor failed; the solitary noble succeeded almost beyond his dreams. After some years of training, disappointments, and delays, he obtained permission from the Pope to found the Society of Jesus.

The new order was only five years old when the Council met at Trent in 1545, but it was already famous. Its early missionary successes, the devotion of Francis Xavier, and the enthusiasm of its members, all combined to make it formidable. Lainez, one of Loyola's earliest disciples, and his successor as head of the Society, whose brain gave the order the shape which it was destined to take, represented his companions at the Council of Trent.

The maxim of the Society was the relentless suppression of heresy, as their one principle was obedience to the Order and to the Pope; and accordingly Lainez made it his business to prevent the Council making any concessions to the Protestants. His address, his subtlety and tenacity, gave him great influence. He was able at the very outset to defeat such liberal Roman Catholics as Cardinals Contarini and Pole, and to persuade the Council to grant no doctrinal reforms.

The successes of Charles in Germany aided the Jesuits. The Pope could never think nor act merely as head of the Church. He was a political power, and statecraft had its share in his actions. At this juncture the interests of the Italian prince were opposed to the existence of a united Christendom. The King of France, Henry II, pointed out that Charles was becoming too powerful, and would remain so if religious concessions reunited Germany. When Charles had overcome the Protestant league and sought concessions from Rome to satisfy the subjects he had beaten, at that very juncture the Pope refused to help him, recalled the Council from Trent, and established it at Bologna in Italy; so the Emperor's plans were again thwarted by the head of the Church that he was striving to keep Catholic. In his anger he turned on the Pope and compelled him to dissolve the Council. It separated, not to meet again until all hope of reconciling the Protestants had gone, and it was free, without thought of Protestantism, to consolidate the external organization of a strictly Papal domination.

Nor was the Emperor more successful in Germany. The cruelties inflicted on the imprisoned princes, Charles' faithlessness in persecuting the Protestants in spite of his proclamations, the presence and exactions of the Spanish troops – all combined to make Germany sullenly hostile, and signs were not wanting that the land would not long endure his tyranny. Maurice the traitor was thoroughly hated and distrusted, or the revolt might have come sooner.

The Emperor was strangely blind to all that was going on. He believed that he had a firm hold on Maurice, whom he had made Elector, and that without Maurice Germany could do nothing.

Meanwhile the princes were coming together again. France was bribed by offers of German land to aid in the enterprise, and at last the confederation was formed, including Maurice, and the princes marched to close the passes of the Tyrol against the imperial troops. Maurice dashed forward and, by a sudden spring, seized the fortress of Ehrenberg, the key to the Tyrol. The Emperor barely escaped by sudden flight, only to find himself at Steiermark, without an army, and driven out of Germany. A mutiny among the confederates' troops alone prevented his capture; for Maurice did his best to catch, as he said, 'the old fox in his den'.

THE RELIGIOUS PEACE OF AUGSBURG

Charles V never recovered from this defeat. The Reformation had at last beaten him, and he acknowledged it, although he did not understand it. He did not stay to treat with the victorious princes, but left that work to his brother Ferdinand. The imprisoned princes, Philip of Hesse and John Frederick of Saxony, were released and restored to their territories, and the preliminaries of a permanent peace were laid down on the old lines of Nürnberg, in the Treaty of Passau, 1552.

At length, after long negotiations, a religious peace was concluded at the Diet of Augsburg in 1555, 'which', said the decree, 'shall be permanent, absolute, and unconditional, and which shall last forever'. The principle of 1526 was recognized, that the supreme civil power in each state was to be at liberty to choose the creed of the country – whether Lutheran or Roman Catholic. This peace, therefore, recognized the right of churches with two separate creeds to exist side by side in Germany, and thus established the Reformation in legal fashion.

The principle which underlay the settlement, *cujus regio ejus religio*, as it was called, was full of difficulties which cannot be described here, and indeed was a fruitful cause of the Thirty Years' War, which brought so much misery to Germany. It did not grant liberty of conscience; it made no provision for any other form of Protestantism save the Lutheran; and all who did not adhere to the Augsburg Confession were still out of the law in strict legal reckoning.

Those who used it at the Diet had to modify it in two ways. The Protestants saw that it permitted the Roman Catholic ecclesiastical princes to persecute their Protestant subjects; and the Roman Catholics saw that it permitted ecclesiastical princes to secularize their states. So the Protestants got a clause inserted which declared that the Protestant subjects of ecclesiastical princes, who had long held by the Augsburg Confession, should not be compelled to forsake their creed; and the Roman Catholics got what was called the 'ecclesiastical reservation' inserted which provided that if any Roman Catholic ecclesiastical state chose to depart from allegiance to Rome, it was to be deprived of its livings and bishoprics.

The Peace of Augsburg closes the history of the struggle for Lutheran Reformation. The Protestant Church of Germany, which adhered to the Confession of Augsburg, had still a long struggle before it to maintain its ground against the Roman Catholic Counter-Reformation, Jesuit intrigues, and the force of arms during the Thirty Years' War; it held its own, but it did no more. The Peace of Augsburg is the flood-tide of the Lutheran Church. In the struggle that followed, it was the younger and more thoroughgoing form of Protestantism that bore the brunt of the attack, and was entitled to the spoils of conquest. Lutheranism held its own, consolidated its ecclesiastical organizations, and perfected its theology; but its history, as a fresh, living, reformation force in Germany, ended here with the Peace of Augsburg.

2

THE LUTHERAN REFORMATION
OUTSIDE GERMANY

Lutheranism beyond Germany, p. 52 – Denmark, p. 53 – Sweden, p. 54.

LUTHERANISM BEYOND GERMANY

*D*uring the earlier years of the Reformation, Luther's influence extended far beyond Germany. The University of Wittenberg attracted many foreign students, who, returning home, secretly or openly spread the new doctrines.

Thus it happened that the beginnings of Reformation in those countries which afterwards separated from Rome and formed national Protestant Churches were almost entirely Lutheran. The early Reformers and martyrs in the Netherlands were Lutheran, and Luther's peculiar doctrinal and ecclesiastical tenets long held their ground in Holland.

The Reformation movements in Hungary, Poland, Bohemia, and Scotland were due to men who were professed disciples of Luther, and even in England Lutheran principles had made progress. But in all these countries another type of Protestant doctrine, the Calvinist, ultimately gained ground, and the Lutheran Reformation passed away.

Two countries only, Denmark and Sweden, with their dependencies, adopted and kept permanently by the Augsburg Confession and the Lutheran principles of Church government.

The Reformation in these countries was more than anywhere else identified with political revolution, and was effected by rulers who felt that good government was unattainable until the power and wealth of the Romish clergy were removed. The history of the Reformation in these countries is the story of a revolution, and the modern political life of Denmark and Sweden begins with the Reformation of their Churches.

In the beginning of the sixteenth century, the countries of Denmark, Sweden, and Norway were united under one King who lived in Denmark, and ruled with only a nominal power over the other two. The countries were almost in a state of anarchy. Two great landed aristocracies, the nobility and the Church, divided between them the wealth and the power of the state, and each baron, bishop, and abbot ruled despotically within his estates. The union of the countries, effected in the end of the fourteenth century, was purely dynastic, and was intensely disliked by the people.

In 1513, Christian II succeeded to the throne – a merciless, fickle, and stupid tyrant, who combined all parties, churchmen, nobles, merchants, and peasants, against him in both countries. A massacre of Swedish nobles at Stockholm, perpetrated in circumstances of peculiar treachery, exhausted the patience of the people, and both Denmark and Sweden rose against the tyrant. The revolt was successful; Christian II was driven from the throne, and then the two countries went their several ways.

Denmark

The people of Denmark offered the crown to Frederick I, Duke of Schleswig-Holstein, an ardent Lutheran, and sovereign of a territory already reformed, and he accepted it. At his coronation he was made by the clergy to sign a bond that he would not forcibly introduce the Reformation, nor attack the Roman Church, in his new dominions. He kept it in the letter, but not in the spirit. He favoured and protected Lutheran preachers and teachers, especially John Jansen, a Danish monk, who had been to Wittenberg; and the new faith made such progress that soon almost all the nobles in Jutland had embraced it, and it had gained a large number of followers in the islands.

Towards the end of 1527, a Diet of the kingdom was convened at Odensee, expressly to discuss the subject of religion, and toleration for Lutheranism was granted. During the years immediately succeeding, the new doctrines spread rapidly among the people. The Roman Catholic party tried to recover their power at the death of Frederick in 1533, but they were beaten, and the power of the bishops was gradually but completely broken. The nobles joined with the king in the overthrow of the ecclesiastical aristocracy, and the lands, which had belonged to the Church for the most part, passed over to the king.

From that time Denmark has been a Protestant country. Its creed is the Augsburg Confession, for the Lutherans in Denmark never adopted the Formula of Concord; its catechism, Luther's; and its form of Church government, although it admits a titular Episcopacy, the Consistorial. Bugenhagen drew up the constitution in the *Ordinatio ecclesiastica regnorum Danicæ et Norwegiæ*. It declared that the King possessed the *jus episcopale*, and was first bishop and supreme ecclesiastical judge; that the nobles were to be the patrons; and that the Church was to be ruled by seven superintendents with the title of bishop. In the great fight between Protestantism and Roman Catholicism in the seventeenth century, the Thirty Years' War, Denmark sent what help the country could to the Protestants in Germany.

SWEDEN

After the massacre of Stockholm, Gustavus Vasa, a young Swedish noble, who had lost almost all his near relations in that slaughter, organized the rebellion against Christian II, and helped greatly in carrying it out to a successful issue. In 1521 he was declared regent of the kingdom, and in 1523 he was called by the voice of the people to the throne. He found himself in the presence of almost insurmountable difficulties. There had been practically no settled government in Sweden for more than a century, and every landowner was an almost independent sovereign. Two-thirds of the land was owned by the Church, and the remaining third almost entirely belonged to the nobles; the peasants were everywhere oppressed; the trade of the country was in the hands of Denmark or the Hanseatic League; and there was no middle class. The nobles and the Churchmen claimed exemption from taxation, and the peasants could not endure further burdens.

In these circumstances, Gustavus Vasa turned his eyes on the Church lands, and planned the overthrow of the ecclesiastical aristocracy with the aid of the Lutheran Reformation.

There seems no reason to believe that the King was not a religious man, thoroughly impressed with the truth and power of evangelical teaching; but he had other motives in his zeal for the Reformation. He wished money to enable him to govern, he desired to free the peasants from their burdens, and he wished to overthrow the powerful ecclesiastical aristocracy which stood in the way of kingly rule. He found it necessary to proceed cautiously. The peasantry did not know Lutheran doctrines, and did not wish to change their faith; the nobles thought that the king was attacking the rights of property, and that their turn might come next if they allowed the Churchmen's lands to be taken from them; the ecclesiastical aristocracy was very powerful.

It should also be remembered that while Gustavus had headed a successful rising against the tyranny of Denmark, that tyranny had been blessed by the Pope, and had been supported by the Swedish bishops. He was now an excommunicated man, outlawed by the Church. This brought him into connection with Lutheran preachers, already to be found in Sweden.

Two brothers, Olaf and Lorenz Petersen, who had studied at Wittenberg, and on their return to Sweden had preached against an indulgence-seller who had penetrated into the country, had fled from the bishops to Lübeck, where Gustavus had made their acquaintance. They and another Swedish Lutheran, Lorenz Andersen, Archdeacon of Strengnäs, were openly protected by the king, and began preaching against saint-worship, pilgrimages, monkish life, and auricular confession. Olaf Petersen especially went about preaching the pure gospel, 'which Ansgar the Apostle of the North had preached seven hundred years before in Sweden'.

The bishops demanded that Olaf Petersen should be silenced. In return, the Reformer challenged them to a disputation, but the challenge was not accepted. The result was the spread of evangelical doctrines. Gustavus made Olaf Petersen preacher at Stockholm, Lorenz Petersen went to Uppsala as professor, while Lorenz Andersen was made chancellor of the kingdom. Disputations were held in public, after the German fashion, in various parts of the kingdom; and at last, in 1524, Olaf Petersen and Dr Galle of Uppsala in public conference discussed the doctrines of Justification by Faith, Indulgences, the Mass, Purgatory, Celibacy, and the Temporal Power of the Pope, with the result that the cause of the Reformation was largely strengthened.

In 1526 Andersen finished the translation of the New Testament into Swedish, and the people, with the book in their hands, were able to compare the teaching of the preachers and of the bishops with the Word of God.

The need of money to carry on the government had been severely felt, and in 1526 two Diets had imposed heavy taxes on church property. The ecclesiastical party, headed by their bishops, instigated a rebellion, which was crushed, and then Gustavus felt that the time had come to carry out his plans. At the Diet at Westeräs he explained the financial condition of the kingdom, and proposed that part of the enormous wealth of the Church should be taken to pay for the national debt, and to yield a settled revenue for the kingdom. The nobles refused to assist him; the clergy declared they would only yield to force. After an eloquent address, Gustavus abdicated the throne. Then the various estates quarrelled, and, after a few days' anarchy, the demands of Gustavus were assented to, and enforced in a decree of the Diet, which really marks the beginning of the modern history of Sweden. It provided, amongst other things, that it was within the King's right to seize the castles and strongholds of the bishops, and to take possession of all ecclesiastical property; and it recognized the lawfulness of the Lutheran Church.

From this time the work of reformation proceeded rapidly, and in a short time Lutheranism became the recognized religion of the country. The church property was confiscated to the State, but enough was left to provide for the support of religion. The episcopal form of government was retained, but the king's supremacy, in Lutheran fashion, was strictly established. Many of the popish ceremonies and usages, such as the use of holy water, pictures, and candles, were retained, but with Protestant explanations. Lorenz Petersen became the first Protestant Archbishop of Uppsala in 1531. A new translation of the whole Bible was completed by the brothers Petersen in 1541. When Gustavus died, the whole country was thoroughly wedded to the Lutheran Church, and showed its attachment to strict Lutheranism by adopting, in 1664, the Formula of Concord.

PART TWO

THE SWISS REFORMATION

LEADING TO THE REFORMED CHURCHES

I

THE SWISS REFORMATION UNDER ZWINGLI

THE SWISS AND GERMAN REFORMATIONS

*T*he Reformation in Germany has commonly attracted much more attention than the revolt against Rome in Switzerland. The conflict with the Emperor which it provoked, its rapid spread, and the number of states and kingdoms which adhered to it, the share which the universities, with their numbers of foreign students, had in the movement, all combined to turn men's eyes, both then and now, to Luther and Germany rather than to Zwingli and Switzerland; but if a reformation be judged by its later consequences rather than by its beginnings, the movement begun in Switzerland was even more important than that which had Wittenberg for its centre. As time went on, it was seen that the principles of the Swiss Reformers, both in doctrine and in church organization, could be readily transplanted to other lands, and accordingly the churches of France, Scotland, Hungary, and a great part of Germany inherited the traditions of Zwingli and Calvin rather than those of Luther and Melanchthon.

This is perhaps due to the fact that the great theologians of the southern Reformation were less inclined to submit to the doctrinal and other traditions of the Mediæval Church, even in matters which to some might seem unimportant to faith, and insisted from the very beginning in following at once what seemed to be the clear teaching of Scripture in all matters, small as well as great. Neither Zwingli nor Calvin wished to keep to a doctrine of the *real presence* because the Mediæval Church had held it, and they did not feel the difficulty, which Luther always felt, in doing other than their fathers had done.

It is probable, however, that there was another reason which was quite as powerful, and which is to be found in the political state and training of the Swiss. In the Mediæval Church the rights of the Christian people had disappeared entirely. When men spoke about the Church, they meant the Pope, bishops, abbots, monks, nuns, and priests; they did not think of the great body of pious Christian people who were really the Church of God.

In Luther's Reformation, although he and the other Reformers knew well enough that the real visible church was the pious people who professed faith in Jesus Christ, they had not been able to give practical expression to this feeling, and the Consistorial system of the Lutherans put the princes and other civil authorities where the bishops and bishops' courts had been.

They might say that the Christian people were the church; but they never tried to give this real church such shape that it could think and act for itself, as the Christian people in apostolic and post-apostolic times had done. They scarcely tried to find out and work into the life of the reformed church the maxims of self-government which had inspired the New Testament Christian community. Their mediæval notion was that the church must be ruled from the outside, and could not rule itself.

In Switzerland from the very outset, the church and the Christian people were known to be one and the same thing, and plans of self-government, not always successful, but still well meant, made part of the proposed reformation. This doubtless came from close study of the New Testament Scriptures; but the free popular life of the Swiss helped them to understand what the New Testament meant, and so set them on the right track from the beginning. A reformation arising in the midst of the free democratic Swiss life was more likely to be able to understand the spiritual democracy of New Testament Christianity than that which had its beginnings in universities and the courts of German princes.

THE POLITICAL CONDITION OF SWITZERLAND

Switzerland in those days was like no other country in Europe. It was as divided as Italy or Germany, and yet it was united as they were not. It was a confederation of states or cantons, each of which was independent of its neighbours, and yet was banded together with them in common league. It was a confederation of independent republics, or rather a 'little republic of communes and towns of the primitive Teutonic type, in which the civil power was vested in the community', and the mode of republican government differed in each.

The Swiss peasants had revolted against their landlords as early as the beginning of the fourteenth century; the battle of Morgarten, where 1300 Swiss had defeated 10,000 Austrians, was fought in 1315. Nearly two centuries later the forest cantons formed a league for mutual defence, and soon after were joined by other little communities of freemen. Their flag had a white cross on a red ground, and bore the motto, ' Each for all, and all for each.'

The forest cantons were independent communes of peasant proprietors, dwelling in almost inaccessible valleys; Zurich belonged to a town which had gathered round an old ecclesiastical settlement; Berne, to what had once been a hamlet, nestling under the fortifications of the palace of a noble family; and so on. The Forest Cantons had a simple patriarchal government; in Zurich the nobles took rank as one of the trade guilds of the town, and the constitution was thoroughly democratic; Berne was an aristocratic republic; and so on; but in all the power belonged to the people, and all the people were freemen.

Another thing worth noting is, that there had been nothing like episcopal government in Switzerland for generations. Their relations to the Papacy had been carried on through legates, and were entirely political. The land was within the jurisdiction of the Archbishops of Mainz and Besançon; but neither they nor neighbouring prelates, as such, had exercised any real sway over the parish priests of the Swiss cantons, and in this way it was not so difficult to introduce reforms.

In the beginning of the sixteenth century foreign culture and intercourse with neighbouring states were changing the old, simple manners of the Swiss. During the Middle Ages the chief strength of an army was supposed to be its heavily-armed cavalry; but the victories of the Swiss over the Austrian and Burgundian troops had shown the superiority of good infantry, if they were well trained. The Swiss troops were supposed to be the best in the world, neighbouring states were glad to get their assistance in their wars, and a bad custom had gradually grown up among the Swiss of hiring out their soldiers for large sums of money to those states who paid best. It was their custom, when a Swiss regiment left to fight on this foreign service, to send along with it as chaplain the parish priest of the district from which the troops came; and some of these chaplains, when they saw the demoralizing tendency of such mercenary warfare, did their best on their return home to make their countrymen give up this bad practice.

ULRICH ZWINGLI

One of the most famous of these patriots was Ulrich Zwingli, parish priest of Glarus, who was to become the Reformer of Switzerland.

Zwingli was born on 1 January 1484 at Wildhaus in Toggenburg, a little district lying so high up amongst the mountains that no fruits ripened in the valley, and no roads ran through it. His father was the head-man or magistrate of the commune, and his uncles were clergymen, and one of them Dean of Wesen.

His father resolved to educate him for the Church, and as he, a well-to-do peasant proprietor, could afford to give his son a good education, Zwingli was sent to school at Basle and at Berne, and thence to the great University of Vienna. There he became a great classical scholar, zealous for the new learning which Italy was teaching Germany and France, and delighted to call himself a *Humanist*.[1] From Vienna he came back to Basle, and studied theology under Thomas Wyttenbach one of those liberal theologians who were accustomed even then to denounce indulgences on the ground that Christ by his death had paid a ransom for all men's sins.

It was the thought of his old master that made Zwingli say long afterwards, 'All deference to Martin Luther; but what we have in common with him we knew long before we had heard his name.'

He took his degree of M.A. in 1506, and was thereafter appointed priest of the small parish of Glarus. He lived there for ten years, reading and studying the Latin classical authors, especially Cicero, Seneca, and

[1] In Scotland this old word for classical learning is retained in the title given to the Latin class in the Universities – the *Humanity* class.

Horace; he also began to learn Greek eagerly, and wrote to a friend: 'Nothing but God shall prevent me from acquiring Greek, not for fame, but for the sake of the Holy Scriptures.' It is said that his favourite books in the New Testament were the Epistles of St Paul. He copied them out in his own hand from more than one manuscript (this book still remains), and he learnt them by heart. His biblical studies led him to declare that the only way to true doctrines was to listen to *the Bible expounding itself,* and that the Papacy had made the Church degenerate. This was his mood of mind at Glarus, while Luther was still a devoted son of the Mediæval Church, and was tormenting himself with fastings and scourgings.

In 1516 he went to be curate at Einsiedeln, where was an abbey which was, and is still, the shrine of a famous winking Madonna, said to work miracles. People came in crowds on pilgrimage to the shrine, and Zwingli's manly piety was indignant at the idolatry and superstition of the crowd, and at the trickery and profanity of the abbot and his ecclesiastics. He began to preach to the pilgrims, and to tell them the folly and sin of image and saint worship. In one of his sermons he said: 'In the hour of death call upon Jesus Christ alone, who bought you with his blood, and is the only Mediator between God and man.' These sermons of his created a great deal of excitement, and reports of them were even sent to Rome, and the Pope's legate was ordered to do his best to silence the preacher by offering him promotion in the Church. He refused all offers of advancement from the legate, but when the council of citizens in Zurich asked him to go there in 1519 as pastor, he went gladly, and soon had great influence in that important town and canton.

Soon after he went to Zurich, a wandering pardon-seller, Bernhard Samson, came to urge the people to buy indulgences. Zwingli preached against him, and prevailed on the authorities to send him out of the country. He also began a famous course of lectures on the New Testament, in which he expounded the doctrines of grace and of justification by faith only. These lectures were attended by great crowds of people, who heard the gospel gladly.

Switzerland had, in virtue of old treaties, supplied the Pope with infantry for his wars against the Emperor; but Zwingli's influence was so great that in 1521 the canton of Zurich refused to hire out its troops as before. This patriotic resistance to an infamous blood traffic raised more opposition than Zwingli's preaching had done, and the popish ecclesiastics in the canton and the neighbouring bishops did what they could to get him silenced. In the previous year the Pope's legate had asked the Swiss Diet to search out and destroy all Lutheran books that had come into their country, and the Diet had given orders accordingly.

The town council of Zurich, influenced by Zwingli, while they apparently obeyed the Diet, issued a mandate enjoining all curates, pastors, and teachers 'to preach the Holy Gospels and Epistles agreeably to the Spirit of God, and to the Holy Scriptures of the Old and New Testaments.' This mandate gave an impetus to the evangelical movement already begun. Zwingli published his treatise on fasting in 1522, and many Zurichers at once used the forbidden kinds of food during Lent. He preached against the celibacy of the clergy, and the people applauded. The Pope, Adrian VI, was very anxious not to quarrel with the Swiss, whose troops were so useful, and tried to win Zwingli over, but it was not to be done. Indeed, when his legates were on the road with flattering messages, Zwingli was writing his *Apologeticus* – an elaborate attack on the corruptions of the Church.

The Bishop of Constance asked the Zurichers to silence the Reformer; Zwingli persuaded them to arrange for a public discussion, and offered to prove all his opinions from the Bible in presence of the people. The council fixed the day, 23 January 1523.

ZWINGLI'S THESES

In order to mark out the subjects to be discussed, Zwingli drew up a list of sixty-seven theses, stating in order the points wherein his teaching differed from that of his accusers, which were really a well-arranged summary of Protestant theology. The statements in the theses, put shortly, are as follows: Jesus Christ, and he alone, is the true object of worship, and is alone to be glorified; and the one thing needful is to lay hold on him and on his gospel. All claims made by the Romish hierarchy to come between Christ and his people, and to add to or take from the gospel, are therefore mere pretensions, and are insulting to Jesus Christ, our sole High Priest. Christ died on the cross once for all for the sins of his people, and therefore the Mass, which professes to continue or repeat that sacrifice, is false, and the Eucharist is only a commemorative rite. Jesus Christ is the only Mediator between God and man, and therefore saint-worship is idolatry. The Holy Scripture says nothing about purgatory, and there is none. 'Nothing is more displeasing to God than hypocrisy; it follows, therefore, that everything which assumes sanctity in the sight of man is folly: this condemns cowls, symbols, vestments, and tonsures.' In similar fashion Zwingli condemned ordination, auricular confession, and absolution, the celibacy of the clergy, all merely ecclesiastical rule, and so on.

A great crowd assembled to hear the disputation, and, in the opinion of the Zurichers, Zwingli easily defeated his opponents. This disputation was followed by another in 1523, and by a third in 1524, and the result of the three was that Zwingli thoroughly won over to his side the canton of Zurich and its magistrates.

THE REFORMATION IN ZURICH

It was resolved to reform the worship and church life in Zurich. It was declared that the Mass was no sacrifice; that images were not to be honoured; that the Lord's Supper was a simple commemoration of Christ's death; that the cup was to be given to the laity; and that the whole service ought to be in the common tongue of the people. The Corpus Christi procession was abolished, and so were fees for extreme unction and for confession. In 1524, Leo Judæus, a friend of Zwingli's, began to translate the Old Testament, and before ten years had passed Switzerland had five versions of the whole Bible in the mother tongue.

In Zurich there was a cathedral, with a dean and chapter, and a large amount of property attached to it to support the canons. The chapter resolved to surrender their benefices. Part of the money was kept for the support of the town's ministers, and the rest of the fund was devoted to educational purposes. Out of the cathedral funds the council of Zurich, following Zwingli's advice, paid schoolmasters and professors. It was also resolved that all monasteries and nunneries should be asked to renounce their property for educational purposes, and many of these establishments did so, the monks and nuns being supported while they lived.

The only hindrance to this reformation in Zurich was the coming of some Anabaptist fanatics from North Germany. Thomas Münzer's disciples soon began to give trouble. They preached in Zurich and gained some disciples. Their doctrines were very extravagant. They taught that all believers, being a spiritual priesthood, were specially taught of God, and did not need any rule of life outside their own hearts and consciences. So they burned their Bibles publicly. They held the most extravagant opinions. Christ had said that his followers must become like little children; and so Anabaptist enthusiasts behaved like children, and played with dolls in the streets of Zurich, and did other things equally absurd. The enthusiasm at last became a sort of madness, and blood was shed in consequence. The council bore long with their vagaries, but were compelled at last to expel them, and then the Reformation went on quietly as before.

From Zurich the Reformation spread to the neighbouring cantons. It appeared at Basle, Berne, Schaffhausen, and Appenzell.

BASLE was the seat of a famous University; learned men resorted to it; Erasmus had made it his headquarters. It was the centre also of papermaking, and Froben's printing press had made it celebrated. It was frequented by artists, and the great Holbein lived there through the Reformation struggle. Many of the scholars residing there were under the influence of Wyttenbach, Zwingli's teacher, and were prepared to welcome the new teaching. Capito, the future Reformer of Strasbourg; Polyhistor, the learned Hebraist and physician; Œcolampadius, the scholar of Reuchlin and future companion of Zwingli; Farel, a young Frenchman from Dauphiné, who was to win over Calvin to active work as a Reformer, were all scholars living at Basle.

The Zurich disputation quickened some of them, and Œcolampadius and Farel began preaching against superstition.

BERNE, the most aristocratic of the little Swiss republics, also sent representatives to the Zurich disputation, and began to feel among its citizens the throb of the Reformation. The council was induced to declare that only the pure gospel was to be preached in the town, and three preachers, Kolb, Haller, and Sebastian Meyer, made use of the permission to preach against the Mass and popish ceremonies.

A similar struggle went on in most of the other cantons, the Reformation slowly but surely gaining ground, and Switzerland was rent into two divisions by the religious question.

THE FOREST CANTONS alone remained unmoved, and formed a centre of opposition to all religious changes. When the Reformation began to make decided progress in other cantons besides Zurich, and Berne and Basle had become wholly reformed, the irritation between the Roman Catholic and the Protestant states grew so strong that war was inevitable. In 1529 both parties were ready for battle, Zwingli for one hoping that the issue would be swift and decisive. The first shock, however, passed off without battle, and the Forest Cantons, without fighting, signed the first treaty of Kappel in 1529, the principal clause was: 'As God's Word and the faith are not things in which it is lawful to use compulsion, both parties shall be free to observe what they think right, and in the common countries or independent territories the majority in the congregations shall determine whether the Mass and other usages be retained or abolished.'

This treaty was not very strictly kept by either party, and led to new disputes, the end of which was that the Forest Cantons came suddenly against Zurich, fell on their army and defeated it, Zwingli being slain. The victory did not advance the Romanist cause. The second treaty of Kappel contains almost the same provisions as the first, and the result was that in Switzerland, as in Germany, each state was left free to choose its own religion.

CHARACTERISTICS OF ZWINGLI'S REFORMATION

Zwingli's death ends the first stage of the Swiss Reformation, and before his death the conference at Marburg, and Luther's dislike to a popular constitution in the church, made it plain that in the Reformation there were to be two distinct movements which could not be wholly united. Great harm came out of this want of union, and the blame must rest not with Zwingli but with Luther. Both men had the same end in view; both believed in the same evangelical principles; their differences were merely a trifle when compared with their agreement. But the characteristic features of Zwingli's Reformation are much better displayed in its later form under Calvin, and we may so compare it with the Lutheran movement.

Zwingli himself and his fellow-Reformers did very little to settle what soon came to be a very important question in the Reformed Church, how the church was to be governed. He himself had very strong ideas about the necessity of keeping clearly before the minds of all that there was no order or class of men who could be called *spiritual* simply because they did certain functions. He wished to impress on all the spiritual priesthood of all believers, whether ministers or laymen. He taught also that it was the duty of all magistrates to rule in Christ's name, and to obey his laws. He was led from these thoroughly good and true ideas to think that there should be no government in the church separate from the civil government which ruled the commonwealth in which the church existed. Hence all the rules and regulations about public worship, about doctrines, and about the discipline of the church, were made in Zwingli's time by the Council of Zurich, which was the chief civil power in the state.

This idea of his, even in his lifetime, was accompanied by many evils, one of the most conspicuous being the connection between the Protestant Reformation and purely political enterprises. Zwingli's idea was that modern states should be like what he thought the old kingdom of Israel was, namely theocratic governments. Had Zwingli's views continued to prevail, it is not likely that the Swiss Reformation would have exercised the power it did beyond Switzerland; for while they worked somewhat smoothly in a small state like Zurich so long as Zwingli's personal influence lasted, they could not have been well applied to larger states, and were quite unsuited to a small Protestant Church struggling for existence against a hostile civil government.

2

THE REFORMATION IN GENEVA
UNDER CALVIN

GENEVA BEFORE THE REFORMATION

*A*fter the death of Zwingli and the second Peace of Kappel in 1531, the centre of interest in the Swiss Reformation was a town which was only slightly connected with Switzerland.

Since the twelfth century, Geneva had been the seat of a bishop, who, like so many other bishops within the German Empire, was also civil ruler. The Dukes of Savoy also claimed the town, and the quarrels between the bishop's party and the duke's followers were frequent.

During the fifteenth century the townsmen had gradually won a certain right of self-government, and a council of citizens ruled the community. In 1513, Pope Leo X appointed a bishop belonging to the house of Savoy, and the ducal and episcopal parties came together. Thus in the beginning of the Reformation two rival factions faced each other in Geneva – a Savoyard and a citizen party. The one party strove to bring the city completely under the control of the house of Savoy; the other aimed at making it a free republic like the cantons of Switzerland, and entered into alliance with Berne and Freiburg for that purpose. The Savoyard partisans, whose military recklessness and licentiousness made them very obnoxious to the quieter citizens, were called by them 'Mamelukes'; while the republican party were nicknamed 'Eidgenossen', *i.e.* confederates. The latter name is interesting, because probably from it comes the name of the great French Protestant party, the Huguenots.

The learning of the Renaissance period had penetrated into the town, and also the Italian pagan licentiousness. The aristocratic party were, notorious for bad living. The bishop's palace and the castle of the Duke of Savoy were both scenes of the most shameless excesses, and these evil examples had made the townspeople very corrupt. The lower clergy followed the example of their superior, and it is said that only one religious house, the convent of the Franciscan nuns, preserved anything like purity of life. The republicans were not free from the vices which disgraced their opponents; their love of liberty was in many cases a love of licence, and their republican enthusiasm had in many cases a pagan origin. They were children of the Renaissance, and had all the faults of that strange movement. The city was full of scepticism, licentiousness, and superstition. Papal indulgences always sold well in Geneva.

FAREL AT GENEVA

In these circumstances, in 1532, William Farel, a young Frenchman, one of the Reformers of Berne, came from that city to Geneva, and began preaching violent, impetuous sermons against 'the Roman Antichrist', and the idolatry and superstitions of the Romish Church. His sermons created a great deal of disturbance; the bishop's partisans denounced him, and the citizens were divided in their opinions.

In 1525 the Eidgenossen had made alliance with Berne and with Freiburg. Berne was Protestant, and had sent Farel to Geneva; Freiburg was Romanist, and sent messengers urging the citizens to expel the impetuous preacher. They deliberated long, and meanwhile asked Farel to leave the city. He did so. At last the council resolved to maintain alliance with Berne, the stronger canton; and to give one of their churches to the Berne people for Protestant worship. Farel came back and occupied the pulpit. Crowds came to hear him preach, and the Reformation made way.

The Duke of Savoy and the canton of Freiburg made common cause against Geneva, attacked it, and were beaten back. The council declared the bishopric abolished, gave Farel full liberty to preach, and his sermons on civil and religious liberty fanned the enthusiasm of the people. In 1535, by order of the council, a public disputation was arranged for, at which Farel with three companions challenged all comers, like knights at a tournament, to dispute with them on the points of theology and morals in debate between the Church of Rome and the Reformers.

The people of Geneva, impetuous and disorderly, unaccustomed to restraining themselves, or to allowing things to be done slowly and in legal fashion, rushed, after the disputation, to the churches, destroyed the relics, dragged down the images, tore the vestments, and committed many other acts of violence. On 27 August following, the council declared that Roman Catholicism was abolished, and commanded all citizens to adopt the Reformed religion.

The conversion of a whole community by force at the bidding of a town council, the supreme civil authority, was not likely to improve the character of the city. There were doubtless many on whom the preaching of Farel had produced a good effect, but the gospel never gains the heart when it is forced in such fashion upon converts. The morals of the city were as bad as when the bishop reigned, and it seemed as if they were going to become worse. Licentious enthusiasts began to preach false and immoral doctrines about the nature of Christian liberty. It seemed impossible to restrain the people. Farel was at his wits' end. He laid hold of a young French student who had come almost by accident to the town, and besought him to stay with him and help him. The young student was John Calvin, and this chance visit was the beginning of Calvin's work in Geneva, so important to all the Reformed Churches in Europe.

CALVIN'S EARLY LIFE

John Calvin, or Cauvin, was born on 10 July 1509, at Noyon, in Picardy. He was therefore a child when Luther and Zwingli began their attacks on the Romanist Church, and may be said to belong to the second generation of the Reformation. His father was procurator-fiscal for the county of Noyon, and secretary to its bishop; his mother, a lady of deep piety, was Jeanne Lefranc of Cambrai. His father's relations with the noble families of the district and with the bishop enabled him to give his son the very best education that was then to be had. The boy was brought up with the children of the noble house of de Montmor, and was destined from the first for an ecclesiastical career.

When the young Calvin was only thirteen years of age, his father got for him the presentation to an ecclesiastical benefice, and sent him to the University of Paris. He went first to the College of La Marche, where he had for his master the celebrated Mathurin Cordier,[1] and then to the College Montaigu, which was soon afterwards to receive an equally celebrated pupil, Ignatius Loyola.

It is said that young Calvin was of an unsocial disposition, and that his fellow-students called him 'the accusative case' because he was always finding fault. When he was eighteen years old his father got him another benefice, and in order to draw the stipend he had to submit to the tonsure, but this was the only approach Calvin made to priesthood in the Roman Church. He was never ordained, and never took the vow of celibacy.

In 1528 his father quarrelled with the bishop, and resolved to make his son a lawyer instead of a priest, and sent him to Orleans to study jurisprudence. The young man obeyed; he became a diligent student of law, though his heart was not in the work; and by studying almost day and night, he kept up his classical and theological studies as well. He was known by this time as the most distinguished student of his day, and it was said that his abilities were such that he might aspire to any position in the legal profession.

His father died in 1531, and Calvin felt free to follow the life he liked best. He left the study of law, went back to Paris in 1532, and quietly attached himself to the small company of Protestants who were accustomed to meet there for the reading and exposition of the Scriptures, and for prayer. He does not tell us why he took this step. It was taken so quietly that it must have been long thought over. Calvin

[1] Cordier, Corderius, or Cordery (1479–1564), was a well-known name in Scottish parish schools half a century ago [early nineteenth century], where his exercises were used in every Latin class. He was converted to the Reformed faith by his great pupil, and did his best to spread evangelical doctrines by means of the sentences to be turned into Latin in his exercises. In the edition published shortly after his conversion, the sentences are short statements of simple evangelical truths, or short pithy attacks on Romanist superstitions. He followed Calvin to Geneva, and died there in his 86th year.

always shrank from speaking about his religious experiences. He was quite different from Luther in this respect. Luther unbosomed himself with the utmost frankness, and told every one all his doubts and fears and faith. It was the nature of the men. Once only does Calvin draw aside the veil. In the preface to his marvellous *Commentary on the Psalms,* he tells us that God drew him to himself by a 'sudden conversion'. It must have happened when Calvin was at Orleans. Henceforward he renounced a brilliant career, gave up his ecclesiastical income, and joined the small evangelical community at Paris, prepared to share their dangers. He settled down to a quiet literary life, and had begun to publish, when he had suddenly to fly Paris, to escape seizure for his religion. He went to Strasbourg, where he became acquainted with Martin Bucer the Reformer, to Basle, and to various other places, leading a wandering student life.

THE *INSTITUTES OF THE CHRISTIAN RELIGION*

In the spring of 1536 he published at Basle the first edition of his *Institutes of the Christian Religion.* It was written in Latin, and then translated into French, for the use, as Calvin said, of his own countrymen. This first edition was smaller, and in every way inferior to the revised editions of 1539 and 1559; but it is probably unmatched as the work of a young man of twenty-six, for Calvin was no older when he published it. It gained for its author the title of the 'Aristotle of the Reformation', and more than any other theological work it has influenced the thought and moulded the character of the Protestant Reformation.

Calvin tells us in his preface that he wrote this book with two distinct purposes. He meant it 'to prepare and qualify students of theology for the reading of the divine Word, that they may have an easy introduction to it, and be enabled to proceed in it without any obstruction'. But he also meant it to be a vindication of the teachings of the Reformers against the calumnies of their enemies, who had urged the King of France to persecute them, and drive them from France. His dedication was: *To His Most Christian Majesty, Francis, King of France and his Sovereign, John Calvin wisheth Peace and Salvation in Christ;* and he said, 'I exhibit my confession to you that you may know the nature of that doctrine, which is the object of such unbounded rage to those madmen who are now disturbing your kingdom with fire and sword.

For I shall not be afraid to acknowledge that this treatise contains a summary of that very doctrine which, according to their clamours, deserves to be punished with imprisonment, banishment, proscription, and flames, and to be exterminated from the face of the earth.'

He meant in cool precise fashion to state what Protestants believed, and he made the statement in such a way as at once to challenge comparison between those beliefs and the teaching of the Mediæval Church. Luther had set great store by the Apostles' Creed, and was never weary of saying that he and all his followers accepted that old and venerated summary of Christian belief, and therefore that Protestants belonged to the Catholic Church of Christ. Calvin made the same claim; but he did more: he showed that the claim was true down to the smallest details, and that when tested by the Apostles' Creed the Protestants were truer Catholics than the Romanists.

To see clearly what Calvin meant to do and did in his *Institutes*, it is necessary to remember what the Apostles' Creed was. Our Lord, before his ascension, told his disciples to go to all nations, baptizing them in the name of the Father, of the Son, and of the Holy Ghost; and so, when Christian pastors in the apostolic and post-apostolic age received converts into the church, they required that they should make this profession of faith: *I believe in God the Father, and in His Son Jesus Christ, and in the Holy Ghost,* and this was the earliest and simplest form of the Creed. A fourth sentence was added, *and in the holy Catholic Church.* These four sentences were repeated by all converts at baptism. The Apostles' Creed and all other early creeds are simply expansions of these four sentences; and the earliest books upon theology which explained the whole round of Christian doctrine were expositions of the Creed, as the Creed was itself an exposition of the baptismal confession. This shows us, among other things, that all true theology rises out of the simple expression of adoring trust in God.

Calvin's *Institutes* is really an exposition of the Creed, and is divided into four parts, each part explaining a portion of the Creed. The first part speaks of God the Creator, or, as the Creed says: 'God the Father Almighty, Maker of heaven and earth'; the second part, of God the Son, the Redeemer, and of his redemption; the third part, of God the Holy Ghost and his means of grace; and the fourth, of the Catholic Church, its nature and marks.

This division and arrangement, borrowed in this way from the Apostles' Creed, shows that Calvin had the same opinion about the Reformation that Luther strove to make clear in his tract on *The Babylonian Captivity of the Church of God.* He did not think that he was helping to found a new church, or that he was making a new creed, or writing a new theology. He did not believe that Protestants were men who held new opinions never before heard of. The theology of the Reformation was the old theology of the church of Christ, and the opinions of the Protestants were views of truth resting on the Word of God, and known to pious people, or at least felt by them, throughout the history of Christendom. The theology which he believed and taught was the old theology of the early creeds, made plain and stripped of the superstitious and false views which had been borrowed by mediæval thinkers from pagan practices and a pagan philosophy. The Reformation, the *Institutes* said, does not invent new opinions, it only strips off the falsehoods and makes plain the old truths.

CALVIN AT GENEVA

The publication of the *Institutes* made Calvin well known to all the leading Reformers; and when in his wanderings he came to Geneva, meaning to stay there one night only, and pass on, Farel begged him to remain with him and help him in his difficulties. Calvin was very unwilling to quit his student life, but he felt it to be his duty to do the work lying to his hand at Geneva, and he remained with Farel.

He says in the preface to his *Commentary on the Psalms:* 'As the most direct route to Strasbourg, to which I then intended to retire, was shut up by the wars, I had resolved to pass quickly by Geneva, without staying longer than a single night in that city . . . Upon this Farel, who burned with an extraordinary zeal to advance the gospel, immediately strained every nerve to detain me. And after having learned that my heart was set upon devoting myself to private studies, for which I wished to keep myself free from other pursuits, and finding that he had gained nothing by entreaties, he proceeded to utter an imprecation that God would curse my retirement and the tranquillity of the studies which I sought, if I should withdraw and refuse assistance when the necessity was so urgent. By this imprecation I was so stricken with terror that I desisted from the journey I had undertaken.'

Calvin was twenty-seven years of age, and Farel twenty years older, when they began to work together in Geneva, and, notwithstanding the difference in age, the two Reformers became strongly attached to each other. 'We had one heart and one soul', Calvin says. Farel introduced him to the ruling citizens. He began his work by giving lectures in the cathedral, and his preaching was at once felt to be attractive and powerful. The council made him pastor, and with Farel he set himself to the serious work of organizing the Reformation. We are told that he drew up articles of faith, and a form of church government, and at all events he wrote his catechism for children soon after his arrival in Geneva. The labours of the Reformers were approved of by the council of citizens, and Geneva became in all outward respects thoroughly reformed.

Farel, however, had long known, and Calvin soon learnt, that what Geneva needed was a reformation of morals. The city was grossly licentious, and had been so for a long time. The rulers of the city for several generations had known this, and had issued laws against licentious behaviour. Sumptuary laws against gaming, drunkenness, masquerades, dances, and extravagances in dress have been found among the records of Geneva during the beginning of the sixteenth and back into the fifteenth century; and the books of the council show entries of punishment for offences against such laws long before Calvin settled there.

This has been forgotten when historians charge Calvin with attempting to reform people, as we should say, by Acts of Parliament. Calvin did not make these laws, nor is there evidence that he considered them to be very important. He had one fixed opinion, however: that people who lived immoral lives, whose walk and conversation were not befitting their Christian profession, should not be allowed to partake in the solemn ordinance of the Lord's Supper, and his views soon brought him into conflict with the people of Geneva.

After many warnings, the Reformers at last resolved to exercise church discipline, and solemnly debar from the Lord's Table unworthy communicants. The magistrates, who had been willing enough to enact laws restraining vice and even luxurious living, would not consent to this simple exercise of church order, and forbade Calvin and Farel to enter the pulpit. They refused to obey; and at Easter 1538 they preached to an excited and armed crowd, and refused then to administer the Lord's Supper to the congregation, lest it should be profaned.

On the following day the council of the city formulated charges against Calvin and Farel. The Reformers were accused of wishing to usurp power by means of their ecclesiastical regulations about the abolition of all holy days save Sunday, the disuse of fonts in baptism, and of unleavened bread in the Lord's Supper.

These charges were evidently mere pretexts, because Calvin had himself declared that all these things named were matters of indifference. The real ground of offence came out in the accusation that Calvin and Farel were setting up a new Papacy; the magistrates wished to retain in their own hands the power of church discipline as well as civil rule. The end was that Calvin and Farel were banished from the city, not by the Papists, but by those men who had hitherto been active in promoting the Reformation.

This dispute between the Reformers and the people of Geneva, occurring so early in the public life of Calvin, reveals one great difference between the Reformed or Calvinist and the Lutheran side of the Reformation. Calvin from the beginning had very clear views about church discipline and the right of the Christian community to rule itself in spiritual matters, and in particular the right of those in authority in the church to debar from church privileges all who were unworthy to share them.

Luther and Melanchthon had the same ideas, but failed to give them practical shape. Luther kept the right of oversight in the hands of the old Episcopal courts, but transferred the nomination of these courts from the bishops to the civil authorities; and the practical though unintentional effect of this was to make the magistrates the judges of fitness to approach the Lord's Table. Calvin, on the other hand, from the very outset saw that, if the church was to exist as a visible community distinct from the state, it must have the right to declare who are fit to become members and to share church privileges, and have the power to rebuke and punish spiritual offences by spiritual censures and deprivation of ordinances.

It does not appear either here or afterwards that Calvin asked for more power than this, that church discipline must be exercised by the church itself, represented by its office-bearers. Calvin in the beginning of his career declared for the spiritual independence of the church in such spiritual things as admission to or exclusion from the Lord's Table.

CALVIN BANISHED FROM GENEVA

Banished from Geneva, Calvin went to Basle, and then to Strasbourg, where he spent three quiet years, acting as pastor to a large congregation of French refugees, and busying himself with literary work. Strasbourg had always occupied a middle place between Germany and Switzerland, and Calvin became acquainted with many of the German theologians. He formed an intimate friendship with Melanchthon, and met him and other German Reformers at the religious conferences which were held at Frankfurt, at Worms, and at Regensburg. In September 1540 he married Idelette de Bure, the widow of John Storder. She was a pious and cultivated lady, *gravis honestaque femina*, says Beza; she bore Calvin three children, all of whom died young. Calvin does not say much about his family life in his correspondence, but the letters he wrote to very intimate friends about her death and the deaths of his children reveal the warm human heart which beat within the stern, courteous Frenchman.

GENEVA CANNOT GET ON WITHOUT CALVIN

Meanwhile at Geneva the turmoil continued. Farel and Calvin had been banished, and were far from the city, but the people felt the need of their presence. There was no commanding influence left, and things were going from bad to worse. Calvin had said that infidelity was at the root of the lawlessness which he had opposed, and the better-minded citizens began to find out the truth of this remark. The social disorders almost led to political disasters. The Bernese tried to get possession of the city; the Roman Catholics, headed by Cardinal Sadoleto, attempted to win it back to Popery; Anabaptists, enemies of all order in church and state, Libertines, Free Spirits, struggled for the mastery in Geneva until the citizens were weary of the turmoil, and longed for the return of their banished ministers.

The council of the city invited Calvin to return. He at first refused. 'There is no place', he wrote to a friend, 'I have such terror of as Geneva.' He was urged to return; many of his friends among the French and German Reformers entreated him to accede to the request of the citizens, and the Swiss towns of Berne, Zurich, and Basle joined them. At length he yielded, and went back to Geneva.

The magistrates gave him a house and garden in the neighbourhood of the great church, made him pastor and professor of theology, and appointed him an annual stipend of five hundred florins, twelve measures of wheat, and two tubs of wine. They also promised that ecclesiastical discipline should be enforced in the Church of Geneva, for Calvin had insisted on that. His acquaintance with the Lutherans had only made him the more earnest in maintaining the right of a church to keep itself pure. He returned to Geneva in triumph, and was received with the most extravagant tokens of welcome. His longing for a quiet literary life was again disappointed, and public life claimed him during his remaining years.

Henceforth he remained in Geneva until his death, and for twenty-four years it is said that he ruled the city. Historians have compared him to a great many very different people. He was the 'Geneva Lycurgus', some say; others, an old Roman Dictator, or Hildebrand, or the caliph of the Muslims. He did a great work, and lived a life of incessant activity, in spite of almost continued illness, headaches, and asthma.

He preached several times a week, and lectured daily. He wrote commentaries on almost all the books of the Bible, composed theological treatises, and conducted an immense correspondence. He was the leader of the Reformed Church all over Europe, and it has been supposed that he was omnipotent in Geneva, and the good and the bad results of the Genevan 'theocracy', as it was called, have been attributed to his influence.

It is unquestionable that during his rule in Geneva the character of the city became altogether changed. The city, which had been one of the most frivolous and licentious in Europe, became the cradle of Puritanism, French and Dutch, English and Scottish. Dances and masquerades were unknown; the taverns and the theatre were empty; and the churches and lecture-rooms were crowded.

The *Ecclesiastical Ordinances*

The instrument which effected all this was the famous ecclesiastical ordinances of the Church of Geneva, and the way in which these were applied by the magistrates. These ordinances are said in the few prefatory words to be 'the spiritual regimen, which God has ordained in his church, reduced to a proper form, to be observed and have place in the city of Geneva', and they have furnished a model for almost every succeeding Presbyterian 'Form of Church Government'.

According to these ordinances, there are four kinds or grades of office in the Christian Church established by God for its government, and these are pastors, teachers, elders, and deacons.

It was the duty of *pastors*, who are also called overseers and bishops, to expound the Word, dispense the Sacraments and, in conjunction with the elders to exercise discipline; they were commonly selected by the ministers already in office and appointed by the magistrates, with the consent of the people; they were made accountable to the quarterly conferences of the church, to the consistory, and to the council of the city.

The *teachers* included all professors in the university, and the schoolmasters. The elders were appointed to exercise discipline. They were not elected by the congregation, but were appointed by the council of the city, advised by the pastors; and all of them had to be members of the councils. In conjunction with the pastors they made a yearly visitation of their districts, and tested in some simple way the faith and conduct of every member of the church.

All the *elders* with all the pastors made the *Consistory*, which was the executive and legislative council of the church. The Consistory met weekly, under the presidency of one of the four syndics or chief magistrates of Geneva, in order to receive and examine reports about irregularities in the life and conduct of any members of the church, and to decide upon the ecclesiastical punishment required, up to exclusion from the Lord's Table. They had no power to inflict any censure or punishment which was not spiritual, but they were required to report misdemeanours to the civil authorities who could punish. As all elders were chosen by the council, and had to be members of the council, the result of this was that the Genevan magistrates sitting as elders in the consistory received information about offences, and reported them to themselves sitting in the council as magistrates.

The *deacons* had charge of the poor and the sick, and were appointed by the council.

This scheme of church government agrees in the main with the principles laid down by Calvin in his *Institutes,* but it differs in so many very important details that it is impossible to believe that the Reformer was wholly responsible for it.

In the *Institutes* Calvin has stated pretty clearly what are the true principles of ecclesiastical government and discipline. He argues that God educates and perfects his people in this life through his church, and that for the edification of the church he has provided a variety of gifts, which are not bestowed indiscriminately on all Christians, but have been given in larger measure to a few. These gifts may be classed under the three heads of instruction, government, and charitable supervision, or, as the Scottish Reformers said, doctrine, discipline, and distribution, and the church can see that certain of its members are specially fitted to instruct, others to rule, and others to look after the collection and distribution of monies. God has given these gifts, and placed men in the church fit to use them, for the edification of his people, and therefore all office in the church is not lordly but ministerial. Office-bearers are men who can best serve the community, and are therefore responsible to God and to the community for such service. Calvin laid great stress on the true nature and value of the office of the eldership, which he considered the most effectual barrier against such an assumption of lordship over the church as that which had been one of the most blameworthy usurpations of the Church of Rome. Through this office the church has that orderly government without which no community can exist, and the Christian community can be preserved from usurped power and ecclesiastical tyranny by means of a truly representative government, where the membership has the power to choose its own office-bearers. Calvin also insisted strongly that this government was spiritual, and had to do with spiritual and not civil offences, and could inflict spiritual and not civil punishments. The highest spiritual punishment, according to him, was excommunication.

How They Differ from the *Institutes*

The *Ecclesiastical Ordinances* differ in many important respects from the Principles laid down in the *Institutes*.

Calvin had expressed himself very strongly against any confusion between civil and ecclesiastical jurisdiction, and had declared that the two must be kept completely separate. In the *Ordinances* this separation is not maintained. The censure of the consistory was continually followed, as we shall see, with fines, banishment, and even death; while, according to Calvin's theory, spiritual offences are to be followed by spiritual punishments only. The elders who exercised rule or discipline were not chosen by the church, nor were they really representative. They were selected by the civil magistrates of the city, and those only were eligible who were already members of a political organization. The rights of the Christian community were practically ignored, although Calvin had declared that all ecclesiastical power really belonged to the whole body of believers. The council chose the pastors, while the church had a right of veto; they chose the elders from among themselves, and they also chose the deacons.

These striking departures from Calvin's principles were made by the magistrates of Geneva in opposition to the wishes of the Reformer. He was specially dissatisfied with the mode of selecting elders, and said that he could not regard the *Ordinances* as a perfect scheme of church government; but he evidently thought that it was the best he could get at the time, and accepted it in the hope that it might afterwards be improved. He was so well pleased with it, not-withstanding all its faults, that he looked upon it as a model that might be copied in other places, and he expressed a hope that Geneva, placed on the borders of France, Germany, and Italy, would incite these countries to a Reformation of a thorough and lasting character.

Nevertheless the points in which the *Ordinances* departed from the principles which Calvin had laid down in his *Institutes,* were the occasion of those characteristics of Genevan rule which have been most blamed by succeeding historians. There is no doubt that the moral corruption rampant in Geneva was stamped out by a rule of the most severe and even cruel character. The old Genevan laws were severe enough in many cases, and were made still more severe against some offences; but after the publication of the *Ecclesiastical Ordinances,* they were applied with a rigour previously unknown.

The consistory sat weekly, every Thursday, and received reports of the manners of the people; and these reports were communicated to the council, which was the consistory over again with civil powers. All noisy games, games of chance, dancing, singing of profane songs, cursing and swearing, were forbidden. Every citizen had to be home by nine o'clock under heavy penalties. Adultery was punished by death. A child that had thrown stones at its mother was publicly whipped and hung up to the gallows by its arms. The old festivities at weddings were entirely done away with; no drums or music were allowed in the processions; no dancing at the feast. The theatre was interdicted save when biblical scenes were represented. Novel-reading was entirely prohibited, and if any one wrote what displeased the consistory he was sent to prison. Free speech was punished, and landlords were ordered to report what their guests had said at table. Landlords were also forbidden to give food or drink to any one who did not say grace before meat. Fasting was forbidden, and a man was punished because he ate no meat on a Friday.

It is impossible to say what share Calvin had in these needlessly severe regulations. Most historians have urged that he was all powerful in Geneva, and could have prevented them had he chosen. He was a Frenchman, and no other nation has in great crises furnished such pitiless logicians. Calvin, too, never abjured the most hateful part of the mediæval theory of church discipline, the principle of appeal by ecclesiastical courts to the secular power for the punishment by fine, imprisonment, or death, of spiritual offences, on the plea that they are crimes against the order and peace of society. Calvin accepted this doctrine; so did Beza. He called liberty of conscience a diabolical doctrine. The Westminster Divines accepted it, and wrecked the Reformation of the Church of England to secure it. Not only Calvin, but all the leading Reformers approved of the death of Servetus because of his denial of the doctrine of the Trinity, and of the blasphemous statements he made in defence of his opinions. All that must be admitted.

THEIR EFFECT ON A REFORMATION OF MANNERS

It must be remembered, however, on the other hand, that we cannot tell what was required to work a reformation of manners in a town so immoral and restless as Geneva.

The Reformation, just because it was a protest against the existing order of things, set loose a whole flood of evil along with it which had to be stemmed. It is almost as impossible for us to understand the pressing danger of Anabaptist and other excesses, as it is to comprehend the moral corruption of the age in which Christianity arose and spread. Pantheistic libertinism was professed as a creed, and the literary records of the Renaissance period reveal an unblushing sensuality which must be taken into account. What Calvin found confronting himself in Geneva, was the renaissance indulgence in all things immoral, fired by a hideous enthusiasm that such indulgence was enjoined by religion because it was natural. There was a dark side of the Reformation which it is not pleasant to look at, but which was there, and which must be taken into account before judgment is passed on the conduct of the Genevan council or on Calvin.

Calvin's government, if it was his, did not cause a tithe of the suffering which Luther hounded on the princes of Germany to inflict on the peasant rebels, and their leaders, the enthusiastic prophets; but suffering caused by blind passion, whether of fear or hate, has curiously always been regarded with more leniency than suffering which is inflicted in pursuance of a stern purpose of reformation.

Apart from all this, however, it is not improbable that Calvin was less omnipotent in Geneva than he is supposed to have been. He was too true a Frenchman, too logical a thinker, to be responsible for the inconsistencies pointed out between the *Institutes* and the *Ecclesiastical Ordinances*. It should not be forgotten that what brought about those punishments which have been so condemned, were those parts of the *Ordinances* for which Calvin was not responsible, and which he wrote against. The real cause of the evil was the relation in which the consistory stood to the civil government of the city. Let us suppose that one of our town councils sat every week as a vigilance committee on morals. It would soon make work for itself. And would not each councillor feel aggrieved if the cases he reported to the committee, and which were censured by them, were not punished? Would he not be tempted, when he sat the same afternoon or next day as a member of a council with power to punish such offences, to insist that punishment should be inflicted? The blame of all these evils ought to be laid at the door, not of Calvin, or even of the Genevan council. They arose naturally out of the thrice hateful confusion between civil and spiritual government, which is the besetting sin against which every church and state must guard themselves.

CALVIN'S DEATH

During Calvin's residence in Geneva the city grew wealthy and influential. The magistrates founded a university, with Theodore Beza as first rector, and eight hundred students thronged its classes during the first year. Protestant refugees from Italy, France, and Scotland crowded into the city, and were received and cared for. 'Calvin made Geneva a second Rome.' His correspondence shows his power and influence. The French Huguenots, the English Reformers, the Scottish Congregation, and the leaders of the Reformation in Germany, all asked and received his advice.

He died young. His constitution, never strong, was worn out by his excessive labours. He preached his last sermon on 6 February 1564, and died on 27 May in the same year, not quite fifty-five years of age.

When he felt death near, he gathered round him first the syndics, or chief magistrates of Geneva, and then all the ministers. He forbade the erection of any monument over his grave, and the spot where he was buried is now unknown.

He was a man of small stature, with a thin face, finely-cut features, a prominent nose, high forehead, and eyes that could flame. He was scrupulously neat in dress, and ate very sparingly.

Unlike Luther, he was an aristocrat by education and taste; a man of great social refinement, who felt much more at ease in good society than among the common people. He has been called hard and cold, but his friends and contemporaries everywhere speak of the cold, shy, stern, polished French gentleman in terms of affectionate tenderness; and young men got on well with him.

Many a writer has sat down to study Calvin's character with aversion, and has risen with the dislike turned to affectionate admiration. Let one example suffice. Here is what Ernest Renan says:

'Calvin was one of those absolute men, cast complete in one mould, who is taken in wholly at a single glance; one letter, one action suffices to judge him . . . Careless of wealth, of titles, of honours; indifferent to pomp, modest in his life, apparently humble, sacrificing everything to the desire of making others like himself. I hardly know any man, save Ignatius Loyola, who could match him in those terrible transports. It is surprising that a man who appears to us in his life and writings so unsympathetic, should have been the centre of an immense movement in his generation, and that this harsh and severe tone should have exercised so great an influence on the minds of his contemporaries. How was it, for example, that one of the most distinguished women of her time, Renée of France, in her court of Ferrara, surrounded by the flower of European wits, was captivated by that stern master, and by him drawn into a course that must have been so thickly strewn with thorns? This kind of austere seduction is exercised only by those who work with sincere conviction. Lacking that deep sympathetic ardour which was one of the secrets of Luther's success, lacking the charm, the perilous languishing tenderness of St Francis de Sales, Calvin succeeded in an age and in a country which called for a reaction towards simply Christianity, because he was the most Christian man of his generation.'

BEZA, CALVIN'S SUCCESSOR

Theodore Beza succeeded Calvin in Geneva, and maintained the reputation which that church had acquired; and down to the middle of the seventeenth century the voice of Geneva was the most powerful among the large circle of Protestant Churches.

CALVIN'S INFLUENCE ON REFORMATION THEOLOGY

Under Calvin's influence, the theological differences in Switzerland were reconciled, and one type of doctrine spread through all the churches calling themselves Reformed. These churches did not, like the Lutheran, adopt one Catechism and one Confession, but unity of thought and feeling pervaded all the various creeds. Calvin himself did not write any confession which has taken a first place among the creeds of churches calling themselves by his name, but his influence is everywhere manifest. He himself lives again in the work of his disciples.

His two most important confessional writings were his *Catechism for Children* and the *Zurich Confession*.

The *Catechism* was meant, he said, to restore to its proper place the godly instruction of children, which had been sadly neglected by the Romanists. Calvin took the Apostles' Creed, the Ten Commandments, and the Lord's Prayer, and wove them into the Catechism called by his name. It gave birth to the two great Catechisms of the Reformed

Church – the *Heidelberg Catechism*, which is the creed of the Reformed Churches of Germany; and the *Shorter Catechism* of the Westminster Assembly.

THE ZURICH CONFESSION

This Confession was very serviceable because it united the Reformed Churches on the doctrine of the sacraments by reconciling in a deeper unity the opinions of Luther and Zwingli. It cast aside the mediæval metaphysic with which Luther had burdened his theory, and at the same time repudiated the shallower view of Zwingli and the earlier Swiss Reformers, who taught that the sacraments were only signs or pictures of spiritual blessings.

Calvin put his doctrine shortly in his exposition of this Confession: 'The sacraments are helps or media by which we are either inserted into the body of Christ, or, being so inserted, coalesce with it more and more till he unites us with himself in full in the heavenly life.'

After all, however, the influence of Calvin and Geneva is best seen in the generation of Protestants it trained and sent forth to battle with Romanism. 'At a time', says Haüsser, 'when Europe had no solid results of reform to show, this little state of Geneva stood up as a great power; year by year it sent forth apostles into the world, who preached its doctrines everywhere, and it became the most dreaded counterpoise to Rome . . . The missionaries from this little community displayed the lofty and dauntless spirit which proceeds from a stoical education and training; they bore the stamp of self-renouncing heroism, which was elsewhere swallowed up in theological narrowness. They were a race for whom nothing was too daring, and who gave a new direction to Protestantism by causing it to separate itself from the old traditional monarchical authority, and to adopt the gospel of democracy as part of its creed . . . A little bit of the world's history was enacted in Geneva, which forms the proudest part of the sixteenth and seventeenth centuries. A number of the most distinguished men in France, the Netherlands, and Great Britain professed her creed; they were sturdy souls, iron characters cast in one mould, in which there was an interfusion of Romanic, Germanic, mediæval, and modern elements; and the national and political consequences of the new faith were carried out by them with the utmost rigour and consistency.'

The Lutheran Reformation made little progress out of Germany. The little republic of Geneva first united the Swiss Reformation, and then gave its distinctive characteristics to the reforming movements in France, Holland, Scotland, Bohemia, Hungary, Moravia, and a great part of Germany. Luther, the man of genial humour, so human on all sides, was after all the Reformer of only part of Germany; Calvin, so unsympathetic, cold, polished, sarcastic, and pitiless in his logic, was the Reformer of a great portion of Christendom.

The Swiss Reformation went far beyond Switzerland and included the great churches of France, Holland, and Great Britain, with all that came out of them.

3

THE REFORMATION IN FRANCE

BEGINNINGS OF THE REFORMATION IN FRANCE

*B*efore the Reformation in France became a great and important movement, two types of Reformed Christianity, stamped with the individualities of two men – Luther and Calvin, the Peter and the Paul of the Reformation – had appeared. In the fierce fighting with Romanism which was to follow, the younger movement became the more important; it was Geneva rather than Wittenberg which matched itself against Rome. The double stream of Reformation life went out through Europe from these two centres, but in times of death-struggle the fierce democracy of Calvinism had twice the strength of the halting conservatism of the Lutheran movement. The history of the progress of the Reformation outside Germany is almost entirely a history of Calvinism, and of the triumph of Calvinist ideas. It was so in France.

The beginnings of the French Reformation lay far back – long before the birth of John Calvin. In the south and south-east there were, in the end of the fifteenth and beginning of the sixteenth centuries, lingering traces of the old Albigenses, and the Vaudois maintained themselves and were protected in right of ancient charters, for a while, amidst the persecutions of the Huguenots. The French Church had always distinguished itself by its opposition to the claims of the Papal court and of the Pope. When the Papacy fell very low in the fifteenth century, and licentious Popes occupied the See of Rome, the French Church, headed by the famous chancellors of the University of Paris, Jean Gerson and Pierre d'Ailly, had been mainly instrumental in summoning the reforming councils of Pisa, Basle, and Constance, and in curbing the Papal curia. The French Church had always stood out bravely against Ultramontanism,[1] and, protected by the Pragmatic Sanction of Bourges, was more truly national than perhaps any other portion of the Mediæval Church in Europe. Many people expected that France, from her past history, would take the lead in a reformation movement in Europe. But the reformation which the ecclesiastical leaders of France promoted in the fifteenth century was no reformation of doctrine or revival of spiritual religion. The reformers of Constance had burnt John Huss.

Just before the Reformation, too, there was in the French Church the same immorality, sloth, and ignorance which disgraced the Mediæval Church of the sixteenth century in Germany and Italy; and the beginnings of the Reformation in France came from the awakening of scholarship and the reading of Scripture in the original tongues.

The earliest reformed preaching was in Meaux, where the bishop, Guillaume Briçonnet, saw that monastic immorality was in urgent need of rebuke, and that the people were longing for earnest religious advice. He had heard of the scholarship of Jacques Lefèvre of Etaples (Faber Stapulensis), and of the persecution which he suffered from the Sorbonne doctors because of his biblical studies; and he invited him and his ardent young disciple, William Farel, Calvin's friend in later life, to come to his diocese and study, teach, and preach under his protection. As early as 1523, Lefèvre published a translation of the New Testament into French, and the people bought and read the book with eagerness.

---

[1] Ultramontanism: from *ultramontane,* beyond the mountains (i.e. the Alps), applied to the Italians: hence, extreme views favouring the Pope's supremacy.

The Franciscans, eager to avenge themselves on Briçonnet for his earlier proceedings against them, accused him of heresy and of favouring heretics. In the storm which ensued the bishop lost courage. Farel fled to Strasbourg, and was soon after followed by Lefèvre and Roussel, another preacher, and the Reformation seemed crushed. But with the Bible in their hands, tracts of Luther to read, and the memories of the sermons of Farel and Roussel, the people held by the evangelical faith. Martyrdoms followed, but the leaven spread in hidden fashion all over France.

FRANCIS I

The King who reigned in these early years of the Reformation was Francis I, to whom Calvin afterwards addressed his *Institutes of the Christian Religion*. High-spirited, and of some intelligence, he had welcomed the revival of letters, had sheltered Lefèvre while that scholar resided in Paris, and had prided himself on his correspondence with such scholars as Erasmus and Budæus. He liked to imagine himself a magnificent patron of letters; he had taken the University of Paris under his special protection, and he had also taken a great interest in Henri Estienne's famous printing press. He had founded new chairs for Greek, for Hebrew, and for Latin oratory. He thought himself a poet, and had written verses. His sister, Margaret of Angoulême, afterwards Queen of Navarre, was one of the wittiest talkers and brightest writers of the time.

Francis had no sympathy with the sloth and ignorance of many of the Churchmen of the day, and privately regarded the Reformation movement as the struggle of mind against dullness. He protected the earlier Reformers, and even assisted them. Francis was a vain, selfish prince, ambitious to shine as an accomplished warrior, and intent on establishing the absolute supremacy of the sovereign. He had no sympathy with the deep spiritual earnestness of the Reformation, and his political necessities soon prevailed over his love of learning.

THE CONCORDAT OF 1516 AND HOW IT SHAPED THE REFORMATION

The independence of the French Church and the rights of the French kingdom against the Papacy had been maintained by the Pragmatic Sanction of Bourges, which asserted the liberties of national churches in a clear and forcible manner. It declared that the Pope was subject to an Ecumenical Council, and that such a council should be held every ten years. It declared that all appointments to high ecclesiastical offices, such as bishoprics and abbacies, were by election and not by Papal nomination. It restricted the costly and troublesome appeals to Rome, declared the exaction of *annates* simony, and finally sanctioned the principle that no interdict can include the innocent as well as the guilty.

The Pragmatic Sanction had always been jealously guarded by the French Church, and by most of the French sovereigns. It was disliked intensely by the Popes, and it could not have been regarded with much favour by a king who aimed at the absolute supremacy of the throne. An independent church must always foster independence among the people. Francis saw that if he could get the church under his own command, his path towards absolutism would be easier. Accordingly, he made a bargain with the Pope, and exchanged the Pragmatic Sanction for a Concordat which was the cause of much future misery to France.

By this Concordat the king gave up the principles of the reforming Councils of Basle and Constance, and consented that the Pope should secure the *annates*, i.e., the first year's stipend from every newly filled benefice, while in return the Pope should give the nomination to all ecclesiastical offices into the king's hands. In other words, the Popes were acknowledged to be the supreme heads of the church, and received a large sum of money annually from France; while the French king was made practically the head of the church within France, and had at his disposal all the archbishoprics, bishoprics, abbeys, and priories in his kingdom.[1] The Act was denounced and opposed in every way, but it was successfully carried through, and remained in force till the Revolution.

The Concordat of 1516 is the key to the history of the French Reformation, and its importance to all French ecclesiastical history since the beginning of the sixteenth century cannot be overrated. On the one hand it secularized the French Church. All the important ecclesiastical offices were in the gift of the king, and had to be

---

[1] Louis XV had the patronage of 18 archbishoprics, 112 bishoprics, 1666 abbeys for men, and 317 abbeys and priories for women.

scrambled for by worldly-minded courtiers. On the other hand, it made the interests of the church and of the throne identical. Opposition to the ecclesiastical system of the French Church could not avoid becoming opposition to the absolutism of the sovereign. From the first this Concordat laid down the lines on which the Reformation struggle had to be carried on in France. The Reformers could not help being also the opponents of absolutism in France; and the king, in order to maintain the hold on the country which his command of the church gave him, was forced to support the Pope, who had bestowed the supremacy on him.

Thus it happened that the Protestants in France had a work to do quite different from Luther's work in Germany, for they had to stand up against both church and state. They had the same work too as the Scottish Reformers and the Protestants of the Netherlands; but in Scotland the Reformation was able in the end to establish a limited monarchy, and the Dutch set up a republic. In France, on the other hand, the kingly power slowly increased; and when it came to a height in the absolutism of Louis XIV, the sovereign was able to stamp out the Protestant Church by bloody persecution.

'A Church under the Cross'

In Germany Luther had his prince on his side, and in Geneva Calvin was aided by the supreme civil authority. In France the Reformers had to struggle against the king's power as well as against that of the church. The Reformed Church in France was therefore entirely unaided by the civil power, and maintained a struggle as severe and testing as that which the Church of the first three centuries had to undergo. The Ante-Nicene Church had two things against it; the established religion, which was paganism, and the state, which was also pagan. The Reformed Church of France had also two things against it: it was persecuted by the established church of the country, which was Romanist; and it was persecuted by the civil authorities, for the kingly power was by the Concordat largely dependent on the recognition of the Papacy. It grew to strength slowly under a double persecution, like the early church of the martyrs and apologists. It had two emblems which it printed on its books and carved on its buildings: the bush burning and not consumed, the anvil smitten and not broken. The great

Beza once said to the King of France, 'Sire, the church of God is an anvil which has broken many a hammer.'

At first Francis did not meddle much with the Protestants in his dominions; but his defeat at Pavia in 1525, and his alliance with the Pope, made it prudent for him, he fancied, to show some desire to clear his dominions of heresy, and persecutions, eagerly urged by the Sorbonne, the Parliament of Paris, many of the bishops, the king's mother Louise, and du Pratt the chancellor of the kingdom, were permitted. It was not, however, until after Francis' second capture and imprisonment, when his wars required money and his people could scarcely raise more by taxation, that the king consented to stamp out heresy by persecution. The clergy offered him large subsidies on condition that he would help them to destroy heretics, and the king actually bought financial help by permitting the torture and slaughter of his Protestant subjects. This was in 1528.

Severe measures were directed against the Protestants. The reading of Protestant literature was forbidden; association with suspected heretics was condemned; and heretics, where discovered, were to be handed over to the civil authorities for punishment. Louis de Berguin, a scholarly noble, and once a friend of the king and a correspondent of Erasmus, was the most notable victim of these regulations.

The varying movements of kingly policy brought about a change. Francis proposed to make an alliance with the German Protestant princes, and he therefore refused to join in a general scheme for the extermination of heresy.

THE YEAR OF PLACARDS

This policy was but short-lived, and persecutions began again. The Protestants on their side did not lack courage. They printed short tracts against the Mass and other Roman Catholic rites, and dropped them silently in the streets, and on staircases in houses. The year 1535 was called the year of the placards. Some reckless partisan had fastened up one of the most severe of these attacks on the Mass within the king's apartments, and Francis' indignation knew no bounds. He at first prohibited all printing, but, recalling this decree, he seriously urged on persecution. The punishment of death for heresy was decreed. Informers against heretics were promised one-fourth of the property of the person informed against if the accusation was found to be true. This led to increased persecution, and all over France Protestants were accused, condemned, and punished by imprisonment, loss of property, and death. It was at this time that Calvin dedicated his *Institutes* to the king.

The closing years of the reign of Francis I were a time of terrible bloodshed and oppression; and yet the Protestants increased in number, and repression, however sanguinary, was proving itself a failure. The blood of the martyrs was the seed of the church. In 1540 the royal Edict of Fontainebleau enjoined upon the officers of the royal courts to institute proceedings against all persons tainted with heresy; the right of appeal was denied to those suspected: negligent judges were threatened with the king's displeasure; and ecclesiastics ordered to show greater zeal. 'Every loyal subject', the edict said, 'must denounce the heretics, and employ all means to extirpate them, just as all men are bound to run to help in extinguishing a public conflagration.' Other edicts followed, of increasing severity, and yet the Reformation spread, and men and women were content to suffer patiently for Christ's sake.

THE VAUDOIS OF THE DURANCE

The most atrocious of the many acts of persecution was the massacre of the Vaudois of the Durance. A portion of Provence skirting the Durance, where that river joined the Rhône had two centuries before been almost depopulated, and the landowners had invited peasants from the Alps to come and settle on their territories. The newcomers were Waldenses, and their industry and thrift soon made the desolate regions full of fertile farms. Their religion was guaranteed protection, for their Roman Catholic landlords had found their services valuable.

When the Reformation began in Germany and Switzerland, these Vaudois villagers sent some of their number to greet the Reformers, and in 1535 they so associated themselves with the movement that they furnished the money required to publish Robert Olivetan's translation of the Holy Scriptures into French, as corrected by Calvin. This act awakened the hostility of some of the French ecclesiastics.

The Bishop of Aix stirred up the local Parliament; arrests were made, and some of the villagers were tortured and slain. In 1540 the Parliament summoned fifteen villagers of Mérindol to appear before it as suspected heretics. The villagers having learned that their death was resolved upon, did not appear; whereupon the Parliament issued the infamous *Arrêt de Mérindol*, which in substance ordered the destruction of the whole village.

The publication of the decree provoked some remonstrance. The king heard of it, and sent an officer to investigate; on his report the king ordered the abandonment of the decree. But he was induced to recall his letters, and in the end an expedition was stealthily organized, and, during seven weeks of slaughter, amid all the accompaniments of treachery and infamous brutality, twenty-two towns and villages were utterly destroyed, 4000 men and women were slain, and 700 sent to the galleys.

Thus a generation passed away, and the Reformation in France was still struggling for existence amid persecutions more dreadful than had visited the Protestants in any other land.

HENRY II AND THE GUISES

In 1547 Francis I died, and was succeeded by his son Henry II, who carried on his father's policy of weakening the Empire in Germany and consolidating the kingly power at home. This implied occasional alliances with the German Protestant princes, and continuous persecution of French Protestants at home. His favourites at court were all enemies of the Protestant faith. The king had married the famous or infamous Catherine of Medici, the niece of Pope Clement VII; and, besides the queen, Protestantism had powerful and unscrupulous enemies in Diana of Poitiers; the Constable de Montmorency, the first minister of the crown, with a great reputation for skill in arms and government; and the Guises, a remarkable family of foreign extraction, who had risen to great power in France. Francis, Duke of Guise, had already won great renown as a general; and his brother, the Cardinal of Lorraine, who was for twenty-three years the adviser of Henry II, was one of the subtlest men in Europe. Their sister had married James V of Scotland, and their niece was Mary Stuart, Queen of Scotland, educated in France under their care, and betrothed by them to the Dauphin of France.

Francis had urged on the persecution of Protestants with such speed that the ordinary courts of justice were hindered in their work. Henry added a new department for the special duty of trying and condemning heretics, and the decrees of these new courts were so severe that they were popularly called *les chambres ardentes*. The martyrs exhibited the utmost heroism, and persecution did not affect the spread of the gospel.

Henry, it is said, once expressed a desire to see with his own eyes and interrogate one of these obstinate heretics. A poor tailor, arrested on the charge of working on a saint's day, was brought before him, and to the astonishment of the court, answered boldly and respectfully all the theological questions put to him. Diana of Poitiers undertook to silence him with raillery; but the tailor, who knew her character and position, said in solemn warning, 'Madam, let it suffice you to have infected France, without desiring to mingle your poison and your filth with so holy and sacred a thing as the true religion of our Lord Jesus Christ.' The king, enraged to hear his mistress so addressed, ordered his instant trial and execution, and resolved to see him burnt. When Henry had posted himself at a window that overlooked the scene of execution, he was seen by the martyr, who fixed his gaze on him. Even after the flames were kindled he continued to look at the king, and for days Henry said that the sight haunted his waking hours and drove sleep from his eyes at night.

It was manifest to the kingdom and even to the court, that these continued executions were not repressing the Reformation. Other martyrs cheerfully stepped forward to take the places of those who had gone before; widow ladies, young men, students, delicate girls, noblemen high in rank, all preferred, and with gladness, cruel martyrdom to denial of Christ. The court could think of nothing but severer measures of repression, and in 1551 a new edict, that of Chateaubriand, was passed, which, like the Edicts of Decius in the early centuries, tried to stamp out Christianity by destroying its literature.

Geneva stood on the borders of France. It was thronged with French refugees. Young men, full of courage and faith, instructed by Calvin and his colleagues in the truths of the gospel, volunteered to carry small books and tracts throughout France, and distribute them. The Edict of Chateaubriand was directed against these pedlars, and the tracts and books that they sold. 'It utterly prohibited the introduction of any books from Geneva and other places notoriously rebellious to the Holy See, the retention of condemned books by booksellers, and all clandestine printing. It instituted a half-yearly visitation of every printing establishment, the examination of all packages from abroad, lest they might contain books, and a special inspection thrice a year at the great fair at Lyons, through which many suspected books found their way into the kingdom. Pedlars were forbidden to sell books at all. Men found with letters from Geneva were to be arrested and punished. All unlettered persons were forbidden to discuss matters of faith at the table, at work, in the field, or in the secret conventicle.'

If edicts and officers of justice could shut out knowledge, the court determined that it should be excluded. But the sowing of the seed went on. From Geneva and from Strasbourg young men taking their lives in their hands went forth through France with tracts and books and Bibles. Beza wrote to Bullinger that it was incredible how many men volunteered to face all these perils in order to build up the church of God.

ORGANIZATION OF THE REFORMED CHURCH

In the midst of these terrible persecutions the Protestants of France began to organize themselves into a church. They had been for more than thirty years either solitary Bible students or little bands of worshippers. Their courage increased with persecution, and they resolved to become a community.

The occasion was simple enough, the birth of a child in the family of La Ferrière, a noble Frenchman, in whose house in Paris a small body of Protestants were accustomed to meet. The father told the little band of worshippers that he was unable to go beyond France to seek a pure sacrament, and that he could not consent to allow his child to be baptized according to the rites of the Roman Church. He implored them to organize themselves into a church, to choose a pastor, and so solve all difficulties.

They consented, and after fasting and prayer Jean le Maçon, surnamed La Rivière, a youth of twenty-two, who had forsaken home and wealth and brilliant prospects for Christ's sake, was chosen to be pastor. The little company then selected elders and deacons, and a church on the Geneva model was established, and a short constitution was adopted.

It seemed as if all France was only waiting for some one to lead the way. In rapid succession communities organized themselves into congregations, with elders and deacons. Three months after La Rivière's election, Paris wrote to Geneva for another minister. A month later Angers had three Protestant pastors; and although persecution went on as fiercely as before, volunteers were found for all these dangerous posts, and the Reformation went on growing.

THE HUGUENOTS: COLIGNY AND THE BROTHERS BOURBON

Finding all efforts to restrain the Reformation to be useless, the Cardinal of Lorraine proposed to establish in France an Inquisition, modelled after the Spanish type, which Philip of Spain had used with such power to stamp heresy out of his dominions. The spirit of constitutional liberty was not yet so dead in France as to permit the utter loss of all legal safeguards of innocence, which the introduction of the Spanish Inquisition involved. The various legal courts, and in particular the Parliaments, protested against the proposal. The king and his advisers forced on the measure, but found to their dismay that the only result was to make several powerful nobles declare themselves Protestants; and from henceforth (1558) a strong Huguenot party confronted the court and the Romanists.

The licentiousness of the French court had disgusted many of the leading nobles, and the profligacy of the clergy sent them to learn Christianity from men of pure life. Some of the highest aristocracy who disliked the Guises had joined the Calvinist opposition – some from policy, but many from conviction. These men formed a moral opposition to the licentiousness of the luxurious court life which Francis I had encouraged, and a political opposition to the absolutist policy of the king and his advisers. At the head of this party were the brothers Bourbon, and Admiral Coligny and his brother Francis d'Andelot.

A son of St Louis had married the heiress of Bourbon, and this family was, in the middle of the sixteenth century, represented by Anthony, Duke of Bourbon (who, failing the king and his sons, was heir to the throne of France), and his brother Louis, Duke of Condé. Anthony Bourbon had married the pious and heroic daughter of Margaret of Angoulême, Jeanne d'Albret, heiress of Navarre, and his son was Henry IV of France. In right of his wife he had become titular King of Navarre, and lived a great deal at Pau, where he attended the preaching of Protestant pastors. On his return to court he began to frequent the gatherings of the Protestants there, and avowed himself a Protestant. The Duke of Condé also declared himself. The younger brother of Admiral Coligny, d'Andelot, 'the fearless knight', as the people called him, took Protestant preachers with him to his castle in Brittany, and their addresses were listened to by large crowds. He was arrested, but was too powerful a noble to be punished.

Henry, baffled by the opposition, concluded a peace with Spain, that he might bend all his energies to the destruction of the Calvinists. Vast schemes were, it is said, prepared. Geneva and Strasbourg were to be destroyed, and heresy crushed at least in France and the Low Countries. In the midst of these preparations Henry died, killed accidentally in a tournament in June 1559.

THE FIRST NATIONAL SYNOD

It is interesting to know that at the very time when new schemes for repression were preparing, the French Protestants were taking another step which showed their growing power. They held their first National Synod with great secrecy in a house in the Faubourg St Germain in Paris. The meeting came about in this fashion: towards the close of 1558 Anthony Chandieu, a pastor in Paris, went to Poitiers to assist at the Communion there. He met, as was common on such occasions, several pastors from various parts of the country, and as they talked together about the state of the church, they lamented the lack of corporate unity in the church, and of any doctrinal standards. Chandieu was commissioned to lay the views of the brethren before the consistory of Paris. The result was, that the Paris congregation sent letters to other congregations, inviting them to send delegates to a conference in Paris. From this sprang the First National Synod. It was a small assembly, representing only eleven congregations; but it gave to the French Church a Confession of Faith and a Book of Discipline.

The Confession, known afterwards as the *Confessio Gallica*, was probably drawn up by Chandieu, and based upon a short Confession to the king composed by Calvin. It was revised more than once afterwards, but may still be called the Confession of the French Protestant Church.

The *Book of Ecclesiastical Discipline* was modelled on Calvin's *Ordinances* for Geneva, but with striking differences, and shows what Calvin's book might have been had he not been hampered by the council of Geneva. The constitution of the French Church was thoroughly democratic and representative in its character. It recognized the consistories, or kirk-sessions, that had already been appointed in each congregation, and it made them thoroughly representative by declaring that elders and deacons were to be re-elected annually. It provided courts of subordinate appeal in the provincial synods, which met twice a year, in which each congregation was to be represented by its pastor and an elder; and it united the whole church under a National Synod or General Assembly, the last court of appeal, and the ultimate ecclesiastical authority. All ministers were required to sign the Confession of Faith, and to acknowledge the *Ecclesiastical Discipline*.

It is interesting to see how in the midst of a country whose government was yearly becoming more arbitrary and absolutist, this 'Church under the Cross' organized for itself a government which reconciled more perfectly, perhaps, than has ever been done since the two principles of popular right and supreme central control. Scottish Presbyterianism borrowed its constitution much more from France than from Geneva, and the early Scottish Church organization, under Knox, was almost an exact reproduction of the French. The later departures from the French model in the election of elders and deacons for life, and the usurpation of exclusive right to send representatives to the General Assembly by the more modern court of the presbytery, has taken from modern Scottish, English, and American Presbyterianism a great deal of the free popular element which was the strength of the early Scottish and French Churches.

ANNE DE BOURG

The death of the king brought no change in the policy of the court. Francis II, a lad of sixteen, succeeded. He was married to Mary, Queen of Scotland, and niece of the Guises, and his accession threw the whole power into the hands of this powerful, fanatical, and unscrupulous party. But the Guises could not do without question what a legitimate sovereign felt to be within his power. They pressed on measures for the repression of the Protestants by extermination, and their eagerness in bloodshed in the end recoiled on themselves. Their party received a severe blow in the trial and execution of Anne de Bourg, nephew of one of the chancellors of France, and himself a judge. His crime had been that he had warned Henry II in open council that it was no small thing to condemn to death those who, in the midst of the flames, called on the name of the Saviour of men.

When brought to trial later by the Guises, he spoke with such eloquence and boldness as to gain a large amount of support among the people. When sentence of condemnation to death by burning was pronounced, he again spoke in words of such pathetic fervour and resolution that it is said he moved even his judges. 'None shall be able to separate us from Christ, whatever snares are laid for us, whatever ills our bodies may endure. We know that we have long been like lambs led to the slaughter. Let them therefore slay us, let them break us in pieces; for all that, the Lord's dead will not cease to live, and we shall rise in a common resurrection . . . And since it is so, why do I tarry? Lay hands on me, executioner, and lead me to the gallows.'

THE SLAUGHTER AT AMBOISE

The execution of de Bourg was the turning point in the history of French Protestantism. The Protestants were learning to know their strength, and from this time forward they began to take counsel together how to act on the defensive, and take advantage of the growing unpopularity of the Guises. Some of the more impetuous wished to raise the standard of revolt at once. Calvin and Beza were consulted, but dissuaded them from open insurrection. Nevertheless a conspiracy was set on foot.

De la Renaudie, a Protestant and an open enemy of the Guises, was made commander, and the civil war which afterwards arose would probably have broken out, had not the plot been betrayed. The Guises took a bloody revenge on the humbler opponents of their policy, and wholesale massacres took place, particularly at Amboise, the memory of which sank deep into the minds of the Huguenots. The Guises accused Condé at court of being the true head of the conspiracy. He demanded an assembly of all the princes and of the members of the privy council, and challenged his enemies to denounce him, and the Duke of Guise felt that he dare not make any further attack.

The slaughter at Amboise, so far from terrifying the Protestants, seemed to give them fresh courage. They began to be known now as *Huguenots*. The origin of the name is obscure; all that we do know for certain about it is that, after the conspiracy of Amboise the name was in every one's mouth. At Valence an armed company seized on the Church of the Franciscans, and Protestant preachers conducted services in the presence of large crowds. Armed companies celebrated the Lord's Supper, 'after the fashion of Geneva', at Nîmes, in Languedoc. The time for secret assemblies had gone by, and in Northern, Central, and Southern France, large open-air meetings showed that great masses of the people had embraced the Reformation.

COLIGNY AT THE ASSEMBLY OF NOTABLES

Still the court thought that the only policy was one of extermination, and there was no abatement of rigorous persecution. The court, however, needed money, for the expenses of the kingdom had been gradually growing larger than the income, and an Assembly of the Notables was convened at Fontainebleau. The Protestants took advantage of the occasion, and the Admiral Coligny, the head of the great house of Chatillon, presented two petitions to the King and to the Queen Mother from the Huguenots of Normandy. They prayed for the cessation of persecution, and for liberty to meet in public for divine worship.

This courageous act on the part of Coligny helped to give others courage. The Bishop of Valence spoke in favour of the Huguenots in his diocese, and demanded that the laws against hymn singing and the reading of Scripture should be revoked, and that a general council should be called. The Archbishop of Vienne made a more daring speech. He asked 'if France was to die in order to please his Holiness the Pope'. The court was obliged to permit the assembling of the States-General.

The Guises did not lose courage. They resolved to crush the Protestants by destroying their leaders, and it appears that they had devised a general massacre of the Huguenots. They caused the King to summon the Bourbons to court, and, heedless of danger, the King of Navarre and his brother Louis, Duke of Condé, went. The younger brother was arrested and condemned to death, and the King of Navarre narrowly escaped assassination. Just as the storm was about to burst, the king fell ill and died.

'Did you ever read or hear', says Calvin in a letter to Sturm, 'of anything more opportune than the death of the king? The evils had reached an extremity for which there was no remedy, when suddenly God shows himself from heaven. He who pierced the eye of the father has now stricken the ear of the son.'

CATHERINE OF MEDICI

The death of Francis left Charles IX, a boy of ten years of age, heir to the throne. The lawful regent was Anthony Bourbon, King of Navarre, and a Protestant. The young king's mother, Catherine of Medici, neglected during her husband's lifetime, overshadowed by the Guises during the reign of her eldest son, now came to the front claiming to rule as her son's natural guardian. The King of Navarre was urged by his friends to assert his rights. Had he done so, France might have had a more peaceful future. Religious toleration might have been secured, and the basis of constitutional monarchy might have been laid; but he weakly resigned his rights, and Catherine seized the power.

The necessities of her position, however, compelled her to make concessions to all parties. She could not afford to lose the support of the Guises, and she was compelled to come to terms with the Huguenots. An edict was passed by which all imprisoned heretics were released, but warned to mend their ways. Meanwhile the States-General, summoned before the death of the late king, met.

Coligny, on behalf of the Huguenots, demanded freedom of religion; a reform in the government of the church, and, in particular, the free election of bishops and clergy; a national council, under the presidency of the king, to discuss the affairs of religion, and, meanwhile, churches for the Protestants; and an assembly of the Notables every two years. He also offered to help the government to pass a law whereby church property could be sold to meet the expenses of the state.

The demands of Coligny, Ranke says, were the programme of the French Revolution of the eighteenth century; and if he could have carried them, that Revolution might have been accomplished without the atheism which disgraced it, and without the destruction of the monarchy and of the aristocracy. The court was not prepared for such sweeping changes, and the utmost that Catherine would consent to was a religious conference at Poissy, where matters of faith could be discussed between Protestant pastors and the Roman Catholic clergy.

The Huguenots had gained toleration, and refugees came trooping back from England, Germany, the Low Countries, and even from Italy. Preachers poured into France from Geneva, and the Protestant congregations found well-instructed pastors able to lead them. It was impossible, however, to change all things by a political compromise. The Guises threatened vengeance. The aged Constable de Montmorency, who thought himself the champion of the old faith, resolved to stem the tide of conciliation, and fanatical mobs rose against the Protestant assemblies. In those parts of the country where the Huguenots were in the majority, it was difficult to restrain them from asserting their principles in open and forcible fashion.

In some towns crowds rushed to the churches, pulled down the images and pictures, and burnt the relics. The Huguenot leaders strove to restrain their followers. Calvin wrote energetically from Geneva against all lawlessness. 'God has never enjoined on any one to destroy idols, save on every man in his own house, or in public on those placed in authority . . . Obedience is better than sacrifice, and we must look to what it is lawful for us to do, and must keep ourselves within bounds.'

THE CONFERENCE AT POISSY

The time appointed for the conference rapidly approached, and everywhere invitation was made to all Frenchmen who had any correction of religious affairs to propose to appear with perfect safety, and to be heard at the approaching assembly at Poissy. The Huguenots were anxious to secure the presence of Beza, and sent urgent messages to him to come and represent them. He was at first unwilling to go, as he did not think any good could come of it. At last he consented, and the Huguenots felt that their interests were safe in his hands.

A Frenchman by birth, born in 1519 at Vezelay, of noble birth, he had given up the most brilliant prospects when he threw in his lot with the Reformation. He was a man of stately presence, great learning, and fascinating manners. Next to Calvin he was the most trusted guide of the Reformed Churches, and the most fitting representative of

French Protestants. He was received by the King of Navarre, and by his brother Louis of Condé, and introduced by them to the Queen Mother and to the Cardinal of Lorraine. His behaviour, readiness, learning, and stately courtesy made a great impression on the court.

When the public discussion took place, the ignorance of the French bishops became painfully manifest, and the Cardinal of Lorraine and others did their best to close the conference, and failing that, to make it a failure. The result of the discussion and deliberation was that delegates from both sides were appointed to meet and confer, and out of these conferences came an Edict of Toleration, published in January 1562.

The Protestants were to give up their churches and secret assemblies, but were allowed to worship openly and by day outside of the towns; and all their pastors were to take an oath, declaring that they would teach only according to Scripture and to the Creed of Nicea. The toleration secured was very limited; but all legal ground of persecution was removed, and Calvin and Beza both thought that although the terms of the compromise were hard, yet they should be accepted. 'If the liberty promised us in the edict lasts', Calvin wrote, 'the Papacy will fall to the ground of itself.'

The Roman Catholics were by no means disposed to come to any terms with the Protestants. The civil authorities in towns and provinces belonged to the state religion, and the parliaments, or permanent courts of justice, were bigoted against Protestantism. It was felt, besides, that the Edict of Toleration was only a ruse of Catherine's to gain time. It was known that the Guises were determinedly opposed to any compromise. Both parties prepared for civil war.

THE MASSACRE AT VASSY, AND OTHERS

The signal was given by the Duke of Guise, who, in the most contemptuous way, violated the Edict of Toleration. On Sunday morning, 1 March 1562, at the head of a band of armed horsemen, he entered the town of Vassy, where a small unarmed congregation of Protestants were worshipping in a barn. In the end a disturbance arose, and the defenceless congregation were almost all massacred. This was the beginning of those frightful civil wars which devastated France until the accession of Henry IV.

The example of massacre given at Vassy was followed in many other districts where the Roman Catholics were in a majority. At Paris, Sens, Rouen, and elsewhere, the Protestant places of worship were attacked, and the worshippers massacred. At Toulouse the Protestants, fearing massacre, shut themselves up in the Capitol; they were attacked by the Roman Catholics, and, after siege, surrendered on the promise that they should be allowed to leave the town in safety. When they came out, they were massacred – men, women, and children, more than 3000 in all. This slaughter of Protestants, under a violation of oath, was celebrated by the Roman Catholics of Toulouse in centenary festivals, held in 1662, in 1762, and would have been celebrated in 1862 had it not been forbidden by the government of Napoleon III.

These bloody massacres provoked reprisals. The Huguenots rushed to the papist churches, and destroyed the images, altars, and relics. Image breaking and bloodshed faced each other in most of the provinces of France.

CIVIL WAR – ICONOCLASM

Out of all these the two parties gradually gathered themselves into two hostile armies, with Francis, Duke of Guise, at the head of the Papists, and Louis, Duke of Condé, with Admiral Coligny, at the head of the Protestants. France was given over to all the horrors of a civil strife, where religious fanaticism added the most atrocious cruelties to the ordinary barbarities of war.

The Venetian ambassador, writing home to the chiefs of his state, was of opinion that this first religious war prevented France from becoming Protestant. The cruelties of the Papists had disgusted a large body of French citizens, who, without any very strong religious feelings, would have gladly allied themselves with the side which, by its moderation, proved itself able to begin and carry out a policy of toleration.

The Huguenot chiefs were anxious to show that their followers could restrain themselves from excesses, and Calvin and Beza wrote urging non-interference with the worship of the Roman Catholics, except in calm judicial fashion. But the Protestants could not be restrained from tearing down the images and destroying the relics in the churches of the Papists.

At Orleans an attack was made on some of the churches. Condé, with Coligny and other leaders, hastened to the Church of the Holy Cross, where the principal tumult was. When they reached the church, Condé saw a Huguenot soldier, who had climbed high on the wall, about to cast down the image of a saint. The Duke seized an harquebus,[1] pointed it at the man, and ordered him to desist and come down. The soldier did not stop for an instant. 'Sir', he said, 'have patience with me until I shall have overthrown this idol, and then let me die if that be your pleasure.' When men were content to die rather than cease image-breaking, the leaders felt that it was vain to expect to check the iconoclasm; and all over France, wherever the Protestant troops went, the churches were dismantled and the relics destroyed. This iconoclasm was everywhere in France taken to mean that the Protestants, if they gained the upper hand, would be as intolerant as the Papists had been, and the rising tide of sympathy for their cause was checked.

The progress of the war was, upon the whole, unfavourable to the Huguenots. Francis, Duke of Guise, was an admirable general, the Papists were well provided with money and with outside help; while the Huguenots had to depend almost exclusively on their own resources, and were scantily provided with funds for prosecuting the war. The Huguenots lost the battle of Dreux (December 1562), mainly owing to the admirable discipline of Guise's Swiss auxiliaries; but, on the other hand, the Papists lost the Duke of Guise, who was assassinated in February 1563.

The death of the Duke gave Catherine more power, and made peace easier. The Huguenots had not been able to overcome the Papists; and as little had the Papists been able to exterminate the Protestants. They were not reconciled, but exhausted; and a truce was agreed upon. The edict of peace secured to the Protestants the privileges granted a year before, and added others, the most important being that, 'In every bailiwick the Protestants on petition shall receive one city in whose suburbs their religious services may be held; and in all cities where the Protestant religion was exercised on the 7th of March of the present year, it should continue in one or two places *inside* the walls to be

---

[1] Harquebus: an old fashioned hand-gun.

designated hereafter by the king, Paris being excluded.' This Edict of Amboise (12 March 1563) was a half-measure irritating to both parties. The Roman Catholics disliked it because it tolerated the Reformed religion, the Protestants because it did not secure as much as they wished. It was the work of Catherine and Condé, both of whom trusted to the future to render the concessions each had made harmless to themselves.

The truce lasted nearly five years, when the second religious war broke out. The opponents fought for more than a year. The only decisive action was the battle of St Denis, at which Montmorency was slain. Then followed the truce of Longjumeaux, whose conditions were the same as those of the Edict of 1562.

This truce lasted only for a few months, when the third religious war began. The Protestants were afraid of the Duke of Alva, Philip II's savage governor in the Netherlands, who was about to aid the French court to exterminate all who refused to submit to the Roman Catholic Church, and they determined to be first in the field. Condé and Coligny had found out that Alva had advised the queen to slay the Huguenot leaders, and then fall on the multitude, and finally suppress the obnoxious faith.

The leaders escaped to La Rochelle, and the war began. The fighting went on through the year 1569 with varying diplomatic and military success. At length came the battle of Jarnac, where the Huguenots were routed, and Condé, with several others, were slain in cold blood on the field. The fortunes of the Huguenots seemed at their lowest ebb. The hereditary leaders of the party were Henry of Navarre, a boy of fifteen, and his cousin Henry of Condé, not much older, and the whole responsibility devolved on Gaspar Coligny. He gathered together the scattered forces, and, notwithstanding some defeats, was able to treat for and obtain better terms of peace than the Huguenots had yet secured. The right of public worship was guaranteed in a large number of towns, and four cities – La Rochelle, Montauban, Cognac, and La Charité – were given to the Protestants as places of refuge.

COLIGNY AND CHARLES IX

The Admiral Coligny was, after this peace, the most trusted leader of the Huguenots. He remained in La Rochelle, in the midst of his co-religionists, and acted as guardian of the two young princes, who were the hopes of the Protestants, Henry of Navarre and Henry of Condé. His main object was to secure to the Reformed the advantages which they had won in the terrible religious wars. He was invited to come to the court, and in spite of warnings he went. 'Better', he said, 'to die a thousand deaths, than by undue solicitude for life to be the occasion of keeping up distrust throughout an entire kingdom.'

Somehow or other, the foolish, weak, and dissolute Charles IX took to the old nobleman. The poor king – he was now twenty years old – had never known such a man. He had been sickly from childhood, surrounded by people whose interest it was to make him dissolute and weak. When he met Coligny, a man who instinctively inspired reverence, saying and doing nothing that was not the result of his convictions, the most famous man in France, the organizer of the Protestant party, and almost worshipped by his friends, commanding the respect due to age, and still in the vigour of life, he could not help trusting him as he had trusted no other.

Catherine, Henry of Anjou her son, and the Guises felt that a new influence was surrounding the king, which they must do their utmost to avert. They were afraid that the king, with an honest man to stand by him, would slip beyond their grasp; and this fluttering fondness of the poor helpless king for Coligny, some historians think, was the cause of the massacre of St Bartholomew.

The queen and Henry of Guise plotted to murder Coligny. The attempt failed. Catherine then went to Charles and told her son that Coligny and all the Huguenots believed that he, the king, had been concerned in the attempt at assassination, and that he would never have peace until the Protestants were exterminated. She then proposed a massacre of the leaders, and forced the king to consent to it.

THE MASSACRE OF ST BARTHOLOMEW

This terrible slaughter of Protestants, which took place on the eve of St Bartholomew (24 August) 1572, was the work of Catherine of Medici, Henry of Anjou, and the Guises. The massacre in Paris was done by 20,000 of the city militia, assisted by some of the soldiers and by the Swiss mercenaries in the pay of the Duke of Guise. The brothers Guise commanded the troops employed.

They first slew Coligny and some of the more prominent leaders, and then the massacre became general. The houses of the Protestants had been previously marked with white crosses, and the murderers wore white scarves and other tokens for mutual recognition. At least 2000 men were slain in Paris alone, of whom half were men of rank. The Protestant historian Crespin says that 10,000 were slain in Paris; and Brantôme, a sceptic and a dissolute man of the world, gives 4000 as the number. Massacres were organized throughout the provinces, and the numbers slain have been variously reckoned at from 30,000 to 100,000. Sully, the prime minister of Henry IV, who had probably very good means of knowing, says that 70,000 fell.

Of late years Roman Catholic writers have not been very proud of this deed, but when the massacre took place many of them were exultant. It is well known that if the deed itself was not instigated at Rome, the Pope and the curia knew about it some days before it took place. Rome was illuminated in honour of the event, the cannons of St Angelo were fired, a procession was made to the Church of St Mark, and a medal was struck to commemorate the *Hugonotorum Strages*. Some of the Roman Catholic princes sent congratulatory messages, and that poor, cankered soul, Philip II of Spain, is said to have smiled for the first and last time in his life when the news reached him.

The massacre had cruelly weakened the power of the Huguenots, and had deprived them of almost all their leaders; but they still existed, and instead of being cowed and broken by the bloody deed, their hearts were steeled to avenge it. A few cities still remained in Protestant hands; La Rochelle, Sancerre, Nîmes, Montauban, and other towns closed their gates, and refused to admit the governors sent from Paris.

La Rochelle was attacked by the royal armies commanded by Henry of Anjou, and the citizens endured all the miseries of a siege, and in the end forced the troops to retire. A like successful resistance on the part of other towns at last forced the court again to come to terms with its hated Protestant subjects, and a peace was agreed upon.

This time the Huguenots felt that they must always be prepared for war. The horrors of St Bartholomew's Eve had told them how merciless their enemies were, and the siege, capitulation, and treachery at Sancerre showed them their utter faithlessness. The Protestants had endured a siege for eight months, during which time at least five hundred men and all the children under twelve had died of hunger. 'Why weep', said a boy of ten, 'to see me die of hunger? I do not ask bread, mother; I know you have none. But since God wills that I die thus, we must accept it cheerfully. Was not that holy man Lazarus hungry? Have I not so read the Bible?' When terms of surrender were arranged, in defiance of oaths, murder and rapine took place.

The Huguenots, without leaders, resolved so to organize themselves that they might be always ready, and in a short period had so perfected their plans that they could readily place 20,000 men in the field at the first call to arms. They met at Montauban to organize, and also prepared a petition to the king, in which they made the old demands for toleration and good government that Coligny had urged in the States-General at the beginning of the religious wars. The court learned that the Huguenot spirit was not dead. Since the Massacre of St Bartholomew another party was slowly rising to importance in France. This was the moderate Roman Catholics or 'Politicians', who were weary of massacre, and who imputed all the evils of the state to the power of foreigners in the realm. They demanded the expulsion of Florentines and Lorrainers, *i.e.* of the Queen Mother and of the Guises; and they urged the restoration of the ancient liberties of the kingdom. These 'Politicians' were strengthened in their opinions by a treacherous attack upon La Rochelle, and by the political programme which the Huguenots put forth at Millau, and they patiently bided their time.

Although the siege of La Rochelle and other Protestant towns, the fourth religious war, as it was called, had been followed by a peace, desultory fighting had gone on since, and the rejection of the Huguenot petition made it evident that another war was imminent. Meanwhile, Charles IX. died, in May 1574, conscience-stricken, of a terrible disease, which caused blood to exude from all the pores of his body, and the people saw in it a punishment for the Massacre of St Bartholomew. He was succeeded by Henry of Anjou, the third and the vilest of the sons of Catherine, and her favourite. He combined the characters of a superstitious Papist and a shameless profligate.

Henry III had, during his brother's lifetime, consorted with the Guises, and had adhered to the strict Papist party; but shortly after his accession, dismayed by the prospect of an alliance between the 'Politicians' and the Huguenots, he issued an edict in which he granted a number of the Protestant demands. He granted unlimited religious liberty, save in Paris, equal social privileges, right of trial before a tribunal composed of an equal number of Romanists and Protestants, and eight fortresses to be held in pledge by the Huguenots.

THE HOLY LEAGUE

This act on the king's part led to the formation of the Holy League, as it was called, a society formed by the Guises and the Jesuits, to unite the French Roman Catholics in political alliance with Philip II of Spain and the Pope. Its immediate objects were to govern France in the interests of the Roman Catholic faith, to come to no terms with the Huguenots, and to overawe the king; its ulterior aim was to destroy the Bourbons, or at least to keep Henry of Navarre from succeeding to the throne.

This led to what were called the Wars of the League, whose varying fortunes need not be followed. The fifth, sixth, and seventh civil wars all ended in treaties of peace favourable to the Protestants.

In the year 1585 the League was remodelled, and the power of the Guises consolidated. The eighth civil war closed in July with the Treaty of Nemours, which was more hostile to the Protestants. The ninth civil war soon followed. It was called the War of the Three Henrys – Henry III, Henry of Guise, and Henry of Navarre, who had become, young as he was, the trusted leader of the Huguenots. It ended in the battle of Coultras, in which the Huguenots were victorious.

The fighting was interrupted by quarrels between the king and the Duke of Guise, the head of the League. The king found his authority fast lessening. The States-General, which met at Blois in October 1588, showed him that the duke was the ruler of France; the insurrection in Paris some weeks earlier taught him how deeply the ramifications of the League had gone. He found the thraldom insupportable, and resolved to get rid of the League by slaying its chiefs. Henry, Duke of Guise, and Charles the Cardinal, were murdered in December 1588, along with many of their friends; but the League was not destroyed. It had established all over France clubs or societies similar to the Jacobin clubs of the Revolution period; and when the Guises were murdered, the mother-club of Paris, the League of the Sixteen, as it was called, seized the government, put its followers into all the positions of trust,

and tried the king by Parliament. Henry III, in abject terror, fled to
the Huguenot army and surrendered to his great rival Henry of Navarre.
A fanatic of the League followed him, a Dominican monk, Jacques
Clement, and contrived to stab him. A few hours afterwards Henry
III died, and the Huguenot general was the legitimate heir to the throne
of France.

HENRY OF NAVARRE

At first he was only recognized by the Protestant part of France. The
League was powerful and resolute to exclude a Huguenot from the
throne. Even the moderate Roman Catholics could with difficulty
admit that a king professing the religion of the minority could reign
over all France. The Pope refused to recognise a Protestant Sovereign,
and Philip II of Spain threatened to pour his troops into the kingdom.
In these circumstances Henry of Navarre intimated his willingness to
be instructed in the doctrines of the Roman Catholic faith. This
brought to his side many of the moderate Romanists, and the king
was able to defeat the League in the battles of Arques and Ivry.

The League was still too powerful for him, and had various projects
to make Charles of Guise, Duke of Mayenne, king; to raise Charles,
Cardinal Bourbon, Henry's uncle, to the throne (he was actually
proclaimed king as Charles X); and to offer the kingdom to Philip II
of Spain, who had married a Valois.

In face of all these complications, Henry took a step which his heroic
mother would never have taken. He became a Roman Catholic. The
effect was that, in a marvellously short time, the League was broken
up, and Henry IV was acknowledged king by almost all France. His
old companions in arms and in faith, although they mourned his
apostasy, did not desert the young man who had from boyhood been
their associate and leader, and who, after the frightful Bartholomew
days, had escaped from court as soon as he could to fight in their midst.
He in return obtained for them what they had been struggling for
during thirty years of civil war.

THE EDICT OF NANTES

In 1598 the famous Edict of Nantes was signed, which went further in
the path of religious toleration than any other edict of the sixteenth

century. Its great fault was, that the circumstances of France made it impossible to guarantee religious liberty without granting to the Protestants political privileges which made them a separate state within the state, and thus in time prevented the complete fusion of the two parties into one government.

This edict granted complete liberty of conscience; henceforth no one was to be persecuted for his religious opinions. All nobles possessing what was called 'superior jurisdiction' were allowed to teach Calvinism, and any one might share their teaching. Nobles not possessing this jurisdiction had the same privilege, and might admit any number of others to their services, unless they lived in places where Roman Catholics possessed the 'superior jurisdiction'. Public worship, after the fashion 'so-called Reformed', was allowed to be continued or restored in all towns where it had been held up to August 1597. Where Protestants were scattered over a country district, a place was appointed in a suburb or village where service might be held. Public worship was forbidden to Protestants in Paris, or within five miles of it, and in the following fanatically Roman Catholic towns: Rheims, Toulouse, Dijon, and Lyons. Elsewhere the Protestants could possess churches, church bells, schools, etc. The chief limitations of religious liberty were, that the Romanist religion was declared the established religion, Protestants had to pay tithes to the established clergy, to refrain from work on festival days, and to conform to the marriage laws of the Romanist Church.

The Protestants, it was also declared, had the same civil obligations and privileges as the Roman Catholics, and had equal claims to all offices and dignities of state. Special courts of justice were established, at which Protestants could be tried. They were also to retain for eight years all the fortresses which had belonged to them before 1597, with all their military stores; and in these towns the governors were appointed by the Huguenots.

4

THE REFORMATION IN THE NETHERLANDS

THE NETHERLANDS

*T*he revolt of the Netherlands from Rome was perhaps the latest, if it is dated from the final triumph, but the land had the honour of furnishing the earliest martyrs to the Protestant faith.

The country of the Netherlands, or Low Countries, lay around the mouths of the Scheldt and Rhine, and in mediæval times was the northern part of the old realm of Lotharingia or Lorraine, the famous middle-kingdom, as it was called. Its situation, with a large extent of sea-coast, and the great rivers which went through it, made it naturally a land of commerce. The sea was continually encroaching, and had to be kept out; the riverbeds silted up, and had to be kept from overflowing their banks and submerging the country.

The perpetual struggle with nature which these dangers forced on the people made them hardy and self-reliant. The land was full of large towns, inhabited by a free and wealthy people. Free burgher life began earlier in the Netherlands than in most of the countries in Europe. Civic liberty was known and valued. In some places the rulers were princes or prince-bishops; in others, a burgher council ruled the district, and, as at Utrecht, considered the bishop of the province their subject.

Other influences helped to preserve the spirit of liberty. The southern portion of the Netherlands had been the land of the Trouvères, and their influence remained strong enough to keep alive an anti-clerical spirit among the people. The Romish clergy never had much power in the larger towns, and even in the country districts they had never been able to put down the 'Chambers of Orators', as they were called, which sometimes, under the guise of archery clubs or singing associations, were really gatherings for the purpose of cultivating the dramatic talents of their members, either in acting the common mediæval miracle plays, or more frequently in composing and declaiming popular satirical and comic verses, in which the vices of churchmen were unsparingly attacked.

The Low Countries, too, had been the scene of the labours of Gerard Groot, the mediæval founder of ragged schools and orphan houses; and his followers, the Brethren of the Common Life, had diffused their feelings of mystical contempt for a mechanical and political Church, and their eagerness for education and heart religion all over the surrounding lands. Thomas à Kempis, John Wessel, John Goch, and other reformers before the Reformation, all belonged to the Netherlands.

THE POLICY OF CHARLES V

In the fifteenth century most of these free states and wealthy towns had come under the sway of the Dukes of Burgundy, who were vassals both of the French crown and of the Empire. It does not concern us to relate how eagerly Philip the Good and his son Charles the Bold strove to make their duchy a kingdom, and how the fierce temper of Charles caused the failure of their policy. The lands saved from the clutches of France were brought by Mary of Burgundy, the daughter of Charles, as a dowry to her Austrian husband, Maximilian, who was the grandfather of Charles V, the Emperor during the earlier Reformation times.

Charles V, who was Count of Holland and Stadtholder of the Netherlands, as well as King of Spain and Emperor of Germany, had been born and educated in the Low Countries, and looked on these provinces as his peculiar possessions. The lifelong policy of the Emperor was to destroy, as far as possible, provincial privileges and civic freedom, and in the Netherlands he did all in his power to centralize the government and remove the old constitutional privileges. The people disliked these measures, but attributed them to Spanish counsels.

THE BEGINNINGS OF THE REFORMATION

When the Reformation began in Germany, and the famous Edict of Worms had been published, putting Luther, his sympathizers, and his writings under the ban of the Empire, Charles issued a decree in the Netherlands containing very similar enactments. The edict was ineffectual in Germany, but Charles was able to enforce obedience in the Low Countries. In 1523 two Augustinian monks, Heinrich Voes and Johann Esch, were seized by the authorities, and, after examination, were burnt at Brussels, being the first martyrs of the Reformation. Luther composed a hymn in their honour, which he entitled, 'A Song of the Two Martyrs of Christ at Brussels, burnt by the Sophists of Louvain'. Religious meetings were forbidden, and the introduction of Luther's writings was prohibited.

In spite of these restrictions, Luther's New Testament was translated into Dutch, and printed at Amsterdam in 1523, and the doctrines of the Reformation became widely known.

The regents who governed the seventeen provinces in the name of Charles, did not make full use of the severe edicts entrusted to them. Margaret of Savoy, Charles' aunt, was inclined to toleration in matters of religion; and Mary of Hungary, Charles' sister, was, it was said, secretly attached to the Reformation. In these circumstances the movement spread rapidly among a people accustomed to read, think, and judge for themselves; for, says an historian, 'even in the Frisian fishermen's huts you might find people who could not only read and write, but discuss scriptural interpretations as if they were scholars'.

The movement received a severe check from an outbreak of Anabaptist fanaticism in 1534. In Leiden the fanatics tried to seize and burn the town. In Amsterdam they ran through the streets uttering mad predictions. In Friesland they seized and occupied a convent, and fought fiercely with the soldiers sent to expel them. The government put them down with relentless severity. They were hunted out, tortured, and slain, until it is said almost thirty thousand had perished, among whom were many quiet Protestants who had no sympathy with Anabaptist zeal. The Reformation, in spite of this check, went on spreading in the Netherlands, until, in 1555, Charles V abdicated in favour of Philip II, his son, and from this event dates the struggle in the Low Countries for political and religious liberty.

PHILIP II AND THE NETHERLANDS

Charles had felt that the Reformation had overthrown his plans and beaten him; his son Philip resolved to pursue his father's policy with even more rigour and severity. 'He undertook to enforce, without limit and unconditionally, the temporal and spiritual despotism at which the restored Papal power was aiming.' It is evident now that the task of Philip was from the beginning hopeless; but the question whether he would or would not succeed kept Europe in anxious suspense for nearly half a century. In the end he failed everywhere but in Spain, and his success in his own land ruined it. The interest which centres round the struggle in the Netherlands comes from the fact that it was the first revolt against the policy of Philip, and in the end so exhausted the power of Spain as to win the safety of Europe.

On his accession to the hereditary dominions of his father, Philip was in the Netherlands. He had observed with distrust the progress of the Reformed religion there. Spain was safe, religious and civil liberty were thoroughly extinguished there; so he could afford to remain in the Netherlands and personally superintend the beginning of the work of repression. He found that the whole Bible had been translated into Dutch (in 1542, by Jacob Liesfeld); that many of the nobles were related to and in constant communication with the Lutheran princes of Germany; and that the Protestants of the Netherlands were in constant communication with the French Huguenots. His measures for the extirpation of heresy were carefully elaborated and then patiently applied. He relied on the presence of Spanish soldiers, a stadtholder devoted to himself and willing to execute his wishes in the minutest details, the establishment of the Spanish Inquisition, and a remodelling of the episcopate of the provinces.

The territories of Spain, including the land south of the Pyrenees and the Low Countries, fronted France on the north as well as on the south, and in war with France Spanish troops had been quartered in the seventeen provinces for the purpose of meeting the French armies on that frontier. Philip determined to retain these troops and use them to enforce his designs. This retention of foreign troops on their soil without their consent was a violation of one of the most cherished privileges of the provinces; the country, besides, was recovering from a severe famine; and the brutality of the soldiers still further exasperated the people, the inhabitants of Zeeland declaring in a remonstrance that they would rather be drowned in the waves than any longer submit to the outrages of the soldiery.

Philip could not always remain in the Netherlands, his presence was required in Spain, and before leaving he had to nominate a stadtholder who should act as regent and govern in his name. The provinces desired to see one of their own nobles in this office, and the names of two members of the aristocracy, who were also princes of the German Empire, William of Orange and Count Egmont, were frequently brought under the notice of the king. Both men had been attached to Charles V and had shown their devotion, and were well fitted for the office. Philip selected instead his half-sister Margaret of Parma, who was entirely dependent on him, who was a stranger to the country, who did not know its language, and who, he supposed, would obey him implicitly. He gave her as her chief adviser Antony Perrenot, best known as Cardinal Granvella, a creature of his, and one or two others on whom he could depend to execute without hesitation any orders he might send.

THE INQUISITION

The most formidable organ of repression, however, was the Inquisition. This terrible institution differed entirely from the organization which went by the same name before the Reformation. The earlier Inquisition, established to quell the Albigenses of the south of France, had inflicted a great deal of suffering on the mediæval recusants; but the functions were usually entrusted to the Dominicans and Franciscans, and mutual jealousies, combined with the fact that these two great orders had been the fruitful home of mediæval heresy, prevented it from being the thoroughgoing instrument of repression that the post-Reformation Popes, the Jesuits, and such monarchs as Philip II required. Accordingly it was remodelled in Rome under the superintendence of Cardinal Caraffa, afterwards Paul IV, detached from the monastic orders, and re-established on an independent basis.

It was designed, according to the Bull of foundation, to extirpate heresy first in Italy, and then in the world in general; and four rules of action were laid down. In matters of faith there was not to be a moment's delay, the Inquisition was to act with the greatest rigour on the slightest suspicion; no respect was to be given towards princes or prelates, however high their rank might be; special strictness was to be shown towards those who screened themselves under the protection of a ruler; and no false toleration was to be shown towards any heresy, and especially towards Calvinism.

Cardinal Caraffa's policy was to ally the Inquisition with the State, asking the civil power to lend all its aid to carry out the orders of the Church, and in return branding as heresy any action or speech which a despotic state deemed hostile to itself. The Inquisition thus became a terrible engine in the hands of a despotic state, and in fact thoroughly strangled all civil and religious liberty where its presence was long endured. Italy and Spain have not yet recovered from the wounds it inflicted.

Charles V had established the Inquisition in the Netherlands as well as in Spain, and, in accordance with its mandate, had published several ferocious edicts, which, in spite of the passive opposition of his regents, were largely enforced. The printing, multiplying, concealing, buying, selling, or giving away any book of Luther, Œcolampadius, Zwingli, Bucer, or Calvin, or any other heretic was forbidden. It was also forbidden to injure in any way the image of any canonized saint, to attend heretical meetings, to read the Scriptures, or engage in religious discussion or controversy. Those who transgressed were, if they recanted, to be put to death by the sword or by burying alive; if they refused to recant, by burning, and their property was to be confiscated.

Informers received a large proportion of the property of heretics convicted on their information. Suspected heretics were required to abjure and, if they came again under suspicion, were to be treated as if convicted. Every year during the reign of Charles a number of executions had taken place, and yet the Reformation had spread. Ten thousand fugitives were living abroad, driven away by the Inquisition, as early as 1550. Philip, who saw and knew all this, only thought that the terrorism had not been great enough; he increased the powers of the Inquisition, and ordered the regent and her council to give the officials every aid.

The New Bishoprics

In the beginning of the sixteenth century four bishoprics Arras, Cambrai, Tournai, and Utrecht, existed in the Netherlands. Philip proposed, in a single stroke, to add fourteen. Cardinal Caraffa, by that time Pope Paul IV, eagerly seconded his plans, on the grounds that heresy was rampant in the Netherlands, that the harvest was plenteous and the labourers few. The clergy of the Netherlands protested against the proposal; the people were indignant, and pointed to their charters, which expressly required the consent of the states to every increase of the clergy. Opposition was in vain. The country, in 1560, was divided into fifteen bishoprics, under three archbishops, of whom the Archbishop of Mechlin was the chief; and Philip secured a large number of willing instruments of repression, as well as of tribunals to try and punish suspected heretics.

Is the Country to Become Spanish?

Meanwhile the country was becoming alarmed. These changes appeared to most of the Netherlanders signs of an intention to reduce the Low Countries to the condition of Spain. The Reformation and patriotism became identified, and the national cause and evangelical religion went on hand in hand.

This gave a great impetus to the Protestant movement. It became the popular cause. Crowds interfered with the ecclesiastical punishments, rescued the victims condemned to death by the Inquisition, made tumults at the Mass, and in some cases attacked the churches and tore down the images.

The nobles became alarmed, and met together to remonstrate. The object of their wrath was Granvella, who was made responsible for every objectionable measure. Philip, pretending to listen to the nobles, removed Granvella; but the old system of terrorism went on, and the nobles found that the king, with his usual duplicity, was making them responsible for the tyranny they had protested against.

The proclamation of the decrees of the Council of Trent roused new resistance. The Prince of Orange spoke against the proposal strongly and courageously; the nobles met together, and it was resolved to send Count Egmont on a special mission to inform the king of the feelings of the people of the provinces; for it was still believed that Philip was ignorant of matters on which he was only too well instructed.

Egmont was a zealous Romanist, and had proved himself a loyal subject to the Spanish monarch. If any man could succeed with Philip, Egmont could, it was thought. He got to Madrid in 1565, was received with apparent cordiality, and dismissed with assurances that the representations of the nobles would be attended to.

As usual, Philip II had no intention of fulfilling his promises. He sent orders to proclaim the Decrees of Trent, the persecuting edicts, and the bloody mandates of the Inquisition, in every town and city in the Low Countries every six months. Historians tell us that the effect of this was almost indescribable; trade ceased, manufactures died out, the country seemed blighted.

Pamphlets containing passionate appeals to the people to put an end to the tyranny were distributed and eagerly read. One of these, which took the form of a public letter to the king, said: 'We are ready to die for the gospel, but we read therein, "Render unto Caesar the things which are Caesar's, and unto God the things that are God's." We thank God that even our enemies are constrained to bear witness to our piety and innocence, for it is a common saying, "He does not swear, for he is a Protestant", "He is not an immoral man nor a drunkard, for he belongs to the new sect"; and yet we are subjected to every kind of punishment that can be invented to torment us.'

The Beggars

The more daring spirits among the younger nobles and burghers resolved to unite to resist the tyranny. The natural leaders, the Prince of Orange and Counts Egmont and Horn, kept aloof, for they thought the enterprise foolhardy. The confederates resolved to begin by a solemn procession to the regent to petition her to abolish the Inquisition, and recall some of the edicts. They met the Duchess on 5 April 1566, and read the prepared address; and the regent, troubled at such an imposing array, consulted anxiously how to answer. Barlaymont, one of her advisers, and a creature of Philip, thought that 'this troop of Beggars' should be driven out of the palace by force. The Duchess dismissed them courteously, but the words of Barlaymont had been reported. Three hundred of the petitioners met at a banquet to deliberate, when one of them, Count Brederode, rose and said: 'They call us Beggars. We accept the name. We pledge ourselves to resist the Inquisition, and keep true to the King and the Beggar's Wallet.' He then strapped round his shoulder the leathern sack of the wandering beggar, and drank prosperity to the cause from a wooden cup.

FIELD-PREACHINGS

The name of Beggars (*Gueux*) was adopted with great enthusiasm, and the badge became almost universally adopted. Everywhere burghers, lawyers, peasants, and nobles could be seen wearing the leathern wallet of the wandering beggar. The people began to feel their power. All at once large conventicles or field-preachings were held all over the country. The people came armed, planted sentinels, the women and children inside, and the armed men on the outside of the crowd, and listened to the preaching of excommunicated ministers. They read the Scriptures, sang hymns, and listened to prayers in their own tongue. The crowds were so large, and the people so watchful and well armed, that the soldiers dared not attack them. The regent felt that unless additional Spanish soldiers were sent, she could not suppress the popular excitement.

The people, encouraged by the immunity of the field-preaching, began attacking Roman Catholic places of worship. When the priests passed through the streets of Antwerp carrying in procession the miraculous image of the Virgin the people jeered – 'Mayken! Mayken! [little Mary] your hour is come!' A mob of sailors invaded the Cathedral Church, and destroyed the relics, images, and pictures. In other places, at Tournai and Valenciennes, similar outbreaks of violence took place.

The regent was powerless to quell the tumults, and in despair conceded to the people the abolition of the Inquisition, and the toleration of the Protestant doctrine. Trusting to this concession, the leading nobles undertook to keep the country quiet and repress the disorders which had arisen, and William of Orange and Count Egmont took a leading part in the work of pacification.

Philip, enraged that his regent should have in any way departed from his policy of ruthless repression, determined on the first opportunity to crush the country and exterminate its leaders. With his usual dissimulation he strove to hide his intentions, and effectually deceived Count Egmont. The Prince of Orange, always well informed and wary by nature, knew and suspected what was in store for his unhappy country, and tried to warn Egmont of his danger. He saw that the king would return to his old policy of repression; that the leading nobles were not sufficiently united to resist; that the less cautious chiefs of the Beggars would revolt; and that the king would take furious and indiscriminate reprisal.

The Beggars made an attempt to seize Walcheren; they assembled in great numbers at Anstruweel, and threatened Antwerp. On their march they had destroyed relics and despoiled churches of images and pictures. Egmont, eager to show his loyalty to the king, fell on these insurgents and defeated them, and the rebellion was put down.

The king, however, had got the pretext he sought for; and the Prince of Orange had so accurately interpreted the course of events that, while he was on his way to voluntary exile in Germany, the Duke of Alva, at the head of a new army of Spanish soldiers, had entered the Netherlands.

THE DUKE OF ALVA IN THE NETHERLANDS

Ferdinand Alvarez of Toledo, Duke of Alva, was the one of the servants of Philip II who most resembled his master. He was a fanatical Spaniard, ignorant in all matters of politics and economics, avaricious, and shamelessly deceitful. Recent publications have proved that he had very little of the ability with which earlier historians have credited him. Ruthless obstinacy, devotion to his master, bigoted attachment to the Roman Catholic Church, and contempt for all constitutional forms and for the promptings of mercy, recommended him to Philip.

Philip, when he had made up his mind to despatch Alva and the Spanish troops, dissimulated as usual. He assured the regent that Alva was not meant to replace her, and he did his best to calm the suspicions of the nobles and the estates of the Netherlands. At the same time he had given Alva orders to put down the Reformation in the most thorough fashion; to take bloody revenge for past disturbances; and to enforce conversion at the point of the sword. Alva's instructions, given him in a secret letter from the king, were: 'To secure the most eminent men who had made themselves suspicious during the earlier disturbances, and to render them incapable of mischief; to imprison and punish the guilty among the people; to extort the wealth of the country for the treasury of Madrid, and to support his troops; to carry out the edicts against heresy with unswerving severity; to finish the organization of the new bishoprics, and to chastise the rebellious cities by the Inquisition, and by imposing subsidies.' His troops were embarked at Carthagena, landed at Genoa, and marched through Savoy, Burgundy, and Lorraine, to Luxemburg and to the Netherlands.

Alva knew well what was expected from him, and he was content to do Philip's work in a fashion congenial to his master. One of his own favourite maxims was, 'It is better to ruin a kingdom by war, if it keeps true to God and the King, than to keep it untouched by war for the benefit of Satan and his followers the heretics.' He entered the Netherlands fully convinced that he could crush the national and religious spirit of the country. 'I, who have tamed a people of iron, shall soon manage these people of butter', he said shortly after he entered the country.

THE IMPRISONMENT OF COUNTS EGMONT AND HORN

His first task was to seize upon the leaders of the people, and to do this he resorted to the grossest dissimulation. He invited them to Brussels, made much of them when they came, and did his best to keep them within reach until he could seize them. He was disappointed that William of Orange had escaped, and he did his best to lure him back again. Suddenly, without warning, he seized and imprisoned Count Egmont and Admiral Horn.

The news created the utmost consternation. Both nobles had proved most loyal to the king. Egmont had incurred the hatred of the populace by his vigour in suppressing insurrection, and Horn had lost land and money in Philip's service. The seizure and imprisonment showed the Netherlands and Europe that the reign of 'thorough' had begun. The escape of William of Orange was openly lamented by the Spaniards. When Granvella, in Rome, was told of Alva's stroke, he asked, Has he caught 'the Silent'? And when he was informed that William was at liberty, he said that Alva had done nothing, for the man who had escaped was worth more than all the rest.

Having secured the two nobles, Alva next set himself to terrify the people. He organized a Council of Disturbances, which superseded the old Council of State, and which began its sittings on 20 September 1567. This council suspended all the ordinary courts of justice, and was called by the people the 'Council of Blood'. Alva presided, and pressed on the work of conviction and punishment. He did his best to prevent lawyers from interfering. 'Lawyers', he said, 'were only accustomed to pass sentence on crime being proved; but that will never do here.' This Council of Disturbances rendered every one's position insecure, and went back on all manner of past offences. The common accusation was the charge of conspiring against the king and the church, or, in the language of the mediæval statute book, treason against God and against the king.

All who had signed petitions from the states or cities in favour of the relaxation of the edicts against heresy, all who had in any way opposed the erection of the new bishoprics, all who had said that the King should respect the liberties of the provinces, were deemed traitors, and punished with fines, imprisonment, and death. All caught singing the Beggars' songs, all who had not actively opposed field-preaching or who had not resisted the destruction of images, were held to be traitors. Suspicion was enough, conviction was not required, and in three months the Council of Blood had sent eighteen hundred people to the scaffold. This went on for years. William of Orange wondered at the patience of his countrymen, who endured without organized resistance, and wrote passionately, 'Where is your spirit of liberty? Where is your old bravery?'

Meanwhile the Beggars were not put down. Bands of them roamed through the country, eluding the Spanish troops, robbing churches, monasteries, and clergy-houses. The land was given over to anarchy.

Civil War – The Prince of Orange

In 1568, the Prince of Orange fancied that the country was ripe for revolt. His brother Louis of Nassau entered Friesland, and held the province successfully against the enemy. The Duke of Alva then marched against the Protestants. Before he set out, in order to terrorize the capital, he executed twenty noblemen, and among them Counts Egmont and Horn. The patriotic troops were no match for Alva's trained soldiers, and Alva completely routed Louis' army, and drove it out of the Netherlands. He then returned to Brussels, and to the sessions of the Council of Blood.

The Prince of Orange, at the head of another army, forded the Meuse, the water, it is said, being up to his soldiers' necks, marched into Brabant, and sought to engage Alva in battle. The Duke, who knew his inferiority, contrived to elude the Prince, to harass his troops with distressing marches, and to dispirit them. The Protestant army, which was for the most part composed of German mercenaries, grew clamorous for their pay, and the Prince, out-manoeuvred by the Spaniards, was forced by the approach of winter to disband his troops. A portion of the army, consisting of Netherlanders, remained with him; and the Prince of Orange, with his two brothers (the third had been slain in battle), marched across the frontier to the assistance of the Huguenots in France.

William the Silent, as his contemporaries called him, had up to this time been a Romanist. He had taken the field against the Spaniards from patriotic rather than from religious motives; but in course of this second banishment, when his country's cause was at its lowest ebb, he became a changed man. He accepted the truths of the Reformed religion, and became an unswerving Protestant. From this time onwards he was a sincerely and deeply religious man, calmly resting on God's guidance and protection.

The Sea Beggars

The most valiant portion of the population of the Netherlands consisted of the sailors and coast people, who were engaged in daily battle with the waves of the North Sea. They had also in largest numbers accepted the teaching of Reformed pastors, and had nourished the love of liberty in spite of the relentless oppression of the Spaniards and of the Inquisition. It is said that Admiral Coligny, the trusted leader of the French Huguenots, pointed out to the Prince of Orange the usefulness of organizing these sailors, fishermen, and sea-traders into a marine force.

When Alva returned to Brussels to continue his work of execution by burning, drowning, and beheading, the Prince found means to communicate with the Dutch sailors and fishermen. He resolved to create a naval force to harass the Spanish ships, and keep alive the national spirit of the provinces. He issued commissions to men in command of armed vessels, and the 'Sea Beggars' soon became the terror of the Spaniards. These Dutch privateers at first recruited and got stores from the English ports, but after remonstrance by the Spanish ambassador, Queen Elizabeth forbade their landing in England. They were forced to commit depredations on the coasts of the Netherlands, and became the terror of the Spaniards both by land and by sea.

The policy of Alva had almost ruined the country. The population was greatly diminished by his prescriptions and executions. Commerce was at an end; agriculture was neglected; manufactures were at a standstill. Alva was distressed for want of money to pay his troops. He had promised when he left Spain to make a stream of wealth fathoms deep flow from Antwerp to Madrid. He knew nothing about political economy, and could not understand that his policy had sapped the springs of wealth, and had in a few years made a rich country poor. He thought that money could still be squeezed from the Netherlanders, and proposed to extort it by new taxes. He bethought him of a Spanish tax which was crushing commercial life out of Spain, and proposed to introduce it into the Netherlands.

His scheme was to levy one per cent on all property; this was called the hundredth penny. In addition, five per cent, or a twentieth penny, was to be levied at every sale or transfer of landed or fixed property; and ten per cent, or a tenth penny, on all sales of goods or moveable property. This new tax, levied in three rates, would have ruined the land completely. Men could not live in a commercial country and pay it. It provoked more resistance than anything else Alva had done. First the province of Utrecht protested, then other provinces joined in the remonstrance. Alva, however, suffered from the want of money. His power depended on his troops, and these had to be paid; but he felt that he had gone too far, and he postponed the collection of the tenth penny for two years. The need of money at length forced him on, and he gave definite orders to collect the tenth and twentieth pennies. The result was that trade and manufacture came to a standstill. The bakers would not bake, the brewers would not brew, the shoemakers refused to make shoes; men would not sell the necessities of life. Nothing was sold, and the tax on things sold could not be levied.

THE CAPTURE OF BRILL

While the states were in passive insurrection, William's fleet of 'Sea Beggars' had been carrying on their ceaseless warfare against the Spaniards, and at length, growing bold by success, they made a sudden descent on the island of Voorn, and took the town of Brill, sometimes called one of the keys of the Netherlands. Its possession secured a point of attack on the whole coast of Holland and Zeeland, and was the beginning of the future State of the Seven Provinces.

From this time onwards the Spaniards were never completely masters of the Netherlands. The fortunes of war wavered long, but there was always some portion of Flemish soil which was independent of Spain. The 'Sea Beggars', secure in Brill, made repeated attacks on the coast towns, and soon all the chief towns of Holland and Zeeland were in their hands, and William Prince of Orange was proclaimed the Stadtholder of the Netherlands. The Prince accepted the dangerous office. He was in France when the news reached him, whereupon, disguising himself as a peasant, he passed through the enemy's lines, and hastened to put himself at the head of the insurgents. Before he reached them, Holland and Zeeland had declared for him. He summoned a meeting of the states at Dordrecht, or Dort, where a new constitution was agreed to, and the Prince was voted unanimously 'the King's legal Stadtholder in Holland, Zeeland, Friesland, and Utrecht'. The assembled states agreed to recognize his authority, to vote taxes, and to prosecute his policy. His first decree was to proclaim freedom of worship to Roman Catholics and Protestants alike.

A fresh army was levied, and the Prince crossed the Meuse and took possession of Oudenarde, Roermonde, and several other cities. He was everywhere welcomed, and his march was so easy that he expected to be soon in Brussels. Once there, he relied on the promise of Coligny to aid him in chasing the Spaniards from Flemish soil. In the midst of his success news came which struck him to the earth, he said, like 'a blow from a sledge hammer'. Coligny and the French Huguenots were massacred on St Bartholomew's Eve. All seemed lost. Mons, which had just been seized by Louis of Nassau, had to be abandoned; the Prince retreated, and his army was disbanded.

Alva came out from Brussels, and wreaked a fearful vengeance on Mons, Mechlin, Tergoes, Naarden, Haarlem, and Zutphen. The terms of the capitulation of Mons were shamefully violated. Mechlin was of set purpose plundered and fired by the Spanish troops. The Spanish commander sent to despoil Zutphen was ordered to burn every house and slay every inhabitant. Haarlem was invested, resisted desperately, and then capitulated on the promise of lenient treatment. When the Spaniards gained possession, they butchered all the Dutch soldiers in cold blood, and with them many hundreds of the citizens; and tying the bodies two and two together, they threw them into the Haarlem lake. It seemed as if the Roman Catholics had resolved to exterminate the Protestants when they found that they could not convert them.

Some towns held out, and the cause of freedom was not altogether lost. Alva's son, Don Frederick, the butcher of Haarlem, was beaten back from the little town of Alkmaar. The 'Sea Beggars' met the Spanish fleet sent to crush them, scattered the ships, and took the admiral prisoner. The nation of fishermen and shopkeepers, once the scorn of Spain and of Europe for their patient endurance of indignities, had at last risen to be a race of heroes determined never again to endure Spanish rule. William the Silent, the soul of the revolt, became all at once an important personage in Europe, worth courting by kings. He published a letter to the princes of Christendom to justify the revolt of his countrymen. 'Alva', he said 'will dye every river and stream with our blood, and hang the corpse of a Dutchman on every tree in the country before he ceases to slake his revenge, and to gloat over our miseries. We have therefore taken up arms against him to snatch our wives and children from his hands. If he is too strong for us, we are ready rather to die an honourable death, and leave a glorious name behind us, than to bow our necks to the yoke and to give up our beloved country to slavery. It is for this that our cities have given their word to stand any siege, to do their very utmost, to bear what it is possible for men to bear, even, if need be, to set fire to their own houses and perish in the flames, rather than ever submit to the mandates of this blood-thirsty hangman.'

The storm was too great even for Alva to withstand. He asked his master to recall him. Like all tyrants, he had great faith in his system, even when it had broken down. Had he been a little more severe, added a few more drops to the sea of blood he had shed, he believed he would have been successful. When Philip agreed to his request, and relieved him from his government, the only policy he could suggest to his successor was to burn to the ground every town which he could not garrison with Spanish troops.

REQUESCENS-Y-ZUNIGA, THE NEW SPANISH STADTHOLDER

The new Spanish Stadtholder selected by the King was Don Louis Requescens-y-Zuniga, a member of the higher Spanish nobility, and a Knight-Commander of Malta. He was a man of noble nature and magnanimous disposition, whose appearance in the Netherlands ten years earlier might have changed the whole current of their history. He came too late, and soon knew it. The Spaniards had as yet an unexhausted treasury and an unlimited number of soldiers. The patriots could not stand against them in the open field; yet the Stadtholder could make no impression on the country. Every fortified town was held with the energy of despair, and on the sea the 'Beggars' were triumphant. Yet the patriots had neither troops nor money. Requescens, seeing all this, and noting it, wrote to Philip: 'Before my arrival, I could not comprehend how the rebels contrived to maintain fleets so con-siderable, while your Majesty could not maintain one. Now I see that men who are fighting for their lives, their families, their property, and their false religion, in short, for their own cause, are content if they only receive rations without pay.' He immediately reversed the policy of Alva. He repealed the hated taxes, dissolved the Council of Blood, and published a general amnesty. He tried, also, to come to terms with the patriots.

The men of Holland and Zeeland had had bitter experience of Spanish amnesties and agreements. 'We have heard too often', William said, 'the words Agreed and Eternal. If I have your word for it, who will answer for it that the king will not deny it, and be absolved for his breach of faith by the Pope?' So the fighting went on, and Requescens, hating the policy of Alva, his predecessor, had to carry on the war which that policy had provoked.

The fortunes of war seemed unchanged. The Spaniards had always been victorious in the open field, and when in the early spring of 1574 William and his brother Louis led an army, largely composed of German mercenaries, into the country, they gained another victory at Mookerheide, which appeared to be even more decisive than any earlier one. The army of William was utterly routed. His brothers Louis and Henry, and with them Christopher, Count Palatine, were slain. Once more the Netherlands seemed prostrate at the feet of the Spaniards. But as before, the patriots routed in battle on land were victorious at sea, and held their fortified towns with such heroic obstinacy that the Spaniards were baffled.

The 'Sea Beggars' dispersed one Spanish fleet in the beginning of the year. They attacked another in the Scheldt, captured forty vessels, and sank almost all the rest.

The Siege of Leiden

The town of Leiden had long been held by the patriots, and its possession was eagerly coveted by the Spaniards. Louis of Nassau had relieved its first siege, but since May 1574 it had been closely invested by the Spaniards. Since the battle of Mooker Haide, William could not face the Spanish troops. He needed all his men for garrison duty in the fortified cities. Leiden was in danger of capture, and no assistance could be sent it. It stood in a plain full of fruitful gardens, of fields where the grain was almost ripe for the harvest, and this plain, like many of the Dutch lands, lay beneath the sea-level, and could be flooded if the dykes that kept the waves out were cut. William could see no means of relief but by bringing the fleet up to the walls of the city, and proposed this to the inhabitants, who consented. The dykes were opened, and the 'Sea Beggars' fleet was to come in with the sea, sailing over buried gardens, orchards, and harvest fields. That was the plan. A host of difficulties arose. It was hard to cut through the dykes; the water flowed in slowly; violent winds swept it towards the sea. Meanwhile food was getting scantier day by day, and from the steeples of Leiden the famished crowds saw the waves daily distant, and the help coming so slowly that it seemed as if it would never come at all, or only when it was too late. The Spaniards, who also knew the danger and the extremities of the townsfolk, promised amnesties and honourable capitulation. 'We have two arms', one of the defenders shouted back from the walls, 'and when hunger forces us, we will eat the left, that the right may wield the sword.' Four weary months passed amid sufferings indescribable, when at last, on the 3rd of October, the sea reached the walls, and with it the Dutch fleet. The Spaniards fled in terror, for the 'Sea Beggars' were upon them, shouting their battle-cry, 'Sooner Turks than Papists.' Townsmen and sailors from the fleet went together to the great church to give thanks for the deliverance which God had brought them from the sea. When the vast congregation were singing a Psalm of deliverance, the voices suddenly ceased, and nothing was heard but low sobs. The whole concourse of people, broken by long watching and famine, overcome by unexpected deliverance, were found weeping.

The good news was brought to Delft by Hans of Brugge, who found the Prince of Orange in church at afternoon service, and the people were told when worship was ended. The Prince, ill as he was, rode off to Leiden to share the general joy. He proposed to found a seat of learning as a thanksgiving, and this was the origin of the famous University of Leiden. The city became the centre of the Protestantism of the provinces. It became to Holland what Wittenberg was to Germany, what Geneva was to Switzerland, what Saumur was to France.

NEGOTIATIONS BETWEEN THE SOUTHERN PROVINCES AND THE NORTHERN

The raising of the Siege of Leiden was the turning-point in the war of independence. The Spanish Stadtholder saw that a new Protestant state was slowly and almost imperceptibly forming, and his difficulties were well-nigh insurmountable. In the midst of them he died quite suddenly on 5 March 1576. His unexpected death was a great blow to Spanish domination, and the events that followed showed the Netherlanders who were Roman Catholics what the Spanish Government could involve them in. The death of the Spanish Stadtholder brought confusion into the Spanish government. Since Alva's days it had been difficult to raise money to pay the troops, and at the death of Requescens the treasury was empty, and the soldiers complained of arrears. Unable to get their pay, they mutinied. 'Ready money or a city', was their cry. The garrison of Aalst began the mutiny, and the soldiers there were joined by most of the garrisons of the fortified towns in the southern provinces. The mutineers seized upon the towns of Aalst, Maestricht, and Antwerp. The most terrible scenes of murder and rapine occurred everywhere, and during three terrible November days the populous and wealthy city of Antwerp suffered all the horrors that could be inflicted on it by a licentious and brutal soldiery.

The Prince of Orange took advantage of this mutiny to push his troops forward, and was soon in possession of the important city of Ghent. The nobles and citizens of the southern provinces had at last seen the horrors inflicted on themselves and their neighbours which their Protestant fellow-subjects in the north had long experienced. Antwerp had suffered; Brussels, more resolute, had taken arms and driven out the Spanish soldiers. The nobles of Flanders and Brabant were eager to unite with the northern provinces; they asked William to save them from the Spaniards. A congress of representatives from the northern and southern Netherlands met together at Ghent, and arranged the preliminaries of a lasting union. The treaty was called *The Pacification of Ghent,* and was signed by the representatives of seventeen provinces.

The treaty provided for the expulsion of the Spaniards, complete freedom of trade and commerce between the northern and southern provinces, the suspension of edicts against the Protestants, the protection of the Roman Catholics, and the union of the provinces under a States-General. It also declared that the Prince of Orange was to remain Stadtholder until the States-General had decided otherwise, after the expulsion of the Spaniards.

DON JUAN OF AUSTRIA IN THE NETHERLANDS

The *Pacification of Ghent* seriously alarmed the politicians of Madrid. Don Juan of Austria, Philip's half-brother, a man of brilliant reputation, was sent down to the Netherlands as Spanish Stadtholder, with full powers. The states refused to acknowledge him until he had expelled the Spanish troops. After some negotiations, the provinces apparently secured from him acquiescence to their demands in the *Edictum Perpetuum,* which granted the expulsion of the troops, the toleration of Protestants, and the States-General; but secret letters intercepted showed that Philip and his regent had not abandoned the old policy of repression, and this intelligence again united the Roman Catholic south with the Protestant north. The States-General disowned his authority, and appointed the Prince of Orange governor of Brabant. It was very difficult, however, for north and south to unite heartily. Toleration was impossible in those days of war to the knife between the rival creeds, and the local jealousies could not be readily overcome. The nobles of Flanders and Brabant played a double part, and their duplicity encouraged Don Juan of Austria to take the field against the Prince of Orange. The war came to an end in the battle of Gemblours, in which the Spaniards were completely victorious. The Prince, however, as before, seemed as formidable in defeat as in victory, and the Spanish Stadtholder despaired of saving the whole of the Netherlands for his master. He died in the midst of his difficulties on 1 October 1578, and Alexander of Parma, perhaps the ablest of Philip's Stadtholders, was sent to succeed him.

ALEXANDER OF PARMA IN THE NETHERLANDS

Alexander Farnese, Prince of Parma, was the son of Margaret of Parma, a former Stadtholder, and, according to some writers, was the last great man whom Spain possessed in the sixteenth century. He was an excellent general, a skilful politician, and a man of tact. He found the affairs in the provinces in great confusion. His one element of strength was the jealousy which existed between the Protestant North and the Roman Catholic South.

The Treaty of Ghent had become a dead letter. The northern provinces thought that Flanders and Brabant had betrayed them in the affairs which resulted in the battle of Gemblours. The southern provinces could not bear to submit to the domination or even equality of the heretics of the north. Alexander skilfully took advantage of this disunion to attach the southern provinces to Spain, with the inevitable result that the Protestants of the north became more closely united with each other, and the more resolute in their determination to remain unsubdued.

THE TREATY OF UTRECHT

In 1579, Holland, Zeeland, Guelders, Zutphen, Utrecht, Overijssel, and Groningen came together and framed the celebrated Treaty of Utrecht, which contained in outline the future constitution of the United Provinces. The Seven Provinces did not sever themselves from Spain. They still professed themselves subjects of the Spanish crown, but they claimed the right of worshipping God and governing themselves after their own fashion. Two years later they threw off the Spanish yoke entirely and proclaimed their independence, choosing William of Orange Stadtholder for life. This was done in July 1581, in answer to a proclamation by Philip, in which he denounced William as an enemy of the human race, and offered a reward of twenty-five thousand golden crowns, with a patent of nobility and a pardon for all past offences, to any one who would assassinate the Prince.

From the Treaty of Utrecht onwards, the United Provinces gradually grew to complete political independence, and became a Protestant power. William of Orange was shot in 1584 by a Roman Catholic fanatic named Gerard, whose heirs claimed and obtained part of the reward promised by Philip. His work did not end with his death. The Seven Provinces elected, as Stadtholder in his place, his son Maurice, a lad of seventeen, but already trained by his father to be a skilful general and a wise political leader. He resolutely set himself to the task of lifelong conflict with Spain. He got aid from Elizabeth of England, which rather hampered than helped him. After the destruction of the Spanish Armada, and the exhaustion of the Spanish monarchy thereby, he obtained signal success against the Roman Catholic troops. The war lasted till 1604, with varying success, until in that year the Dutch struck a final blow at Spanish domination by the capture of the Spanish treasure fleets from the East and West Indies. A suspension of arms was agreed to in 1607, and a truce for twelve years, which became a lasting peace, was arranged in 1609. The Dutch had won their independence, and had become a strong Protestant power, whose supremacy on the sea was challenged only by England.

THE DUTCH CHURCH – ITS ORGANIZATION AND CONFESSION

During the years of fierce persecution which attended Protestantism in the Netherlands from the beginning of its existence, the Protestants, notwithstanding the severities practised against them, were able to organize themselves into a Church and publish a confession. This was not done without difficulties within the ranks of the Protestants themselves. The people of the Netherlands had received the new faith from various sources, and each party was tenacious of the Reformation in the precise form in which it first reached them. The earliest Reformers in the Low Countries had learned the gospel at Wittenberg from Luther, and Lutherans were numerous in the northern provinces. Somewhat later the opinions of Zwingli found their way into Holland, and were adopted by many earnest-minded persons. In the southern provinces French Reformers, whose training was Calvinistic, taught the people the Genevan Reformation. Thus Luther, Zwingli, and Calvin all found disciples in the Netherlands. The partisans of each Reformer differed from each other, principally in their views of church government; and although these differences were almost overcome, they reappeared later in the contest which emerged between the church and the Protestant State about the independence of church life and government. Gradually, however, Calvinism pushed aside Lutheranism and Zwinglianism, and the church of the Netherlands became Calvinist in doctrine and discipline.

THE DUTCH CONFESSION (*CONFESSIO BELGICA*)

As early as 1559 (some give 1561 as the date), a young Flemish pastor, Guido de Brès, in conjunction with Adrien de Saravia, Modetus, chaplain to William of Orange, and Wingen, prepared a Confession of Faith, in order, they said, to prove the Reformed faith from Scripture.

Guido de Brès, who was one of the foremost evangelists and martyrs of the Netherlands, was born in 1540 at the town of Mons. He had been trained for the church, and was converted from the errors of Romanism by studying the Holy Scriptures. After his conversion he fled to England, where, in the days of Edward VI, he was trained in Protestant theology. He went afterwards to Switzerland, and returned to become an ardent evangelist in Northern France and in the Southern Netherlands. He was a warm admirer of the Confession of the French Church, and modelled his Confession for the Flemish Church upon the celebrated *Confessio Gallica*.

This Confession, the Belgic Confession, as it was called, was revised by Francis Junius, a disciple of Calvin, in 1561, and was presented to the king, Philip II, in 1562, in the same manner as the Augsburg Confession had been presented to his father Charles V. The eloquent address which accompanied the Confession may be compared with the dedication to Francis I which prefaced the *Institutes* of Calvin. The Protestants deny that they are rebels to the government, and profess that they only desire leave to worship God according to conscience and to the Word of God. Rather than deny Christ, they say they are ready to 'offer their backs to stripes, their tongues to knives, and their whole bodies to the fire, well knowing that those who follow Christ must take his cross, and deny themselves'.

This Confession, gradually adopted by the Protestants of the Low Countries, made Calvinism the creed of the churches there.

The Constitution of the Dutch Church

As early as 1563, in the midst of persecution, delegates from various Protestant communities met in synod, and agreed upon a system of church government, which borrowed its principles largely from the *Ecclesiastical Ordinances* of Geneva; and the constitution of the church, almost from the beginning, was based on the Geneva model. This Presbyterian organization, with pastors, teachers, elders, and deacons, was not adopted without protest from the Lutherans in the Low Countries; but when the fierce persecution under the Duke of Alva burst upon them, the Presbyterian form of church government proved most able to hold its ground, and therefore prevailed in the end. The consistorial system of Luther is only possible when the State is favourably inclined towards the church; but Presbyterianism, as France, Scotland, and the Netherlands have shown, can maintain itself in a 'Church under the Cross'.

At an assembly of the church held at Dordrecht in 1574, the first General Assembly of the Dutch Church, a set of Articles formerly agreed to at a meeting at Emden, and embodying the leading principles of Presbyterian organization, were revised, enlarged, and formally adopted. All ministers were required to yield obedience to the *classical assemblies*, or presbyteries; elders and deacons were required to subscribe to the Confession of Faith and those articles of Church Government.

Two peculiarities of Dutch Presbyterianism require to be explained. Their kirk-sessions are not, as in most other Presbyterian Churches, congregational courts for the direction and rule of one congregation. The kirk-session is composed of ministers and elders from a number of congregations, and in some respects resembles a presbytery. Yet, like the kirk-session of other Presbyterian Churches, it is the primary court.

The other peculiarity of the organization of the Dutch Church is, that it was seldom able to deliberate as a Church. This was due partly to the jealousy of the Protestant state, and partly to the political constitution of the United Provinces. Holland, or the United Provinces, was a confederation of states, in many respects independent of each other. The Reformation tended to decentralize the church, and produce a separate ecclesiastical organization for each independent political state. The same tendency in Holland worked towards the formation of as many separate churches as there were provinces.

The Seven Provinces had not come together as a nation; they were rather a confederation. They had bound themselves to protect each other in war, and so to maintain a common army, and to contribute to a common military treasury; but they were not one state. The internal affairs of each province were left under the control of each separate state.

When William of Orange was elected Stadtholder for life, one of the laws which bound him was a proviso that he should not acknowledge any ecclesiastical council or consistory which had not the approval of the province in which it proposed to meet. The religious affairs of each particular province were to be regulated by that province.

This gave an aspect of division to the Dutch Church, and actually prevented corporate and united action. The Church could only meet in General Assembly when all the Seven Provinces agreed to give permission. This political entanglement did much to hinder the usefulness and power of the Dutch Reformed Church, and caused a continual struggle between church and state in Holland.

STRENGTH OF THE CHURCH IN HOLLAND

The long fight of forty-five years against Spain and Popery seemed to stimulate the energies of the Dutch Church and its Universities, and its theological schools soon rivalled older seats of learning. The

University of Leiden, a thank-offering for wonderful deliverance, was founded in 1575; Franeker came into being ten years later (1585); the Universities of Groningen (1612), Utrecht (1636), and Harderwijk (1648) followed in succession after some years of interval. These Universities were all theological schools, attended by students from most of the Protestant countries in Europe.

The Dutch theologians of the seventeenth century became famous for their learning, zeal, and theological acumen. When the great Arminian controversy, which agitated the Dutch Church later, broke out, the theologians of Holland were the most celebrated in Europe both for learning and orthodoxy.

The Westminster Confession, which became the creed of most Presbyterian Churches in English-speaking lands, is largely based upon the old Dutch Confession; and the theologians who framed its articles borrowed largely from the stores of those Dutch Reformers who had just emerged from their terrible and prolonged struggle with Spanish Popery.

5

THE REFORMATION IN SCOTLAND

PREPARATION FOR REFORMATION

Scotland, far from the centre of European life in the sixteenth century, nevertheless received the Reformation almost as early as, and accepted it more thoroughly than, most other countries.

The land had been well prepared for it by the education of the people, by the constant intercourse between Scotland and the continental nations, especially France and Germany, and by the sympathy of Scottish students with the earlier religious movements in England and in Bohemia; while the condition of the Romish Church, the poverty of the nobility, and the political situation of the country aided to some extent the efforts of those who longed for a reformation of religion in Scotland.

THE OLD CELTIC CHURCH AND EDUCATION

The old Celtic Church in Scotland, which had maintained its hold on the country for nearly seven centuries, had always looked upon the education of the people as a religious duty. Its rules declare that it is as important to teach boys and girls to read and write as it is to dispense the sacraments or take part in *soul-friendship*, which was its name for confession.

The Celtic monastery was always an educational centre, and in some cases the instruction given was as good as could then be found out of Constantinople. When Charles the Great [Charlemagne] established those high schools which afterwards grew to be the older universities of Europe, he sent to Celtic monasteries for the first teachers. When the Celtic Church of Scotland gave place to the Roman Church, her educational system was in large measure taken over, and education in Scotland continued to be very much better than could have been expected from the state of civilization.

The cathedral and monastery schools produced a large number of teachers and pupils who desired to see their work carried on at a great university like those which at that time were rising all over Europe. At first the poverty of the country prevented the erection of universities in Scotland, and elaborate provision was made by the king and by the bishops to send the best Scottish students to Oxford, Cambridge, and Paris. Travelling tutors passed from Scotland with a number of students under their care to the English and continental seats of learning. Frequently the young Scotsmen remained abroad as lecturers or as wandering students.

SCOTLAND AND LOLLARDY

This scholastic intercourse brought Scotland very near the great intellectual movements of Europe. At the very period when Scottish students went in large numbers to Oxford, Wycliffe was teaching, and Lollardy was triumphant in the great English University. Scotch students came back infected with the constitutional maxims and religious aspirations of the great Englishman, and Lollardy spread in Scotland. After the Universities of Aberdeen, Glasgow, and St Andrews were founded in the fifteenth century, the old records tell us how the ecclesiastical authorities made visitations to purge the teaching staff of Lollard errors.

In due time Lollardy passed from the universities to the people, and the earlier historians of the Reformation never fail to tell of the Lollards or Bible-men of Kyle, and their interview with James IV.

There were Scottish students in Paris when Peter Dubois, Marsilius of Padua, and William of Ockham were publicly teaching that the church is the Christian people, and that there can be a church without Pope or priest.

SCOTLAND AND HUSS

Bohemia and John Huss's doings there were well known in Scotland. Calderwood tells us about Paul Craw [Pavel Kravar], a Bohemian, who was convicted of heresy at the instance of Henry Wardlaw, Bishop of St Andrews, before several doctors of divinity, for teaching the doctrine of John Huss and Wycliffe: 'For denying any change to be made in the substance of bread and wine at the Lord's Supper, auricular confession to priests, and prayer to saints departed.' He was condemned to be burned, and at the execution 'they put a ball of brass in his mouth that the people might not understand his just defence against their unjust condemnation'. Recent archaeological research has brought out evidence of a closer connection between Scotland and Bohemia than had before been suspected.

THE ROMISH CHURCH IN SCOTLAND AND THE POLITICAL SITUATION

The Romish Church in Scotland was very wealthy, and was perhaps more corrupt than anywhere out of Italy. The heritage bequeathed it by the Celtic Church was not all good; satirists had begun to point out the contrast between the professions and the lives of ecclesiastics, and their books had a great effect on the common people. 'As for the more particular means', says John Row, 'whereby many in Scotland got some knowledge of God's truth, in the time of great darkness, there were some books set out, such as *Sir David Lindsay, his Poesie upon the Four Monarchies,* wherein many other treatises are contained, opening up the abuses among the clergy at that time: *Wedderburn's Psalms* and *Godlie Ballads,* changing many of the old Popish songs unto godly purposes: *a Complaint,* given in by the halt, blind, and poor of England against the prelates, priests, friars, and other kirkmen who prodigally wasted all the tithes and kirk livings upon their unlawful pleasures, so that they could get no sustentation nor relief as God had ordained. This was printed, and came to Scotland. There were also some theatrical plays, comedies, and other notable histories acted in public; for Sir David Lindsay his *Satire* was acted in the amphitheatre of St Johnston (Perth), before King James V, and a great part of the nobility and gentry, from morn to even, which made the people sensible of the darkness wherein they lay, of the wickedness of their kirkmen, and did let them see how God's Kirk should have been otherwise guided nor it was; all which did much good for that time.'

The wealth of the Romanist Church in Scotland had long excited the envy of the barons, who waited for the time when they might safely seize some of the ecclesiastical property. For long no such opportunity occurred. The clergy had been popular landlords. Church vassals were much better off, and lived much easier lives, than their neighbours who held their land under the barons and lesser gentry. The Scottish peasants might laugh at Sir David Lindsay's *Satires*, but they liked the church, and overlooked its faults.

When Scottish preachers who had been at Wittenberg, or who had studied the writings of Luther and of the other Reformers, or who had learned from Scripture what it was to be in earnest after pardon and salvation, began preaching a reformed gospel, then, and not till then, the people began to feel the bitter meaning in the satires of the age against the clergy. The ecclesiastical authorities did their best to suppress these Reformers. First Patrick Hamilton, then George Wishart, and many other earnest and spiritually-minded preachers were martyred; and these cruelties did more than the preaching or the satires to make the Scottish people dislike the Roman Church. Bloody Mary had made England Protestant; and Cardinal Beaton, by his judicial murders, and especially by the murder of old Walter Mill, made the people in Scotland ready for Knox and for the Lords of the Congregation.

For generations the foreign policy of Scotland had been enmity to England and friendship for France. The French alliance had led to the marriage of James V to a princess of the house of Guise, and later to the betrothal and marriage of the heiress of the Scottish throne with the Dauphin of France. James V died, leaving his French Queen regent, and her conduct filled the minds of many Scotsmen with the fear that Scotland was about to become a province of France. Frenchmen had been appointed to offices of trust in Scotland; Dunbar Castle was held by French troops; and the regent was scheming to create a standing army after the French fashion. This alarm so increased that the national party, who in the end triumphed, actually reversed the hereditary policy of Scotland, and had for their aim alliance with England and war with France. England was Protestant, while the real rulers in France were the Guises, the leaders of the fanatically Romish party, the men who planned the Massacre of St Bartholomew.

This was the state of matters in Scotland when John Knox began his wonderful work as a Reformer.

The people were educated beyond their civilization, and could understand and welcome new views, while their manners were coarse and their lives rough. The church had forfeited the confidence of the nation by the immorality of the clergy, and latterly had stirred the passions of the people against it by its cruel persecution of men of blameless lives who preached a pure gospel. Some of the barons had shared in the religious revival begun by the Reformed preachers; others were anxious to save the country from French domination, and still more of them were eager to follow the example of England, and enrich themselves at the expense of the church. All these motives, pure and other, were stirring the people of Scotland in the years preceding 1560.

JOHN KNOX

John Knox, born at Giffordsgate, a suburb of Haddington, in 1505,[1] educated at Glasgow University, ordained priest in 1542, first became known to the people of Scotland when as a young man he went about with George Wishart in 1547 to protect the Reformed preacher while he addressed crowded audiences. After the martyrdom of Wishart, and the assassination of Cardinal Beaten, Knox joined the party who had stormed and were holding the Castle of St Andrews. When the defenders were forced to capitulate, the few chief members of the garrison, including Knox, were sent to France and condemned to slavery in the galleys. While tugging at the oars, a wooden image of the Virgin was handed to him to kiss by way of adoration. Knox refused to honour the 'painted board', and threw the image into the water, saying that,

---

[1] At the time of writing it was commonly held among scholars that Knox was born in 1505. It was not until the early twentieth century that historians agreed upon a later date for the Scottish reformer's birth (*circa* 1514).

being of wood, 'Our lady could swim.' After a captivity of nineteen months he, along with the others taken at St Andrews, was released at the request of Edward VI of England. Restored to freedom in February 1549, he went straight to England, where he was employed as an itinerating preacher. His eloquence, zeal, and matchless courage soon brought him to the front. He was offered the bishopric of Rochester, but declined it on the ground that he did not believe that there was scriptural authority for the office. He was consulted about the revision of the *Articles of Religion*, and suggested the celebrated *Declaration on the subject of kneeling at Communion*, which was inserted in the Second Prayer Book of Edward VI in 1552. The accession of Mary forced him, after a bold attempt to carry on his work as wandering preacher, to retire to the Continent.

A year was spent in visiting various places in France and Switzerland. In Geneva he became the fast friend of Calvin. After a short stay in Frankfurt-am-Main, where he was pastor to the congregation of English refugees gathered there, he became the pastor of the English congregation at Geneva in 1555. During his short stay there he took part in the composition of that directory for public worship, which, under the various names of Book of Common Order, Book of Geneva, and Knox's Liturgy, guided the public worship of the Reformed Church of Scotland down till the publication and adoption of the Directory of the Westminster Divines. He also had a share in the translation of the most popular of the earlier English versions of Holy Scripture, the Geneva Bible.

In his absence he gradually became regarded as the man alone fit to guide the efforts of the reforming party in Scotland to a successful issue, and in the autumn of 1555 he returned to his native land. With his usual courage he at once began preaching in his lodgings in Edinburgh, and went on several preaching tours – to Forfarshire under the protection of Erskine of Dun; to West Lothian under the protection of Lord Torphichen, and elsewhere. It was during this visit also that Knox began to dispense the Lord's Supper after the reformed fashion. The first celebration was in the Earl of Glencairn's house in the spring of 1556.

The Reformer probably did not feel the country ripe for any great movement towards reformation, and he left Scotland for Geneva in

July 1556. He complained of the slowness, timidity, and want of union among the Protestants, when a few of the nobles invited him to return in March 1557, and then sent word that he had better delay his coming. This rebuke led to a confederation of nobles, who were afterwards well known in Scotland under the title of the Lords of the Congregation.

THE CONGREGATION AND THE FIRST COVENANT

The turbulent character of the Scottish barons, and the weakness of the central authority, whether of King or Estates, led to constant confederations of nobles and others to carry out with safety enterprises sometimes legal, sometimes outside law. The confederates promised to aid each other in the work proposed, and to defend each other from the consequences following. Such agreements were commonly drawn in legal fashion by public notaries, and made binding by all the forms of legal security known. These Lords of the Congregation followed a prevailing custom of confederation, when they covenanted with each other to maintain and further the blessed Word of God and his Congregation, and to renounce the congregation of Satan with all the superstitious abominations and idolatry thereof; but they put new spiritual meaning into it when their covenant of federation became also, as it did, a public promise to God after Old Testament fashion to be true and faithful to his Word and guidance. This 'band subscrived (*sic*) by the Lords', as Calderwood calls it, was the first of the five Covenants famous in the history of the Reformed Church of Scotland.

To this Covenant were attached two resolutions, in which the confederates resolved to insist on the use of King Edward's Prayer Book in parishes under their control, and to further the exposition of Scripture privately in houses until the authorities permitted public preaching by 'true and faithful ministers'.

This Act gave great encouragement to all who desired a reformation, and emboldened the people to express their distaste for the superstitious ceremonies of the Roman Catholic Church. The Court in 1559 prohibited all persons from preaching who had not the authority of the bishops; and as this was disregarded, the preachers were summoned before the Justiciary Court at Stirling.

Meanwhile Knox returned to Scotland. He landed at Leith on 2 May, and went to Perth, where the Lords of the Congregation were assembled to protect their preacher. The news came to Perth while Knox was preaching that the Reformed ministers were outlawed, and next day after sermon, while a priest attempted to say Mass before an excited crowd, a tumult broke out, and the 'rascal multitude', as Knox calls them, broke into and sacked the monastery of the Grey Friars and of the Carthusians. The Queen-Regent marched to attack the rioters; the Earl of Glencairn came to protect the Reformed; civil war seemed at hand. All at once the Queen yielded; negotiations went on on both sides without mutual confidence. At length the Lords of the Congregation marched on Edinburgh and took possession of the city in October 1559, and there, convening the Estates, deposed the regent. A treaty was concluded with England, and Elizabeth sent English troops to assist the Congregation. A battle was fought between the Romanist faction, aided by French troops, and the Congregation, aided by soldiers from England, in which the French were repulsed. The Queen-Regent died in the following June (1560) and the Congregation were masters in Scotland.

The Estates of the realm met, and were asked to consider a petition from the Congregation, demanding reforms in doctrine, discipline, the administration of the sacraments, and the distribution of the patrimony of the church. In answer, the Estates asked for a summary of the doctrinal reforms desired; and within four days a document, afterwards known as the *Scots Confession*, was presented. It was considered, the prelates made few objections, and when put to the vote it was adopted almost unanimously. Three other Acts were passed which abolished the Pope's jurisdiction within the realm, repealed all former Acts of Parliament contrary to the Word of God and the Confession of Faith recently adopted, and forbade attendance at Mass and other idolatrous ceremonies. And the Reformed became the religion recognized in Scotland by legal authority. The authority, however, was the power of the Estates apart from the sovereign; for the Queen-Regent was dead, and her daughter, Mary Queen of Scots, had not yet returned from France.

THE SCOTS CONFESSION

The Scots Confession, or *Confessio Scotica*, presented to the Estates, and engrossed in their Acts when adopted by them, was the work of six Scottish Reformers – Knox, Spottiswood, Willock, Row, Douglas, and Winram. It is said that Maitland of Lethington, accounted one of the ablest statesmen of his time, revised the book, and softened some of its statements. Drawn up in haste by a small number of theologians, it is more sympathetic and human than most creeds, and for that reason has commended itself to some who object to the 'impersonal logic' of the Westminster Confession. The first sentence of the preface gives tone to the whole: 'Long have we thirsted, dear brethren, to have notified unto the world the sum of that doctrine which we profess, and for which we have sustained infamy and danger. But such has been the rage of Satan against us, and against Christ Jesus his (*sic*) eternal verity lately born among us, that to this day no time has been granted unto us, to clear our consciences, as most gladly we would have done.' The preface also puts more clearly than almost any other similar Confession the reverence felt by the leaders of the Reformation for the Word of God. It says: 'Protesting, that if any man will note in this our Confession any article or sentence repugning (*sic*) to God's Holy Word, that it would please him, of his gentleness, and for Christian charity's sake, to admonish us of the same in writ, and we of our honours and fidelity do promise unto him satisfaction from the mouth of God; that is, from his Holy Scripture, or else reformation of that which he shall prove to be amiss. In God we take to record in our consciences, that from our hearts we abhor all sects of heresy, and all teachers of erroneous doctrines; and that with all humility we embrace the purity of Christ's evangel, which is the only food of our souls.'

The Confession itself contains the truths common to the Reformed creeds of the Reformation. It contains all the ecumenical doctrines, as they have been called – that is, the truths taught in the early Ecumenical Councils, and embodied in the Apostles' and Nicene Creeds; and adds those doctrines of grace, of pardon, and of enlightenment through Word and Spirit which were brought into special prominence by the Reformation revival of religion. The Confession is more remarkable for quaint suggestiveness of titles than for any peculiarity of doctrine. Thus, the doctrine of revelation is defined by itself, apart from the doctrine of Scripture, under the title of 'The Revelation of the Promise'. Election is treated according to the view of earlier Calvinism as a means of grace, and an evidence of the 'invincible power' of the Godhead in salvation. The 'notes by which the true Kirk is discerned from the false' are said to be the true preaching of the Word of God, the right administration of the sacraments, and ecclesiastical discipline rightly administered. The authority of the Scriptures is said to come from God, and to depend neither 'on man nor angels'; and the church knows them to be true because the 'true kirk always heareth and obeyeth the voice of her own spouse and pastor'.

This Confession was first read over in Parliament, and then reread clause by clause. Randolph, the English ambassador, who witnessed the same, described it to Cecil, Elizabeth's great minister, and among other things he tells how, when the articles were read, some of the barons were so moved that they started forward, offering 'to shed their blood in defence of the same', and that old Lord Lindsay, 'as grave and as godly a man as I ever saw', said, 'I have lived many years; I am the oldest in this company of my sort; now that it hath pleased God to let me see this day, where so many nobles and others have allowed so worthy a work, I will say with Simeon, *Nunc dimittis.*'

QUEEN MARY AND THE REFORMATION

The Reformation was not to triumph in Scotland so suddenly and so easily. A messenger, Sir James Sandilands, despatched to Paris with the Confession of Faith, not only failed to receive the young queen's signature, but was informed of her displeasure at the events which had taken place in Scotland; and seven years of struggle, ending in the deposition of the monarch, lay before the final ratification of the Confession and the full legal recognition of the Reformed Church in Scotland.

Francis II, the husband of Mary, died in 1561, and the young Queen came to Scotland in August of the same year. She was accompanied by a large and brilliant circle of friends and attendants, among whom were three of her uncles, members of the house of Guise, and the son of the famous Constable de Montmorency. The Duke of Guise himself, and the Cardinal of Lorraine, had come with her from Paris as far as Calais. The Scottish Reformers knew well the men who surrounded their queen, and came so ostentatiously to protect her. The Duke of Guise was known to be at the head of that party in France who wished to exterminate the French Protestants by wholesale slaughter. He, it was believed, had instigated the judicial murder of Anne de Bourg, and had planned the slaughter of Amboise. The licentiousness of the Guises was only excelled by their cold-blooded cruelty. These were the men who descended on Scotland to surround and counsel the young queen.

It is scarcely wonderful that, with all this in their minds, Knox and his friends regarded the coming of the queen as a great calamity, and that they should have seen in the two days' mist and rain that hung over the east coast of Scotland 'the very face of the heavens manifestly speaking what comfort was brought into this country with her – to wit, sorrow, darkness, dolour, and all impiety'.

The beauty, the bright wit, the misfortunes, and the dark end of the unfortunate young queen have surrounded Mary with the halo of romance. And yet even her admirers have scarce done justice to her indubitable courage and to her great intellectual gifts. She was almost alone when she returned to her native land, and she found out at once that her strength lay in expecting nothing from France, and relying entirely on a queen's party which she herself had to create. She was a girl of nineteen when she quitted France; and yet Knox, after interviews with her shortly after her arrival, seems to have felt her power, and known that it was so much to be feared that either the queen or the Reformation must go down. Her single-handed struggle with the Reformation in Scotland was watched with anxiety all over Europe; and had she not been trained in such a tainted court, and been overweighted with the odium of such relations as the Guises, it is possible that she might have succeeded. It seems cruel to think of it, now that the danger is centuries old, but quiet, pious families in Holland, in France, in the Rhineland even, as well as in her own Scotland and England, breathed freely at last when the axe at Fotheringay brought her sad troubled life to an end.

The struggle began at her coming. She and her court ostentatiously went to Mass on the first Sunday after her arrival, although the saying and hearing of Mass had been forbidden under severe penalties. She challenged at once the legality of the proceedings of the Estates which had legalized the Reformation. To tell the story in detail would fill too many pages. After seven years of struggle Mary was imprisoned in Loch Leven Castle, deposed, and her infant son, James VI, was placed on the throne, while her half-brother, James Stewart, Earl of Moray, was made Lord Regent. The Estates, or Scottish Parliament, again voted the Confession of Faith, engrossed it in their Acts; the regent for the sovereign signed it; and, thus ratified, it became part of the law of the land, and the Reformed religion was the form of Christianity legally recognized in Scotland.

THE BOOK OF DISCIPLINE AND THE FIRST GENERAL ASSEMBLY

Shortly after the Parliament of 1560 had separated, the authors of the Confession were asked to draw up a short statement showing how a Reformed Church could best be governed. The result was the remarkable document which was afterwards called the First Book of Discipline, and which was the earliest Form of Church Government in Scotland.

It provided for the government of the church by kirk-sessions, synods, and general assemblies; and recognized as office-bearers in the church ministers, teachers, elders, deacons, superintendents, and readers. The authors of this Book of Discipline professed to go directly to Scripture for the outlines of the system of church government which they advised their countrymen to adopt, and their profession was undoubtedly sincere and likewise just. They were, however, all of them men in sympathy with the church at Geneva, and had had personal intercourse with the Protestants of France. Their form of government is clearly inspired by Calvin's ideas, and follows closely the Ecclesiastical Ordinances of the French Church. The offices of superintendent and reader were added to the usual threefold or fourfold Presbyterian form of government. The office of superintendent was due to the unsettled state of the country and the scarcity of Protestant pastors. The superintendents took charge of districts of country corresponding not very exactly with the Episcopal dioceses, and were ordered to make annual reports to the General Assembly of the ecclesiastical and religious state of their provinces. The readers owed their existence to the small number of Protestant pastors, to the great importance attached by the early Scottish Reformers to an educated ministry, and also to the difficulty of procuring funds for the support of pastors in every parish. The Book of Discipline contains a chapter on the patrimony of the church which urges the necessity of preserving monies possessed by the church for the maintenance of religion, the support of education, and the help of the poor. The presence of this chapter prevented the book being accepted by the Estates in the same way as the Confession of Faith. The barons, greater and lesser, who sat there had in too many cases appropriated the 'patrimony of the Kirk' to their own private uses, and were unwilling to sign a document which condemned their conduct. The Book of Discipline approved by the General Assembly, and signed by a large number of the nobles and burgesses, never received the legal sanction accorded to the Confession.

The General Assembly of the Reformed Church of Scotland met for the first time in 1560, and in spite of the struggle in which the church was involved, meetings were held at least once a year, and sometimes oftener, and the church was organized for active work.

Calvin's *Catechism for the Young* was translated, and ordered to be used. The Book of Common Order, or Knox's Liturgy, gradually displaced the Liturgy of King Edward VI, and the Reformed Church of Scotland, with its confession, ecclesiastical constitution, order of public worship, and scheme of instruction for the young, spread itself over the land, planting churches, improving morals, and educating the people.

One of the chief difficulties which the struggling church had to contend with was the want of money to pay its ministers. The Roman Catholic Church had been legally abolished, and yet no provision had been made for the maintenance of the Reformed clergy. Ecclesiastical property was in a strange condition. Previous to 1560 the Roman Catholic Church in Scotland had been very wealthy, and had in its grasp a very large proportion of the landed property of the country. While the church was struggling against Mary and her efforts to bring back the Romanist religion and hierarchy, large portions of the old estates of the church had been made over by the prelates to their friends and dependants, a still larger proportion had been seized by the nobles, and what remained and nominally belonged to the church was in the hands of men who called themselves bishops, abbots, priors, deans, and parsons, but who had never received orders, who were nominal Protestants, and who took these ecclesiastical titles in order to have some legal claim to the property which belonged to these offices. After a great deal of expostulation, the Assembly prevailed upon the Estates to decree that all such persons who held the church lands still nominally belonging to the church, were to keep for their own use two-thirds of the income of the benefices, and with the remaining third were to provide for the ministry, for education, and for the support of the poor. The Reformed Church, however, found it very difficult to enforce the law, and the ministry and schools in Scotland during the earlier years of the Reformation were mainly supported by free-will contributions from the better disposed of the people, by 'benevolences', as Knox graphically calls these subsidies.

EDUCATION

The democratic ideas of Presbyterianism, enforced by the practical necessity of trusting in the people, made the Scottish Reformers pay great attention to the education of the people. All the leaders of the Reformation, whether in Germany, France, or Holland, had felt the importance of enlightening the people; but perhaps Scotland and Holland were the two countries where the attempt was most successful. The education of the people was no new thing in Scotland, and although in the troublous times before the Reformation high schools had disappeared, and the universities had decayed, still the craving for learning had not altogether died out. Knox and his friend George Buchanan had a magnificent scheme of endowing schools in every parish, with high schools or colleges in all important towns, and of increasing the power and influence of the universities. Their scheme, owing to the greed of the barons who had seized the church property, was little more than a devout imagination, but it laid hold on the mind of Scotland, and the lack of endowments was more than compensated by the craving of the people for education.

The three universities of St Andrews, Glasgow, and Aberdeen took new life, and a fourth, the University of Edinburgh, was founded. Scotch students who had been trained in the continental schools of learning, and who had embraced the Reformed faith, were employed to superintend the newly-organized educational system of the country, and the whole organization was brought into sympathy with the everyday life of the people by the preference given to day schools over boarding schools, and by a system of inspection by the most pious and learned men in each circle of parishes. Knox also was prepared to order compulsory attendance at school on the part of two classes of society, the upper and the lower – the middle class he thought might be trusted to its own natural desire for learning; and he wished to see the state so exercise power and patronage as to lay hold on all youths 'of parts', and compel them to proceed to the high schools and universities that the commonwealth might get the greatest good of their service.

THE DEATH OF KNOX

John Knox died in November 1572. The assassination of his friend the Earl of Moray, the Good Regent, had made a deep impression on him, and the news of the Massacre of St Bartholomew lately come to Scotland, almost took the heart out of him. He had never been a robust man, and had undergone in his lifetime no ordinary hardships, but his dauntless spirit had carried him through all. 'I know not', says Smeaton, 'if ever God placed in a fraile, weake, little bodie a more godlie and greater spirit.' He had been in a very weak state long before his death, and yet he had struggled against his weakness, and scarce ever failed to preach and exhort according to his wont. James Melville gives us a picture of him shortly before his death, as he saw him while a student at St Andrews: 'Being in St Andrews, he was very weak. I saw him every day of his teaching go hailie and fairly (cautiously), with a furring of mattricks about his neck, a staff in the one hand, and good godly Richard Ballanden, his servant, holding up the other oxter, from the Abbay to the parish kirk: and by the said Richard and another servant, lifted up to the pulpit, where he behoved to lean at his first entry; but ere he had done with his sermon, he was so active and vigorous, that he was like to ding that pulpit in blads, and fly out of it.'

He died before his work was quite done, for the Reformed Church had a severe fight before it, which was the harder for it that Knox was not there to do his part in the battle. He had not the learning of Calvin, nor the genial sympathy of Luther, but no man could match him in courage. 'He neither feared nor flattered any flesh.' And that made him the Reformer for Scotland.

Like his French contemporaries, he was quite as much a statesman as an ecclesiastical leader, and while he lived he was, and was known to be, the leader of the Scottish people. The nobles would gladly have laid hands on the movement, and diverted it into channels more congenial to themselves; but Knox had made the pulpit the power in Scotland, and by his fearless free speech had created a public opinion which had to be reckoned with. He was a man of deep personal piety, 'fearing God, and without any other fear.'

THE TULCHAN BISHOPS

The power of the Reformed Church of Scotland was greatly strength-ened and consolidated by the representative character of her courts, and more especially of her General Assembly, and the freedom with which all the concerns of the nation were spoken about and discussed there gave to the Assembly of the Church the character of a national Parliament able to speak for the people of Scotland in more thorough fashion than the Estates of the realm. While Mary was still queen, her keen eye had detected this power of the Church, and she had made various efforts, always unsuccessful, to prevent the meeting of the General Assembly. After the death of the Good Regent, the Earl of Moray, during the regencies of Lennox, Mar, and Morton, and during the reign of James, the Assembly was felt to be specially obnoxious to rulers who loved the exercise of power. It was seen, however, to be dangerous to attack the Assembly directly, and those in power in the State tried to weaken its authority by creating and upholding ecclesiastics who from their position might sit in the Estates and speak for the church there. After the death of the Regent Moray, the constant policy of the nobility was to try and force, not Episcopal government, but bishops upon the church.

Another and perhaps the more visible cause why those in authority were not content with the simple Presbyterian constitution which the Book of Discipline had assigned to the church was, that it gave them small chance of plundering the revenues, while the appointment of bishops gathered a large proportion of the monies of the church into few hands, so enabling the patrons to make bargains with the ecclesiastics they appointed to these offices, and thus to divert a large portion of the ecclesiastical funds still remaining in the church's possession into the pockets of the leading nobles.

Shortly before Knox's death, the Assembly, not without protest, had, on the insistence of the Lords of Council, agreed to accept ecclesiastics with the title of bishop on certain conditions, the chief of which were, that these bishops were to have no more rule than the superintendent, that they were to be subject to the General Assembly, and that they were not to be appointed without due provision being made for the support of the ordinary ministry. This arrangement, called the *Convention of Leith*, had been come to mainly by the exertions of John Erskine of Dun, the ancient friend of Knox, one of the original superintendents, and more than once Moderator of the Assembly. A few years' experience showed the Scottish Church the dangers resulting to her free, democratic life from the provisions of this convention, and shortly after Knox's death there were symptoms of a coming struggle.

The most flagrant instance of the use made of these bishops by the greater nobles to defraud the church occurred in 1581, when Boyd, the Archbishop of St Andrews, died. On the death of the aged prelate, the Duke of Lennox determined to appropriate to himself the properties of the See. It was impossible to do this unless by some legal artifice, and the plan chosen was to induce Robert Montgomery, minister at Stirling, to accept the office of Archbishop, serve himself heir to the property of the See, and then cause him to hand over the revenues to Lennox. This case was perhaps the worst; but all over Scotland this sort of thing went on, and titular bishops, abbots, etc., were appointed in order to get a legal hold on the monies of the Church, and divert them from their proper uses into the pockets of the lay patrons. The people called these bishops, and other dignitaries, who permitted themselves to be so used, Tulchans, and the first struggle against bishops in Scotland was not a contest between Presbytery and Episcopacy, but between the Church, anxious to keep its patrimony, and these Tulchans. When Montgomery's case was discussed in the Assembly, 'the moderator, Mr David Dickson, craved liberty to expone [set forth] what was meant by Tulchan bishops. It was a Scots word, used in their common language. When a cow will not let down her milk, they stuff a calf's skin full of straw, and set it down before the cow, and that was called a *tulchan*. So these bishops possessing the title and the benefice without the office, they wist not what name to give them, and so they called them Tulchan bishops.'

ANDREW MELVILLE

John Knox died when this struggle between the court and the church was beginning, and a new leader had to be found to take his place. Among the learned Scots attracted to their native land by the triumph of the Reformation and by the revival of letters, Andrew Melville was the most distinguished. Born in 1545 at Baldovy, near Montrose, he was educated at the Grammar School of that town, and at St Mary's College in St Andrews. Thence he went to Paris, and was a student of the famous Peter Ramus. When his student life was over he became professor of Latin in Geneva, and in 1574 returned to Scotland with the reputation of one of the most distinguished scholars in Europe. Soon after his return he was made Principal of the University of Glasgow, and under his rule that College attracted not only crowds of Scotch students, but large numbers of foreigners.

He was a member of the Assembly of 1575, in which the question of Episcopacy *versus* Presbytery was for the first time seriously raised; and he was one of the committee appointed by that Assembly to consider the scriptural warrant for the name and duties of bishop (if bishops as they were at that time in the Kirk of Scotland had a lawful calling or office by the Word of God). The resolution come to was that the name bishop belonged to all parties of the church who had been placed over congregations, but that it might also be applied to ministers chosen by their brethren to be commissioners for the inspection and planting of churches; and the general feeling of the church on the subject may be gathered from the common saying that there were those three kinds of bishops – My Lord Bishop, my Lord's Bishop, and the Lord's Bishop; the first Roman Catholic bishops, the second tulchan, and the third pastors of congregations.

THE SECOND BOOK OF DISCIPLINE

When the Reformed Church of Scotland found itself face to face with these new ecclesiastical problems, it felt the need of a more distinct and compact scheme of Church government than was contained in the First Book of Discipline. That form of church government had been hurriedly prepared, and made mention of several matters which were outside the scope of a book of ecclesiastical ordinances. The Assembly of 1576 appointed a committee to consider the question, and frame a new book which might supersede the work of Knox and Row. The work was done slowly and patiently, and at length in 1578 the *Second Book of Discipline* was ordered to be printed for criticism and correction. Three years were spent in weighing every point and sentence, and the Book of Policy, as it was called, was accepted by the Assembly, and ordered to be engrossed among its Acts.

This book, which gives in short and clear form the outline of Scotch Presbyterian Church government, begins by distinguishing ecclesiastical from civil rule, and claims for the Kirk a 'policy different from the civil policy'. The whole government of the church, it says, consists in doctrine, discipline, and in distribution; and for this threefold government there is a threefold office of pastor or bishop, elder, and deacon. The Book of Discipline adds a fourth office, that of doctor or teacher. A short chapter states the nature of calling, election, and ordination of pastors. Each office with the duties belonging thereto is described, and the various assemblies in which the office-bearers meet to exercise their rule. It is singular that in the year preceding the adoption of the Book of Discipline by the Assembly, the Presbyterian organization of the Scottish Church was completed by the universal recognition of the presbytery as a court above the kirk-session, but inferior to the synod; and that this book of policy makes no mention of this court, which now exercises such important functions in the Scottish presbyterial organization.

With the publication of the *Second Book of Discipline* the Reformed Church of Scotland completed her ecclesiastical organization, and ended the first portion of her history. The Reformation was by that time firmly established, and Protestantism had taken firm hold upon the people of Scotland. The church had a long struggle before it; but the contest was not with Popery, but with the state; not to reform religion, but to develop and preserve that democratic form of church government which commended itself to her people as the most agreeable to the Word of God, and the best fitted to enable her to do her duty as a church of Christ.

In 1574 the ecclesiastical condition of Scotland was somewhat curious. The old pre-Reformation parishes had been retained, and numbered somewhat over a thousand. To supply these, there were 289 ministers and 715 readers, many of these readers being the Roman Catholic priests, who had come over to the Reformed faith, but had not education sufficient to warrant their ordination as Protestant pastors. These parishes were classed together in what afterwards became presbyteries. The presbyteries were grouped into synods, and the whole was ruled by the General Assembly. The Presbyterian organization was in a measure complete. But side by side with this there remained the old pre-Reformation dioceses, thirteen in number, for the most part filled by men who were Protestant ministers, who took the title of bishop, but exercised no ecclesiastical episcopal functions. Three of these bishops – only those of St Andrews, Glasgow, and Aberdeen – had even attempted to exercise episcopal jurisdiction, and they had done so not as bishops, but as superintendents. These bishops sat in the Scottish Parliament, and their chief duties were to manage the cathedral revenues, and to perform the judicial functions which had belonged to the bishops in pre-Reformation times.

This episcopal organization lived on side by side with the active aggressive Presbyterian polity of the Church. The state of matters was made still more anomalous by the fact that three of the old super-intendents still survived and exercised their functions of oversight; and the districts of the other superintendents were ruled over by temporary commissioners appointed by the Assembly, and removable at its pleasure.

The aim of the church in the struggle which lasted from 1574 to 1638 was to do away entirely with what it considered the useless and mischievous episcopal organization, which had no connection with the living work of the church, and to supersede the superintendents and commissioners by presbyteries, and thus unite the church in one harmonious whole. The aim of the court was to retain the old episcopal system, and gradually by means of it to break up the church into a number of fragments, ruled over by a bishop responsible only to Parliament; and, latterly, to restore Episcopacy in the old sense of the word, and overthrow the whole Presbyterian constitution.

The year 1638 witnessed the triumph of the church, but this whole struggle is beyond the limits of our present task.

PART THREE

THE ANGLICAN REFORMATION

I

THE CHURCH OF ENGLAND DURING THE REIGN OF HENRY VIII

THE EXCEPTIONAL CHARACTER OF THE BEGINNING OF THE ENGLISH REFORMATION

*T*he English Church and people broke away from the mediæval Papal ecclesiastical system under circumstances so very exceptional that it is impossible to describe the rupture as part of the Reformation, or as having much in common with contemporary movements in Germany and France. While the reign of Henry VIII lasted, the Church of England, which had separated itself from the Papacy, had little or nothing in common with the Reformation. The work done in that reign was simply to demolish the Mediæval Church in England. The real Reformation began in the reign of Edward VI, and was carried out into successful issue under Elizabeth. Henry VIII destroyed Papal supremacy, spiritual and temporal; he pulled down the ecclesiastical framework which united the Church of England with the great Western Church ruled by the Bishop of Rome, but he put nothing lasting in its place. His aim was to build up a kingly Papacy, as despotic as and even more secular than the one he was destroying, on the ruins of the jurisdiction of the Bishop of Rome. The church framed after his model did not last longer than his own lifetime; but his work had enough of permanence in it to give the Reformation of the Church of England, when it afterwards came about, a character of its own, marking it off from similar movements in other countries. It was Henry's object to change the ecclesiastical state of England in such a way that the king might take the place of the Pope; might rule as spiritual as well as temporal monarch, and so obtain through the church absolute dominion over his subjects. All reformation of doctrine or worship or morals was as hateful to Henry as to the Bishop of Rome.

ANTICIPATIONS OF THE REFORMATION IN ENGLAND

Church historians have usually traced the beginnings of the English Reformation back to John Wycliffe, who, in the fourteenth century, was the mouth of England, disowning the temporal and spiritual supremacy of the Pope within the realm; but it is very doubtful indeed whether his influence lasted among the English people down to the sixteenth century in such force at least as to count for much in the longings for reformation which were filling the minds of many pious people.

Like Francis of Assisi, and many other mediæval reformers and revivalists, Wycliffe had passionately embraced the idea that the benefits of Christ's salvation can only be appropriated by those who imitate Christ, and that this imitation of the Lord Jesus is possible only to those who live a life of poverty like the Master's. He therefore found himself at war with the well-endowed clergy of the wealthy Church of England, and preached that the church in order to be Christ-like must be poor. He taught that the state can best help the church by taking from it its wealth, which can only prevent it being like its Master. And he organized a body of travelling evangelists, called poor preachers, who, in a fashion not unlike the itinerating preachers of the Wesleyan movement, went throughout all England preaching the doctrine of evangelical poverty. He was a fervent admirer of the great mediæval jurists, of William of Ockham, Luther's 'dear master', of Marsilius of Padua, and of Peter Dubois of Paris. They had taught, long before the times, that the state is nothing but the people; and Wycliffe, following them, taught that the church is nothing but the people. This preaching of his attacked the whole mediæval system of church life, for that was founded on the idea that the clergy are the real church, and that the laity are included within the circle of the church only when they are brought into contact with the clergy, in whose hands are the sacraments. It led also to his translation of the Bible, the book of the church, and therefore of the Christian people, and not of the clergy only. Wycliffe's views were eagerly adopted by a large proportion of the English people, and his followers, the Lollards, were for some time a formidable body.

Lollardy was undoubtedly a preparation for the Reformation, and the Bible-men, as they were called, must have exercised great influence in preparing the people of England for a revival of heart-religion, if they had been in actual communication with the generation in whose midst the Reformation arose. It seems difficult, however, to trace any such direct connection, and, at all events, no trace of widespread sympathy with Bible-reading or the poor preachers is visible in England either during the reign of Henry VII or at the accession of Henry VIII. The English people as a whole seem to have had very little sympathy with the Reformation until the time of Elizabeth.

THE ECCLESIASTICAL STATE OF ENGLAND AT THE BEGINNING OF THE REFORMATION

When the Reformation movement began in Germany, there were undoubtedly a few Englishmen who sympathized with the Saxon Reformer, and desired to see the creed of the church made simpler and more in harmony with the Bible, and its government and worship more consonant with apostolic practice; but the vast majority of Englishmen had no such views. Most people, no doubt, desired to see some reformation in the manners of the clergy, and especially in the morals of the monks, and would have gladly witnessed the imposition of taxes on church lands, or the lessening of the wealth of the bishoprics and abbeys. There were, moreover, an increasing number who were disgusted with the gross ignorance of the clergy, and who wished, from political and social reasons, to lessen the influence of the Bishop of

Rome. They disliked his interference in political affairs, and they were indignant that he took so much money out of the kingdom.

It is not probable that the morals of the Romish clergy were worse in England than they were elsewhere, but they were bad enough to bring the Church into discredit. The clergy were, as a rule, grossly ignorant, and it is probable that a knowledge of Scripture was rarer in England than in France or Germany, because, since the days of Lollardy, Bible-reading had been accounted a crime. The Bible was an unknown book to most of the clergy, and Erasmus tells us that he saw a copy of the Gospel of Nicodemus chained to a pillar in Canterbury Cathedral and read as part of canonical Scripture.

The higher clergy had very little church work to do, and were employed in administering the affairs of state, or in presiding over the courts of justice. The Archbishop of Canterbury was Lord Chancellor, the Bishop of Winchester Lord High Treasurer, the Bishop of Durham was a Secretary of State, and the Bishop of London was Master of the Rolls. The Bishops of Bath, Hereford, Llandaff, and Worcester did not even reside in the kingdom.

In these circumstances it was to be expected that men, influenced by the new learning of the Renaissance, should be indignant at the ignorance of the clergy, and were anxious to enlighten both clergy and laity; and that patriotic Englishmen remembering the ancient traditions of a country which for centuries had maintained a haughty and distant attitude towards the pretensions of the Roman See, should have been anxious to disown the power of the Pope in England. Accordingly a band of young scholars appeared, at the head of whom were Colet, Dean of St Paul's, and Thomas More, who aimed at purifying the church by educating the people and the clergy, and by inciting the national Church of England to hold her own against the encroachments of the Bishop of Rome.

ENGLAND'S RELATIONS TO THE PAPACY

The Bishops of Rome in the later Middle Ages laid claim both to temporal and spiritual supremacy, and these claims had been over and over again resisted by the English people. The Popes, since the time of Innocent III, held that all kings and princes were their vassals in matters civil as well as in things sacred. This claim had been enforced in the reign of King John, who had paid tribute to Rome in acknowledgment of the Pope's supremacy. But when the poll-tax had been demanded from John's successors, it had been indignantly refused. England, without ceasing to belong to the mediæval Catholic Church, had repudiated the Pope's right to interfere in her national concerns. No English King, save King John, had ever acknowledged himself the Pope's vassal. It was no new thing in England to disown the Pope's supremacy in temporal affairs.

The Popes, from the beginning of the Middle Ages, had claimed to be supreme in all spiritual affairs, and therefore to be supreme ecclesiastical rulers over the English Church. These claims had in practice amounted very much to this. They claimed to give final decision in all ecclesiastical appointments, *i.e.* they held that no bishop or abbot, or other church dignitary, could be appointed to office without the sanction of the Pope in the last resort, and this supremacy of theirs they wished to be acknowledged in a practical fashion by the payment to the Pope of the first year's income from every ecclesiastical office. They claimed to give final decision in every disputed question raised within the English Church. And this practically meant that every churchman, bishop, abbot, priest, monk, or nun could only be tried before Church courts and not in the King's courts, and that the complainant or defendant had always the right of appeal from the English court to the Pope's court in Rome. They also claimed that canon law, that is, the law of the church made by decisions of Councils and of Popes, should be recognized in England, and exist there in power side by side with the common law of England.

This spiritual supremacy of the Pope had been repeatedly challenged by the English people. Kings of England had declared over and over again that no appeal could be taken in any case from English courts to the Roman Curia. These declarations had taken the shape of legal enactments, and during the reign of Richard II, had grown into the famous statute of *Praemunire.* This statute made all appeals from an English law court to a foreign court of justice, whether Roman or other, a crime to be severely punished. It asserted in the strongest fashion that the king was supreme in all disputes, ecclesiastical as well as civil, and it punished any appeal from the civil courts to ecclesiastical courts of justice either in England or in Italy.

Besides the protests of the king and of the Parliament embodied in this statute, the English people on one great occasion at least had solemnly disowned the supremacy of the Pope, and had asserted the independence of the English Church. The *Magna Charta* was meant to restrict the Pope's power, as well as to curb that of the King; and its first clause had vindicated the independence of the Church of England – *Quod ecclesia Anglicana libera sit et habeat omnia jura sua integra et libertates suas illaesas*, that the English Church should be free and have all its laws and liberties intact and unharmed.

The English church and people had been accustomed to protest against Papal interference, and reformers who wished merely to raise the standard of learning among the clergy, and to curb the Pope's power in England, could say with historical accuracy that they were teaching no new thing.

The aspirations of such reformers may be seen in the political romance written by the ablest of their number, the *Utopia* of Sir Thomas More. To these men reformation was simply an intellectual and political movement. It was not a religious revival. They could sympathize with the reforming Councils of the fifteenth century, but they had little in common with Wittenberg or Geneva.

THE EARLY RELATIONS OF HENRY VIII WITH THE PAPACY

These reformers of the study and council chamber hailed with delight the accession of Henry VIII to the throne of England. The young King, like his contemporary Francis I of France, was supposed to be a friend of the new learning, and a sovereign set on uprooting abuses. They were soon disappointed. At first Henry proved himself a most devoted upholder of the Papal supremacy. His position was strange, and requires explanation.

Henry VII, the first king of the house of Tudor, had won the throne of England on Bosworth field, and held it by a precarious tenure. He was anxious to strengthen his position by foreign alliance, and looking around Europe, decided that Ferdinand of Spain could render him most help. He therefore concluded, with some difficulty, a marriage between his eldest son Arthur and Catherine of Aragon, one of Ferdinand's daughters. Arthur died early; and eager to preserve the Spanish alliance, Henry was anxious to marry Catherine to his second son Henry, afterwards

Henry VIII, now his heir. The Pope granted a dispensation, and the marriage took place. Henry VIII had married his brother's widow.

It was always a question whether Arthur and Catherine had been really or only legally married. If the marriage had been a mere legal marriage, then the power of the Pope to grant dispensation could be easily acknowledged even by those who had no very strong ideas of Papal supremacy; but if the marriage had been a real one, then the Pope's dispensation meant that the Pope had power to grant a dispensation to Henry and Catherine in the face of the divine laws of kinship. Common report said that the marriage had been a real one, and that Henry had married his brother's widow, and that for such an act dispensation could only be granted by the Pope if he actually possessed the supreme powers which Ultramontanes[1] declare the Pope possesses. Thus the legality of Henry's marriage, and the legitimacy of his child Mary, rested upon the supremacy of the Pope in the widest and loftiest sense of the terms. It need not cause any wonder, therefore, that Henry VIII, at the beginning of his reign, adopted views of the Papal supremacy more akin to the teachings of Italian Ultramontanes than to the traditions of the English crown. The validity of Henry's marriage, the legitimacy of his children, and their right to succeed to the throne, depended upon the supremacy of the Pope.

When Luther attacked the Pope, Henry ostentatiously defended the cause of the Bishop of Rome, and no king since King John had more absolutely acknowledged the claims of the Pope than Henry VIII. His own personal interests, and the interests of his wife and children, depended on such acknowledgment. England under Henry VIII, in the beginning of the king's reign, was the devoted vassal of the See of Rome. However Henry might be inclined, from training and education, to adopt the views of Colet, More, and Erasmus, his peculiar position forced him to take up a position of uncompromising hostility, and his defence of the Pope against Luther gained for him the title of Defender of the Faith.

HENRY'S CHANGE OF OPINION

Henry maintained this acknowledgment of the supremacy of the Pope in all matters during the first eighteen years of his reign. He changed

[1] See p. 90.

it suddenly, and many reasons may be given for the change. There seems to be evidence for supposing that Henry had always had doubts about the legitimacy of his marriage with Catherine, and that these doubts increased as he saw himself without male heirs. He had no son to succeed him, and he seems to have really believed that the lack of an heir-male was a divine punishment for marrying his brother's widow. During all these years, however, the Spanish alliance, first with Ferdinand and then with his grandson Charles V, the Emperor, seemed to be of the utmost importance to Henry and to England; and this Spanish alliance, he believed, would be powerful enough to secure the throne to his daughter, whose legitimacy, declared by the Pope, would be upheld by the Emperor.

But Charles V was busy with his schemes for putting down the Reformation and restoring the mediæval Empire, and the Pope was eager to maintain his independent secular position as the first of Italian princes, and neither was so true to the English alliance as Henry had hoped. He could not trust the succession to the throne to their fidelity to him and his house. His position was perplexing, and as the shortest way out of his difficulties he resolved to ask the Pope to divorce him from Catherine of Aragon. If he had scruples of conscience about his marriage with his brother's widow, this would end them; he could marry again, and might hope for a son and lawful successor. Cardinal Wolsey, his minister, entered into his plans, and the Pope was asked to grant a divorce.

Just then, however, the Pope was loath to quarrel with Charles V, Catherine's nephew, and refused to grant the divorce, and Henry, a man of strong passions and great obstinacy, resolved to obtain the divorce in spite of the Pope. All the personal interests which had once united to make Henry uphold the Papal supremacy now were in league to make him disown it. Had the Pope granted the divorce, there would probably have been no break with Rome, for then the King would still have been interested in maintaining the Papal supremacy; as matters stood, Henry's interests and his desires prompted him to take another road, and he took it.

Thomas Cromwell suggested that the universities of Europe should be asked to decide whether Henry's marriage was a lawful one, and Henry eagerly adopted the suggestion. The case was stated, and the learned faculties were asked to decide according to canon law and with due regard to the king's tender conscience. After some time and much expenditure of money, the universities, by a very small majority, declared that the marriage between Henry and Catherine was invalid, and was no real marriage, and the decision implied that Henry had no legitimate heir.

Fortified with this opinion, Henry resolved either to frighten the Pope into granting the divorce, or to defy him and repudiate his supreme authority.

Many minor reasons helped him to come to this resolution. Henry loved lavish display; he had long before exhausted the hoarded treasures of his father, and he could not increase the taxation of the country. His treasuries were empty, he wished to refill them, and the monasteries might be despoiled. That was one reason. There was another which appealed still more strongly to his vanity.

HENRY VIII, FRANCIS I, AND CHARLES V, AND THEIR RIVALRY

The three great nations in Europe at the time of the Reformation were Spain, France, and England, and their kings could not help being rivals. The king of Spain, the most powerful of the three, was also Emperor of Germany, and his policy was to restore the Empire to its mediæval splendour. According to old mediæval ideas, Christendom was one, the Emperor was the supreme sovereign, and other kings were dependent princes. If Charles had succeeded, the positions of Francis and Henry would have been inferior to what they were, and their policy was to prevent the restoration. A mediæval Christendom implied one undivided church, centralized in the Pope, the Bishop of Rome. It was therefore the policy of the kings of France and England to prevent such ecclesiastical centralization, and to make the churches of their respective nations as independent of Rome as possible.

Francis had accomplished this for France, not in the old French fashion, but in a manner which helped largely to increase his personal power in his own kingdom. The Pope, by the Concordat of 1516, had, on condition that the *annates* (incomes from the first year of new benefices) were paid regularly and some other privileges secured, practically made the king of France head of the French Church, for he had made him the sole dispenser of clerical preferment.

Henry, the rival of Francis, was also his imitator, and it must have been difficult for him to avoid envying the position Francis had acquired in gift from the Pope. What Francis received by the Concordat of 1516, the English Parliament gave to Henry when it declared him to be the one supreme head on earth of the Church of England. It thus fell out that the kingly supremacy over the Church in France made the French court support the Papal claims; while it set England in revolt against Rome. France, rescued from Papal domination by the Pope's own act, could rest there, and in all other respects maintain the old religion. England having secured her independence in spite of the Pope, and by an act of rebellion against his authority, could not rest there; the logical necessities of her position drove her farther and farther from Rome.

Thus it came to pass that the Reformation in England is the almost unwilling advance of a nation in revolt against Rome, because resistance to Rome had come to be the way of achieving, first, the personal aggrandisement of an imperious monarch, and then the independence of the people. France, in spite of the Huguenots, remained Roman Catholic; England, in spite of Henry VIII, became a Protestant nation.

THE SUBMISSION OF THE CLERGY

Henry soon discovered that the Pope was not to be terrified into granting the divorce, but he determined to frighten the clergy of the Church of England into conformity with his schemes. Cardinal Wolsey had been appointed Papal legate in England, and had been received as such by the bishops and clergy. In 1531 the king suddenly accused him of breaking the statute of *Praemunire* by accepting that office and presuming to fulfil its duties; and the accusation included the charge that all the clergy in England were partakers in his crime, because they had received him as the Pope's ambassador. It was also declared that both Wolsey and the clergy of the English Church had forfeited their whole ecclesiastical property in punishment for the crime. The clergy were seriously alarmed, and bought themselves off by a gift of £118,000, and an acknowledgment somewhat unwillingly made that the king was the 'singular protector and the only supreme lord, and, *as far as that is permitted by the law of Christ*, the supreme head of the Church and of the clergy'. The ambiguity in the acknowledgment was intentional. It left a loophole for weak consciences, but the king was satisfied with the phrase, feeling confident that he could force his own interpretation of the acknowledgment upon the church.

He proceeded without delay to show how he understood the concession which had been made, for he expanded the declaration into three articles, which he required the clergy to subscribe. They were asked to declare implicitly that no ecclesiastical law or ordinance could be thereafter enacted and published by the clergy without the king's consent; to approve of the appointment of a committee of thirty-two persons to revise the ancient canons of the church, and to expunge all those prejudicial to the king's authority; and, finally, to declare that ecclesiastical canons were to stand good only when ratified by the king's consent. These propositions were submitted to the Convocation or General Assembly of the Church of England, and, after some hesitation, they were accepted by the assembled clergy. Convocation went a little further than the king, for it petitioned that the *annates* should no longer be paid by the English clergy to the See of Rome.

This act of Convocation, which practically declared that the Church of England could make no laws for its own guidance or government without the king's sanction and ratification, has been called the *Submission of the Clergy*. Thus, in the year 1532 the Church of England, at the bidding of king and Parliament, renounced her allegiance to Rome. This renunciation of Papal rule included (1) the acknowledgment of kingly supremacy; (2) submission to the crown by surrendering the right to make laws; and (3) the withholding from the Pope of the revenues which had been paid him for generations. The church remained the same in doctrine, government, and worship, only the king took the place which the Pope had held.

The clergy had hoped to be allowed to retain the *annates* in their own possession, but the king showed that he meant the kingly supremacy to be as real as the old supremacy of the Bishop of Rome, and insisted on the Papal tax being paid into the royal treasury.

THE PROGRESS OF THE SEPARATION FROM ROME

During the earlier years of the reign of Henry VIII, when it was in the king's interest to stand well with the Pope and the king of Spain, all complaints against the church had been repressed. Now that Henry desired to terrify the Pope into granting him the divorce, complaints were encouraged. Henry used his Parliament as Charles V might have used the German Diet. All nations had accusations to bring against the church. The Germans published their *Hundred Grievances;* the English Parliament summoned to meet in 1529 had also complaints to make about the freedom of the clergy from the jurisdiction of the law courts of the land, about the absolute control exercised by ecclesiastical courts over laymen in disputed cases of marriage, wills and succession, slander, and so forth, about the avarice of the clergy and the heavy charges made for funeral and baptismal fees, and so on. The Parliament formulated these complaints, and in so doing terrified the clergy not a little, and made them more submissive to the imperious orders of the King.

In January 1532–3, Henry VIII married Anne Boleyn, and so personally defied the Pope. His marriage with Catherine of Aragon was declared null and void by the Archbishop of Canterbury, speaking in the name of the Church of England, and by Act of Parliament. The king and the nation, and somewhat unwillingly the church, had thus joined in unitedly bidding defiance to the Pope, and had revolted from the ecclesiastical empire of the Middle Ages. Parliament followed this act of defiance by passing laws intended to make the separation complete, and politically harmless to Englishmen. Seven Acts of Parliament were specially important.

(1) In 1533 the Parliament forbade the clergy to pay the *annates,* or first year's income on entrance to a new benefice. This 'first-fruits' had always been considered a homage due to the Pope's supremacy.

(2) In the same session Parliament abolished appeals to Rome. This *Statue for Restraint of Appeals* declared that no English subject was to appeal from an English court to a court beyond the realm, and asserted that any such appeal to a foreign, *i.e.* Papal or other, law court, was a defiance of the statute of *Praemunire,* and was to be treated as such. All disputed cases, where the church was the acknowledged judge, were to be settled by church courts *within the realm of England.* Appeals were possible as formerly from archdeacon to bishop, and from bishop to archbishop or dean of arches; but there the right of appeal stopped,

and the archbishop's court was declared to be the final court of appeal. Only the king could appeal from this highest church court, and he could carry his appeal to Convocation, and not beyond the kingdom.

(3) In 1534 *the Submission of the Clergy* was ratified by Parliament. It was declared that the king's consent was necessary to all ecclesiastical ordinances; and to give this practical value it was provided that in all disputed cases there was right of appeal from the highest spiritual court, the archbishop's, to the king in Chancery.

(4) Parliament further declared that the Pope had no right to interfere in the election of bishops, and whatever power the Pope was supposed to have really belonged to the king. This power was defined in such fashion as to give the whole right of nomination to the king, while the shadow of ancient ecclesiastical usage was preserved. When a see became vacant, the king had a right to send down to dean and chapter leave to elect *(congé d'élire)* some one mentioned in the letter of licence to the vacant office. Papal dispensations were also declared illegal, and the dispensing power once acknowledged to belong to the Pope was declared to reside in the Church of England, and its exercise to belong to the Archbishops of Canterbury and York.

(5) To show, however, that all these Acts had in view no reformation, but only the political severance of the Church of England from the Papacy, Parliament passed an Act on heresy, which declared that heretics were to be burned as formerly under the old statute *De haeretico comburendo*, and the king, as head of the church, was asked to take charge to purge it from false doctrines. Only it was declared that it was no act of heresy to speak evil of the Pope.

(6) Finally, this remarkable Parliament passed the *Act of Succession* and the *Treason Act*. The first declared the Princess Mary, the daughter of Catherine of Aragon, to be illegitimate, and settled the succession on the Princess Elizabeth, the infant daughter of Anne Boleyn. The *Treason Act* provided for the punishment by death of all who refused to accept the *Act of Succession* or to acknowledge the new title and prerogatives of the king.

THE SEPARATION FROM ROME NOT REFORMATION

In all the Acts of this Parliament, and in all the decisions of a submissive Convocation, there was nothing which was not purely political. England had not become Protestant or Lutheran, and men could not speak of a Reformed Church in England. What was done was that England had unitedly broken away from that confederacy of nations, presided over by Emperor and Pope, which was the mediæval ideal of civil and ecclesiastical government. What makes the Acts of this Parliament of so much importance was that England was the first nation which, as a nation, broke away from mediævalism and disowned utterly the old ecclesiastical empire of the Middle Ages.

Heretics, that is, pious men who had accepted the doctrines of Luther, or who had learned a purer Christianity by private study of the Bible, were sought out, persecuted, and slain with as much energy and vindictiveness as if England had been the obedient slave of the Pope. It is said that Wolsey had on his death-bed entreated the king to root out every trace of Lutheranism; and, in spite of the mild tolerance of Sir Thomas More, heretics were sought after and punished. Tyndale, who had translated Erasmus' New Testament into English, was hunted from place to place like a wild beast. All who ventured to speak against the Mass, Transubstantiation, Saint-worship, and the Efficacy of Good Works, were liable to be seized and burnt as heretics. The Acts of Parliament had not brought liberty of conscience, they had simply created new occasions for persecution and death. In addition to the old theological crimes there came a new one. Whoever refused to take the oath of supremacy, whoever dared say that Catherine of Aragon was the king's lawful wife, or that the Princess Mary was the heir to the throne, was liable to be seized, persecuted, and brought to execution. England was in a strange troubled state, and conscientious men could only suffer for conscience' sake.

THE EXECUTION OF SIR THOMAS MORE

Sir Thomas More was Lord Chancellor while the Parliament summoned in 1529 was by successive Acts severing the nation from the ecclesiastical empire of Rome. In his youth he had been a distinguished student, and had been fired with love for the 'new studies' of Latin, Greek, and Hebrew when attending at Oxford the lectures of Linacre, one of the early English humanists, who had trained himself in Italy for his scholastic work in England. He had devoted himself to the legal profession, had become under-sheriff of London, and was known as the friend of Dean Colet and of Erasmus. His book *Utopia* bears witness that he had adopted many of the views of Marsilius of Padua and other liberal jurists of the later Middle Ages.

He thought that both church and state existed for the people, and he yearned for a reformation of morals in the church. When he became Lord Chancellor, he was noted for the lenient way in which he dealt with heresy; but he remained attached to the doctrines of the Roman Catholic Church, and abandoned some of his earlier opinions in favour of stricter views about the divine origin of the supremacy of the Pope. He disapproved, therefore, of the whole of the proceedings of the English court and Parliament after the fall of Wolsey. He had warned the king that he could be no party to the divorce of Catherine of Aragon. He had refused to attend the marriage and the coronation of Anne Boleyn, and when threatened with the consequences, he had told the king that threats were for children and not for him. Henry had a strong affection for his Chancellor; but nothing was more calculated to deepen the distrust of the validity of the divorce, of the new marriage, and of the succession to the throne depending thereon, than the refusal of the highest legal authority in the land to regard Catherine of Aragon as any other than the lawful wife of Henry VIII.

More was accordingly summoned to take the coronation oath to the new queen, acknowledging Anne Boleyn to be the lawful wife of Henry VIII, and to admit the lawfulness of the *Act of Succession*. He had to choose between his conscience and his life, and he made up his mind calmly to die. His wife came to him in prison to beg him to yield. 'Mistress Alice', he said to her gently, 'tell me one thing, Is not this house as nigh heaven as mine own?' His daughter, Margaret Roper, famed for her learning, her gentleness, and her beauty, came to see him, and her visits seemed to strengthen his calm courage. He died in July 1535. The news reached Erasmus, who was finishing his book on the *Purity of the Church*, and he stayed to write a preface, in which he described his old friend More 'a soul purer than snow'.

The judicial murder of More and of Bishop Fisher, a fellow-sufferer, showed men into what a strange pass Henry and his Parliament had brought England, when men were burnt for Lutheranism on the one hand, and were executed for maintaining the Pope's authority in morals and doctrine on the other.

The Suppression of the Monasteries and the Confiscation of Church Lands

Henry VIII had been always a lavish spender of money. His father's hoards had disappeared in the French war in the beginning of his reign. The king and the court were in great need of funds. Thomas Cromwell pointed out that money might be got by the suppression of some of the monasteries.

No portion of the clergy were more justly attacked than the monks during the period of the Reformation. Their laziness, their wealth, their greed, and their bad living were notorious all over Europe. Popular writers had satirized them, and grave statesmen had remonstrated with the Pope, and urged a reformation of the various orders.

Cromwell urged a visitation of the monasteries to find out whether the complaints made were really justifiable. Three visitations took place, and the visitors undertook to prove that the lives of the monks and nuns were not what they ought to have been, that the monastic property had been badly managed, and that many monks and nuns wished to get rid of their vows. Parliament passed bills ordering the suppression of the smaller houses, and finally of all the monastic establishments. The property was confiscated for the king's use.

The great sum of money thus handed over to the king might have led, in the hands of a thrifty and sagacious sovereign, to the formation of a vast crown estate, yielding revenues so large that the king might have dispensed with taxes, and therefore with Parliaments, and this might have ruined the liberties of England. Henry had all the will to rule as a despotic monarch, but he was unable to exercise the self-denial needed to accomplish his desires. His one aim was to get abundance of ready money, and the properties confiscated from the monks were thrown into the market and sold to the highest bidder. The result was a vast increase in the numbers and prosperity of the landowners of England. In a few years Henry had squandered the money obtained, and was as poor and as dependent on his people's subsidies as before.

THE TEN ARTICLES

Cranmer, who was Archbishop of Canterbury, and who had been a facile instrument in the king's hands while Henry was making himself supreme over the church's liberties and master of much of its wealth, had a secret preference for the reformed doctrines of Luther and Zwingli. Thomas Cromwell, who since the death of Wolsey had been the king's political adviser, was also an admirer of the leaders of the Reformation. They were both desirous, after the political separation of England from the Papacy had been achieved, and the suppression of the monasteries had been effected, to introduce a reformation in doctrine and religion, and to bring the Church in England into harmony with the Reformed Churches in Germany and Switzerland.

Cromwell's political idea was that Henry should place himself at the head of a Protestant confederation which might rival in power the mediæval empire of Charles V. This could only be done, however, if the Church of England embraced the doctrines of the Reformation and encouraged the men who had hitherto been persecuted as heretics.

The king had a strong objection to the proposal, but he yielded for a time, and a short creed called the *Ten Articles* was published in 1536, and approved by Convocation. These Articles asserted the authority of Scripture, of the three great ancient Creeds, and of the first four Ecumenical Councils; they taught that baptism was necessary to salvation; that penance with confession and absolution was expedient and necessary; that Christ's body and blood were substantially, really, and corporeally present in the bread and wine of the Eucharist; that justification was by faith, joined with charity and obedience; that images might be used in churches; that the Virgin was to be honoured and the saints invoked; that the various rites and holy days of the Mediæval Church, with vestments, crucifixes, and holy water, were to be retained; that there was a purgatory; and that prayers might be offered for the dead.

These Articles scarcely pretend to approach the Protestant faith. Some church historians have called them a judicious and salutary compromise between the teaching of the more pronounced scriptural Reformers and the old superstitions; but they have been better described as essentially 'Romish, with the Pope left out in the cold'. Old Fuller says that they were meant for 'weaklings scarce weaned from their mother's milk of Rome'.

While these events had been taking place, Catherine of Aragon died in 1536, and the king got rid of Anne Boleyn by causing her to be beheaded on a charge of unfaithfulness. Her daughter, the Princess Elizabeth, was declared by Parliament to be illegitimate, and the succession was again uncertain.

The king then married Jane Seymour, to whose offspring the crown was secured.

THE PILGRIMAGE OF GRACE

The execution of Sir Thomas More and of Bishop Fisher had embittered a large number of the king's subjects who were attached to Rome, and these, taking heart at the declaration of the illegitimacy of Elizabeth and the unsettled state of the succession, rose in rebellion in Yorkshire and Lincolnshire. The rebels expected Spanish aid, and they relied also on the effect of the Bull of excommunication which had been published by the Pope against the king.

Their plans, however, suffered easy defeat, and the birth of a son to Jane Seymour, whom the king had married after the death of Catherine of Aragon, gave the king the coveted lawful succession and quelled all anarchy among the people. Unfortunately, the queen died in giving birth to her child.

Cromwell and Cranmer again introduced their ideas of a Protestant union. Cranmer and a committee of prelates in 1537 drew up what was called the *Bishops' Book*, or the *Institution of a Christian Man*, which contained an exposition of theology much more Protestant than the *Ten Articles*.

Next year Cranmer, who had been in negotiation with the Wittenberg theologians, constructed another creed called the *Thirteen Articles*, which was largely based on the Augsburg Confession.

The king refused to sanction these Articles, and gradually withdrew from the plan of a Protestant alliance. Cromwell aroused his master's displeasure by his persistent advocacy of the scheme, and by his plan of marrying Henry to Anne of Cleves in order to cement the alliance. He perished on the scaffold, as More and Fisher had done, and the king became more and more reactionary.

THE BLOODY STATUTE, OR THE SIX ARTICLES

The first sign of this was the publication of the *King's Book* or the *Necessary Doctrine and Erudition for any Christian Man,* a Romanist revision of the *Bishops' Book.* In 1539 Henry resolved to go back to the policy of the earlier period of his reign, and opened communications with Charles V. The change in the foreign policy of the king reacted on his home administration. He issued the *Six Articles* 'for the abolishing of diversity of opinion', and revoked his permission to read the Bible in Tyndale's translation.

These Articles required all Englishmen, on pain of confiscation of property, and death, to believe in Transubstantiation, to deny that it was necessary for the laity to partake of the cup at Communion, to accept the celibacy of the clergy, the binding obligation of vows of chastity, the necessity of masses and of auricular confession.

The doctrines of the Reformed Churches of Germany and Switzerland had made some progress in England in spite of previous persecutions, and had been embraced by a large number of the people during those years of toleration when Cranmer and Cromwell guided the policy of the king, and this statute of the Six Articles gave rise to a great deal of persecution. The people called it the *Bloody Statute* and the *Whip with Six Strings.* It began a reign of terror which ended only with the king's death. Fortunately for the nation, that was not long delayed.

THE STATE OF THE CHURCH IN ENGLAND IN 1547

Henry died in 1547, leaving three children – Mary, daughter of Catherine of Aragon, 31 years of age; Elizabeth, daughter of Anne Boleyn, a girl of 14; and Edward, a boy of 10, the son of Jane Seymour. Mary and Elizabeth had been declared illegitimate by different Parliaments. Edward succeeded his father on the throne.

Henry left behind him a chaos which it cost the nation a severe struggle to emerge from. He had, while he lived, kept a firm grasp on the extreme Romanist and on the Protestant party, and to the end maintained his own ideal – the Roman Church without the Pope. He had done this by placing himself in the position previously held by the Pope. He had an authority over the church much more absolute than over the nation. The position was difficult to fill, and more difficult for men who came after him than for Henry, for reformed opinions were spreading. He left also difficult political problems waiting for solution. The treasury was empty. His foreign policy had been shifty, and was full of difficulties for his successors. The sale of the church lands had brought about social and economic changes, full of difficulties.

The most pressing question, however, was: Shall England go forward to Reformation or back into Roman Catholicism? The church could not remain where Henry had left it.

2

THE REFORMATION UNDER EDWARD VI AND THE REACTION UNDER MARY

Is There to Be a Reformation?

When Henry died, Edward VI, a boy of ten, succeeded to the throne. Shortly before his death, Henry had made a will in which he nominated a Council of Regency consisting of sixteen nobles, who at once assumed the function entrusted to their care, and began to govern. They chose the Earl of Hertford, one of their number, to be Lord Protector of the Realm, and in accordance, it was said, with the terms of Henry's will, he was created Duke of Somerset.

The most serious question which had to be faced by this Council of Regency was the religious one. England could not stand where it did. Either the church must reform, or England must fall back into its old alliance with Rome. It is probable that had the opinion of the people been asked, there would have been a large majority for a return to Romanism. The last years of Henry's life had been a reign of terror, and the odium had been laid, and that justly, on the royal supremacy in matters of religion. The people of England, besides, knew very little about the reformed doctrines, and the Bible had scarcely been circulated. The reformed faith had not been preached in England as it had been in Germany or in France. There was no popular enthusiasm for the Reformation.

The suppression of the monasteries had also made many of the peasantry long for a return to the old paths. The English had opposed no obstacles to the suppression of these monasteries and to the confiscation of the church lands when that was first decreed; but the peasantry had since discovered that the great result to them was that they had exchanged easy landlords for harsh ones. All over the land the new proprietors were enclosing commons, throwing small farms into large ones, growing grass for sheep-grazing rather than corn, and thus diminishing at once the property and the work of the labouring classes. They sighed for the return of what they regarded as the good old times.

The suppression of the monasteries had set loose a host of men brought up to no profession and unable to work for their living, and these had to be provided for. The government had found that they could do this in the cheapest fashion by giving these disbanded monks work as parish priests, vicars, or curates. In this way the church became filled with men who had little heart in their work, and who hated the new order of things which had ruined their lives.

All these things made it doubtful whether or not England would advance towards Reformation or go back again to Rome.

On the other hand, there were in the kingdom a number of earnest and resolute men, who were prepared to give their goods and lives to further the cause of the Reformation, which they believed to be the cause of Christ, in England.

Among these men were the Lord Protector Somerset, and several members of the Council of Regency, and they determined to force the Reformation upon England. The first intimation given of the intention to maintain the royal supremacy came in the shape of a notice served upon all the bishops, requiring them to take out new licences from the new sovereign. This had been an invention of Cromwell's to guard the royal supremacy.

THE ROYAL VISITATION – THE BOOK OF HOMILIES – THE BOOK OF COMMON PRAYER

A *Royal Visitation* of the whole kingdom was ordered. The country was divided into six circuits, and commissioners were sent into each to see that the church services were properly conducted. The episcopal jurisdiction was for the time virtually suspended, for the visitors went in the king's name. Provision was also made for the better conduct of church services in places where these were found to be deficient. Archbishop Cranmer, who had always been a Lutheran at heart, and who encouraged the Council of Regency in all their plans, composed a *Book of Homilies*, which was given to the parish clergy and appointed to be read in the churches. Erasmus' *Paraphrase of the New Testament* was translated into English, and ordered to be used also in public worship.

These measures were not taken without opposition. Gardiner, Bishop of Winchester, who had acquired great influence over Henry VIII in the later years of his life, and who was one of the authors of the Bloody Statute, was at the head of the reactionary party, and protested against all the proposals of the visitors.

Meanwhile Parliament met, abolished the *Six Articles*, declared that the clergy were released from the vow of celibacy, that in the Lord's Supper the wine, as well as the bread, should be administered to the laity, and approved of the ecclesiastical policy of Protector Somerset.

The visitations went on. In order to render the service in church simpler, more attractive, and more uniform, the *Book of Common Prayer*, compiled by Cranmer out of the old service books, was ordered to be used in churches. This is the *First Prayer Book of Edward VI*, and although afterward somewhat altered and added to, it is in the main the same as that used by the Church of England to-day.

Other signs of departure from Romanism were soon to be seen. The images and relics in the churches were destroyed. The old Fast-days were abolished, and Archbishop Cranmer set the example by openly eating meat in Lent.

All this was very distasteful to a large number, perhaps the majority, of the people and of the clergy, and yet no open resistance could be made. Bonner, Bishop of London, tried indirectly to stem the tide by declaring that the new Prayer Book could be taken in a Romish sense;

but this only led to more decided definition of its theological terms, to the removal of altars from churches and the substitution of tables, and to the preparation of a new *Book of Order*.

In a short time the whole face of the church was changed, and in doctrine and worship the Church of England had become Protestant. The changes which had been made had caused great dissatisfaction with Somerset: there were attempts at rebellion; and although these were put down, still the Lord Protector's want of success, both in his foreign and in his home policy, combined with the dissatisfaction produced by his religious measures, brought about his overthrow, and the Earl of Warwick succeeded.

ALLIANCE WITH CONTINENTAL PROTESTANTISM

The accession of Edward, and the Protestant policy of Somerset and Warwick, encouraged Archbishop Cranmer to revive his old scheme of an alliance between the English Church and the Protestant Churches of the continent. Under the congenial patronage of Somerset, Cranmer's plan seems to have included the assembling in England of delegates from all the Protestant Churches to hold a Protestant Council which might act as an answer to the Council of Trent, and construct a common Protestant creed.

This was never carried out; but Cranmer got the aid of several foreign theologians to help him to instruct the people of England in the Reformed faith. Martin Bucer and Paul Fagius came from Strasbourg to England and were settled at Cambridge, where they gave lectures on theology and on the Old Testament Scriptures. Two distinguished Italians, Peter Martyr from Florence, and Bernardino Ochino from Siena, taught at Oxford. These foreign theologians, all of them accomplished scholars, trained numbers of students in the articles of the Reformed faith, and prepared a generation of teachers for the future Church of England. In continental fashion, too, they held public disputations on controverted points of theology, such as on Transubstantiation, on the Celibacy of the Clergy, on Purgatory, and so on.

All these theologians were Calvinist rather than Lutheran, and from them the Church of England got that inclination for the Calvinist as opposed to the Lutheran mode of stating the doctrines of the Christian faith which has moulded its articles.

THE FORTY-TWO ARTICLES

One result of these doctrinal discussions and disputes was the publication in 1553 of the *Forty-two Articles,* designed to express in confessional form the creed of the Reformed Church of England. They were the work of Cranmer, assisted by the bishops and other learned men. Cranmer had begun work on them as early as 1549; he finished them in 1552.

The appearance of these Forty-two Articles was very opportune. The rivalry of the Romanist and advanced Protestant parties in England, the public disputations conducted by the foreign divines, and the labours of itinerating preachers like John Knox, made many people eager for some authoritative statement of doctrine which these articles supplied. They defined with great clearness the limits of the changes which the church had made upon her mediæval theology.

These articles of religion are in almost all points the same as the Thirty-nine Articles, the present creed of the Church of England. Cranmer's own sympathies had always been Lutheran, and he borrowed no less than three of his articles directly from the Augsburg Confession. These were omitted in the Elizabethan revision, but in the main the Forty-two Articles of Edward and the Thirty-nine Articles of Elizabeth are one and the same document.

THE BEGINNINGS OF PURITANISM

The free discussion of Reformed theology and of Reformation ideas had for one of its results the origin and growth in England of a theology which accepted thoroughly the main principles of the Reformation revival of religion. One of these principles was that God had brought himself so near man in the revelation of himself in Jesus Christ that men, burdened as they were by sin, could nevertheless go directly to God for pardon and, according to his promises, receive it. Luther's theses had stated this great Reformation principle, and the possibility of going directly to God without the need of any human mediation had been insisted upon by every reformed theologian. The Mediæval Church, on the other hand, had denied this 'spiritual priesthood of believers' – for priesthood means right of direct access to God – and had placed between God and the people the priesthood of the church. It had also made the priesthood of the clergy visible by insisting that the clergy should, when engaged in public worship, wear a special dress symbolical of their priestly office, and had erected in every church an altar or special place of meeting between God and the priest.

Men who felt the truth and grandeur of the Reformation doctrine that all believers are priests with right of approach to God through faith, and that every spot of ground where the waiting soul seeks its pardoning and redeeming God is an altar, could not bear any doctrine or visible symbol of the special priesthood of the clergy. They were not content with the doctrinal statement of the Reformation truth; they could not bear to see the people misled by any outward symbol or rite which had in the days of superstition been used to teach the false mediæval theory of mediation. They objected, therefore, to the retention of all such ecclesiastical usages as might mislead the people in this important doctrine. They specially objected to the use of ecclesiastical vestments and to altars in churches. These men were the forerunners of the English Puritans.

It should always be remembered that Puritanism at the beginning did not mean a system of church government, and had nothing to do with either Presbyterianism or Congregationalism. The early Puritans in England did not protest against episcopacy as a system of government.

They might have fared better in the end had they done so. Their protest was against everything in creed or worship which would detract from the doctrine of the universal priesthood of believers. They believed that clerical vestments and altars in the churches obscured this vital truth, and they refused themselves to wear the robes, and to stand at altars with their backs to the worshipping congregation.

The question very early took definite shape. John Hooper, who had been a Cistercian monk, and had adopted Reformation views, became a noted preacher in the English Church. During the last years of Henry's reign his life had been in danger, and he had fled the kingdom to Geneva. His intercourse with the Swiss theologians had confirmed his principles, and when he returned to England he was resolute to oppose all rites which savoured of mediæval superstition. He was recommended to the King to be made Bishop of Gloucester in 1550. Unlike John Knox, he had no objection to government by bishops, and he accepted the appointment, but he would not wear the episcopal vestments; nor would he take the oath in which the phrase 'all the saints' occurred: 'So help me God and all the saints.'

Many theologians, including Calvin, had been inclined to regard such things as matters of indifference, but Hooper could not do this. Martin Bucer and Peter Martyr shared Calvin's opinions, and tried to shake Hooper's resolution by argument. They could not persuade him, and he was ordered by the court to keep his house and refrain from preaching. He obeyed, but in his forced retirement he wrote and published a *Godly Confession and Protestation,* in which he set forth with great plainness his reasons for refusing to wear vestments. For this act he was imprisoned. After some time a compromise was effected about the vestments; the words 'all the saints' were left out of the oath, and Hooper was consecrated Bishop of Gloucester. But what had occurred was significant of coming troubles.

Ridley also, one of the ablest of the leaders of the Reformation party in Edward's time, a man of learning, breadth of view, and tolerance – he pled that the Princess Mary should be allowed to worship God as she pleased – when he was made Bishop of London on Bonner's deprivation, cleansed all the churches in his diocese of images, relics, and holy water, and insisted that all the altars should be removed, and communion tables put in their stead.

These things boded ill for the timid compromise between Romanism and the Reformation, which was Cranmer's idea of what the Church of England should be. They awakened a sterner opposition on the part of men who had always been attached to the Mediæval Church. When Hooper and Ridley showed how far the Reformation would carry them, Gardiner and Bonner grew fiercer in the opposition. The government had to restrain both parties. Hooper had been imprisoned for his Reformation principles. Gardiner and Bonner were sent to the Tower for their mediæval views.

THE DEATH OF EDWARD VI

The young king had never been very robust, and before the close of 1552 the state of his health gave serious alarm to the Protestant leaders. The next heir was the Princess Mary, daughter of Catherine of Aragon. Parliament and Convocation had declared her to be illegitimate, but these resolutions carried no moral weight. Every one believed that

Catherine had been Henry's lawful wedded wife, and that Mary was his daughter, and failing Edward, his heir. Besides, according to the settlement of the succession under Henry VIII, she was to succeed Edward on his death without heirs.

Mary was a rigid Roman Catholic, of Spanish descent, who never forgot her mother's wrongs, and who looked on the Reformation as rebellion against God and a personal insult to herself. She was cousin to Charles V, the Emperor of Germany, had the greatest admiration of his talents and policy, and would render herself wholly subservient to him.

The knowledge of these things filled the minds of the counsellors of Edward with anxiety. The succession of Mary would turn back the Reformation, and it would destroy them. They felt that they must secure a Protestant successor.

Edward VI had as a boy firmly embraced the Reformation, and desired to secure to England a Protestant monarch. When he felt that he had not long to live he determined to name his successor. Nothing would persuade him that he had not the power to do so; and nothing would induce him to nominate one of his sisters. He believed that they were both illegitimate, as Parliament had declared, and that they were out of the succession. The dying boy had all the Tudor tenacity. He deliberately set aside Elizabeth as well as Mary; he also as deliberately set aside the young queen of Scotland, Mary, the representative of Margaret, his father's elder sister, and selected Lady Jane Grey, the representative (eldest child of eldest child) of Mary, his father's younger sister. Lady Jane had married the eldest son of the Earl of Northumberland, and was a Protestant. Edward believed that the people would accept the successor he named. His counsellors believed that the feeling in the country was so strongly Protestant that no Roman Catholic could succeed. They were both mistaken.

On Edward's death, Queen Jane was duly proclaimed; but the people, taken by surprise, did not respond. The Princess Mary escaped. Men gathered round her; the people responded to her appeals. After a few weeks all opposition was at an end, and the throne was Mary's.

The high-spirited, beautiful, and learned young queen was imprisoned and beheaded, and a Roman Catholic ruler sat secure on the throne.

THE STATE OF ENGLAND AT MARY'S ACCESSION (1553)

When Mary succeeded, the Reformation, as a political and visible edifice, reared with such pains by Edward and his counsellors, simply disappeared as a thing of no substance. It had really been forced on England from the outside by the government, and had not, as in other lands, been forced on the government by the people, or been equally acceptable both to rulers and ruled.

The country, too, was in a very impoverished state, partly owing to changes in the trade and economic conditions of Europe, but due mostly to the reckless extravagance of the reign of Henry VIII, and to the debased state of the coinage. The people were ready to blame the government and any outstanding act of the authorities for their poverty. The suppression of the monasteries and the sale of church lands, was at once fastened on as the measure which had brought distress on the country; and the ousted monks, scattered over the country as rectors, vicars, and curates, fanned the flames of discontent with the Reformation, and prepared the people for a reactionary policy in ecclesiastical matters.

Gardiner, Bishop of Winchester, who had been released from the Tower on Mary's accession, and had become her favourite minister, perfectly understood the situation. He knew that the country upon the whole preferred the old religion, but that it had always disliked the Pope. His policy, therefore, was to go back to the position in the end of the reign of Henry VIII, without insisting on the royal supremacy in the same high-handed fashion.

Mary, although she allowed herself to be guided by Gardiner, had more enthusiastic ideas. The ease with which she, after long years of disgrace and neglect, had come to the throne, seemed to her an indication that the people hailed a return to the old religion with delight, and had felt the past years as great an incubus on them as they had been on her.

As the daughter of Henry, and the Queen of England, she felt it to be her duty to make atonement to the Pope for the insults which the Roman Church had suffered at the hands of English statesmen. As the daughter of Catherine of Aragon, and the cousin of Charles V, she felt that she must help the Spanish, and make England and Spain one in foreign, and especially in ecclesiastical, policy.

SPAIN NEEDED ENGLAND'S HELP

Mary came to the throne in 1553. The Treaty of Passau between the Protestant princes of Germany and Charles V was signed in 1552. Charles was forcing himself to confess that the Reformation had beaten him, when Mary sent him word of her accession and entreaties for his advice. The English alliance was the one thing that might reverse the triumph of the Reformation, and restore success to the Austro-Spanish policy. Charles instantly answered, and his advice showed his anxiety.

Mary, he wrote, should first secure her throne; then she should secure a Spanish alliance by marrying Philip, the Emperor's heir; and these two things done, peace might be made with the Pope.

The Pope was as anxious to congratulate Mary as Charles could be; but the Emperor did not wish to rouse the anti-Papal feelings of the English people; the interests at stake were too mighty. So Cardinal Pole, the legate, was ordered to remain in the Netherlands until the country was prepared for him.

HOW MARY SECURED HER THRONE

At first this was a matter of little difficulty. The attempt to set Lady Jane Grey on the throne had discredited and discouraged the Protestant leaders, and few of them appeared. It was easy, therefore, for Gardiner to get the Parliament to repeal all the enactments which had to do with Catherine's divorce and Mary's illegitimacy. The Act of Parliament establishing the royal supremacy in matters ecclesiastical became an easy instrument for changing the religion of the country. The queen on her accession attended the Mass according to the old usage. Cranmer protested, and was sent to the Tower, where he was soon joined by Latimer and Ridley. The Prayer Book was abolished, and all the changes in worship introduced in the reign of Edward were swept away. The Church of England was restored to the condition in which Henry VIII had left it.

THE SPANISH ALLIANCE

The English people did not like the Spanish alliance, and were specially hostile to the marriage of their queen with Philip of Spain. Bishop Gardiner, who knew the temper of the nation, did his best to dissuade the queen, but she was bent on marrying Philip. When Gardiner knew that the marriage must go on, he drew up such terms of marriage settlement as gave Philip no royal title in England, no rights of succession, and no legal influence over English affairs. That Charles and his son accepted these terms shows the value placed on a stable alliance with England.

The English people hated the marriage, and manifested their feelings by rising in rebellion in several places – Sir Peter Carew in Cornwall and Devon, the Earl of Suffolk in the Midland Counties, and Sir Thomas Wyatt in Kent. Wyatt's was the only formidable rebellion and it was quelled by the courage of the queen. The nation also felt that Mary was her father's daughter, and the rightful heir, and had no great sympathy with rebellions against her. Philip came over, primed with careful instructions from his father to do his best to please the English people, which he in his uncouth way did his best to follow, by drinking English ale and otherwise, and the marriage was celebrated with all pomp. The Spanish alliance was secured.

THE REUNION WITH ROME

Philip and Mary were both earnestly devoted to the Roman Catholic faith, and longed to see England released from the Papal ban under which it had lain since the marriage of Henry with Anne Boleyn; but there were difficulties. The English people had never liked to acknowledge the Papal supremacy, and the best traditions of English history warned them against easy submission to the Pope. Charles advised his son and daughter-in-law to go to work very warily. There was, however, a still greater difficulty – the abbey lands which had been wrested from the church and sold to private individuals. On the one hand it was difficult for the Pope not to insist on their restitution, and on the other to restore them would have provoked rebellion. Few of these lands remained in the hands of the Crown; most of them had been sold, and the money had been spent. The queen could not buy them back from the present possessors and restore them to the church.

Charles V, after some difficulty, induced the Pope to waive all claims to these lost abbey lands, and it only remained to prepare the English people for the arrival of a Papal legate.

The legate selected by the Pope was Reginald Pole, grand-nephew of Edward IV. He was an English nobleman, therefore, but had gone

into exile rather than acknowledge the royal supremacy of Henry VIII
or the legality of the divorce of Catherine of Aragon. He was Mary's
kinsman, and one who had suffered for the sake of her mother's honour.
Parliament was asked to reverse his attainder. This was done, and Pole
was received in England as an English noble. He then presented his
credentials as the Pope's legate. The news was heard with indifference.
At last Parliament passed a resolution in favour of reunion with Rome.
On St Andrew's Day (30 November) 1554 the cardinal-legate gave his
solemn absolution to the nation. Philip and Mary, with both Houses
of Parliament, knelt in the cardinal's presence while he restored them
to the communion of the Holy Church. The Parliament repealed all
the laws affirming the royal supremacy and disowning the supremacy
of the Pope. The clergy, on the other hand, solemnly renounced all
claims to the abbey and other church lands which had been seized.
The union with Rome was again completely restored.

WHY THE PAPAL REACTION DID NOT SUCCEED

Within the space of two years England was to all appearance
completely reconciled with Rome. It seemed as if the reign of Edward
had never existed, and as if Henry had lived in harmony with the Pope
to the end of his life. The Roman Catholic reaction had set in, and
seemed about to carry all before it; but within a very short period this
whole reactionary movement was arrested, and within a few years
England stood forth as the great Protestant nation. How did this come
about?

It is perhaps impossible to tell all the causes, but three appear on the
surface of history – the persecutions which took place during the reign
of Mary, disputes about the church lands, and the spread of
Reformation opinion through the results of the teaching during the
short reign of Edward.

THE PERSECUTIONS IN MARY'S REIGN

The Protestants in England in the time of Mary were never harassed
with such dreadful persecutions as decimated the Huguenots of France
or slew the Reformers of the Netherlands. Yet they roused in the
country such a horror of the Papacy as survives to the present day. The
cause of this was partly due to the martyrs themselves and the way in

which they met their fate, partly to the deep-rooted idea that those executions were instigated by Philip, and were part of a wider scheme to make England Spanish.

The policy of Mary and her advisers was to strike down the leaders of the Reformation during the previous reign. The men selected were well known, conspicuous for their rank, eloquence, learning, and piety – Cranmer, the aged primate; Hooper, well known for his fervid eloquence; Ridley, one of the wisest and most tolerant of Reformed theologians. The people knew the men who were struck down, and were concerned in their death. England saw its wisest and most capable men handed over to the executioner, and burnt at the stake.

And for what? it was asked. For the sake of Spain and the Spanish alliance. For the sake of Philip, a cold-hearted bigot; and to stand well with that nation which had allowed its own sons and daughters to be tortured by the Inquisition, and which had tamely submitted to the most crushing despotism.

The martyrs, too, met their fate with Christian fortitude. In their lifetime their policy had not awakened universal confidence, but their deaths showed that they had been in earnest, and forced home on the hearts of the people the truth of the opinions they had striven to make dominant while they could, and for which they were now content to die.

THE CHURCH LANDS

Mary had been warned by Charles V not to attempt the restoration of the abbey lands to the church. They had been sold, and by their sale had been distributed among nearly forty thousand purchasers. To touch them would make all property insecure. The church and the Pope had expressly renounced all claim to them ere Parliament had consented to abolish the laws against the Pope and the Roman Catholic faith. Yet Mary was uneasy in her heart. She felt the weight of them on her conscience. How could England be blessed while so many of her subjects and she herself profited by thefts from the church?

Pope Paul IV, who had been consecrated in 1555, had not approved of his predecessor's policy in this matter, and made continual appeals to the queen to make restoration to the church. At last Mary yielded personally to his threats, and with some difficulty got Parliament to consent that the church lands still held by the Crown should be given back. This awakened great discontent. It made the possessors of the rest of the abbey lands feel that their title was insecure, and the loss of the money compelled the queen to add to the taxation. The church was felt to be relentless, and the people grew to hate it.

THE EFFECT OF THE REFORMATION TEACHING IN THE REIGN OF EDWARD VI

The foreign theologians brought over during the last reign to teach in Oxford and Cambridge had trained a generation of younger scholars who accepted their opinions with a conviction of their truth, who spread them among the people, and who were now content to suffer for them. Hitherto there had been little in the English Reformation to awaken enthusiasm. The people had shifted back and forward in easy fashion from one national profession of faith to another. Mary's persecutions made the Reformation heroic; and young preachers, trained by Martin Bucer and Peter Martyr, were glad to take their lives in their hands if they could only win their countrymen to acknowledge the scriptural creed of the Reformers. The translations of the Bible, especially Tyndale's and Coverdale's, had been read by hundreds, and England was being taught what the Reformation meant.

The people were heartily tired of the persecutions, and indignant with the church that had occasioned them; they despised the eagerness for property which the church showed when it risked so much to get back its lands, and they were now better taught in the Scriptures and in Reformation doctrine. There were signs that the force of the Roman Catholic reaction had spent itself.

MARY'S END

Mary died in 1558, of a dropsy, just in time perhaps to escape being the victim of a revolution. 'The unhappiest of queens and wives and women', she had been born amidst the rejoicings of a nation, her mother a princess of the haughtiest house in Europe. In her childhood she had been treated as the future sovereign of England, and in her girlhood as the bride-elect of the Emperor of Germany – a lovely, winning young creature, all men say. Then in her seventeenth year the crushing stroke, darkening her whole life, fell on her. Her father, Parliament, and the church of her country, called her illegitimate, and, branded in this cruel fashion, she was sent into solitude to brood over her disgrace. When all England saluted her as queen in her thirty-seventh year, she was already an old woman with sallow face, harsh voice, only dark bright eyes remaining to tell how beautiful she had been. But her people seemed to love her, who had been so long yearning for affection; she married the man of her choice, and she felt herself the instrument selected by heaven to restore an excommunicated nation to divine favour. Her husband, whom she idolized, tired of living with her in a year or two, and went back to Spain. The child she passionately longed for never came. The church and Pope she had sacrificed so much for disregarded her entreaties, and seemed careless of her troubles. And the people who had welcomed her, and whom she really loved, called her Bloody Mary, and taught the English nation to call her so still. Each disappointment she took as a warning from heaven that she had not yet paid full atonement for England's crimes, and the fires of persecution were lighted afresh, and new victims burned to appease the God of sixteenth-century Romanism.

3

THE REFORMATION UNDER ELIZABETH

ELIZABETH'S SUCCESSION

On Mary's death, Elizabeth was proclaimed queen without any opposition. The Roman Catholic party, which might have opposed her succession, was powerless, for England was at war with France, and Elizabeth's only rival was the Dauphiness, Mary, Queen of Scots. Yet her legitimacy was to all Roman Catholics extremely doubtful. She was Anne Boleyn's daughter, and Catherine of Aragon was living when she was born.

England was in a woeful condition when she succeeded. The treasury was empty, the revenue had been anticipated, and the country was engaged in a ruinous war with France. The queen's own position was most precarious. Her legitimacy was more than doubtful. France, at the first opportunity, would promote the claims of Mary Stuart. Spain, at first apparently her only friend, was hated in England. The strength of Protestantism in the country was doubtful. The religious question confronted her at the outset, and she temporized. She went to Mass to please the Roman Catholics. She forbade the elevation of the Host to please the Protestants. She waited to know what Spain and England would say.

Spain seemed friendly. Philip II offered himself in marriage; but the Spanish alliance depended quite as much on the Pope as on Philip, and Elizabeth soon found that the Papacy would never accept the daughter of Anne Boleyn. When the English ambassador announced her accession to the Pope, he was told: 'Elizabeth being illegitimate, cannot ascend the throne without my consent; it is impertinent on her part to do so. Let her, in the first place, submit her claims to my decision.' That was enough: Elizabeth could not count on Spain.

Nor had she to wait long for England's answer. Her first Parliament was almost unanimously Protestant. It met in 1559, and re-established the royal supremacy over the church, though in a modified form. Henry VIII had called himself 'the only supreme head on earth of the Church of England'. Elizabeth was content to be the 'Chief Governor', and Parliament enacted that all clergy and magistrates should take an oath recognizing her as queen, 'unto whom the chief government of all estates, whether they be ecclesiastical or civil, in all causes doth appertain'.

A commission of divines had been appointed to revise King Edward's Prayer Book, and they had so modified it as to make it more conformable to Roman Catholic usage, and this revision was on their recommendation adopted.

England had chosen to be Protestant, and Elizabeth, deprived of the alliance of France by Mary of Scotland, of Spain by the Pope, had to throw herself on the sympathies of the English people, and become Protestant also.

HOW THE RELIGIOUS QUESTION WAS SETTLED

Elizabeth herself was by no means what is called a good Protestant. She had no strong religious convictions. She was very like the great mass of the people and clergy she was called to rule over. When Edward ascended the throne she was a girl of fourteen; but young as she was, she knew how to take care of herself, and she conformed to the religion which was in favour at court. When Mary came to the throne she was a strong-minded young woman of twenty. She conformed again to the Roman Catholic worship. She was in her heart her father's daughter, and preferred Roman Catholic doctrine and worship, with the sovereign in the place of the Pope.

She was a Tudor, and loved pageantry. Her family instincts made her love authority, and the Roman Catholic Church was the living picture of authoritative rule which the world then gave. She was a scholar, and had read and liked to read the old Greek fathers. She liked the church to reverence patristic opinions and practices. She was fond of show and ceremonial, and preferred the gorgeous ritual of the Church of Rome. Only, no Pope must meddle with her.

She hated John Knox, and through Knox, Calvin and the whole Genevan school. She did not like the doctrine of justification by faith, the plainness of Genevan worship, and above all she hated those democratic principles of church government which were enshrined in Presbyterianism. The Reformer of Knox's stamp, with his doctrines of predestination, free pardon from God directly, and the spiritual priesthood of all believers, feared God, and nothing else. Elizabeth liked men to fear the king also, and she fancied that fear of the church was a good preparative for fear of the monarch. She had not the wit to put it as her successor did, 'No bishop, no King', but that was what she thought.

Her Parliament had told her that England was more Protestant than she liked, so she submitted, and accepted the Prayer Book and other Protestant usages.

The Roman Catholic bishops appointed in Mary's time had the courage to protest against these changes. They resigned or were deprived, and in 1559 all the Episcopal Sees in England save Llandaff were vacant.

A new episcopate was appointed, and at its head Elizabeth placed Matthew Parker, who in early days had been her mother's chaplain. The requisite number of bishops required to make a lawful consecration was got by bringing out of their retirement some of Edward VI's bishops who had been deprived of their sees by Mary. Parker's views were much more Protestant than her own, but he did not care to introduce innovations. Other bishops were chosen of a similar character. The idea was a Protestant Church resting on, and remaining true to, a visible Roman Catholic foundation.

Elizabeth soon found out, however, that her bishops were much more Protestant than she liked. The persecutions under Mary had sent a great many English families across the seas. They had gathered together in Frankfurt, in Geneva, and elsewhere; they had become intimate with Calvinist theologians, and they came back to England Calvinists. They were men who could not be silenced; they had suffered, and the martyrs of the last reign were to be held in honour: they had opinions, and could give reasons for their faith. The bishops knew that the Church of England could not be what Elizabeth wished it, and must have some authoritative statement of doctrine, some creed which in all its main outlines should be Calvinist. The queen was forced to give way, and the bishops prepared a creed called the *Eleven Articles*. Elizabeth would have images, crucifixes, and vestments retained, while the bishops knew that the people would not permit them. The quarrel was so much prolonged that on one occasion the bishops threatened to resign in a body. So the Eleventh Article declared that 'images are vain things'.

THE THIRTY-NINE ARTICLES

This short creed was soon found to be insufficient, and the queen besides insisted on keeping the church too much like the Roman Catholic. She wished to enforce the celibacy of the clergy, for instance. The bishops found it necessary to have an authoritative creed or exhibition of the dogmatic beliefs of the church. Archbishop Parker, assisted by the Bishops of Ely and Rochester, took Cranmer's *Forty-two Articles*, omitted three, and revised the remainder. The revision was presented to, and revised by, the Houses of Convocation. The queen 'diligently read and sifted' the Articles before giving her consent, and made at least two very characteristic changes. She inserted the first clause in Article XX: 'The Church hath power to decree rites or ceremonies, and authority in controversies on faith'; and she deleted Article XXIX: 'Of the wicked, which do not eat the body of Christ in the use of the Lord's Supper'. The bishops, however, insisted on the restoration of that Article, and the queen submitted. These Articles are, and were intended to be, Calvinist in their theology. Bishop Jewel, who finally revised them in 1561, wrote to Peter Martyr at Zurich: 'As to matters of doctrine, we have pared away everything to the very quick, and do not differ from you by a nail's breadth.' Thus the church, which had altered its Prayer Book to suit Roman Catholic tastes, framed its articles of religion or creed to bring itself into conformity with the Reformed Churches of Switzerland.

PURITANISM AND VESTMENTS

The queen did not like the Thirty-nine Articles, and had made this manifest. Their sanction was a victory to the Protestant party which she could scarcely forgive. Emboldened by their success, the Puritans made a vigorous attempt to overthrow the Prayer Book and to get rid of all the rites and vestments which had descended from the Mediæval Church, and almost succeeded. Elizabeth resisted with all the force and tenacity of her nature, and in the end was successful.

This Puritan struggle began about the year 1564, and lasted all Elizabeth's lifetime. At first the principal point in debate was the wearing of copes and surplices,[1] for Elizabeth's Puritans occupied the same position as their brethren in the reign of Edward VI. They held that office in the Christian Church is neither sacerdotal nor lordly; they were made bishops or clergymen not because they were priests, who could get nearer God than the laity, nor because they were rulers appointed by authority outside the church, but because the offices of overseer and pastor are of use to the church, and because the church had called them to be of service to her in this way. They refused to wear the vestments, because vestments meant something in which they did not believe.

The contest soon became embittered. The bishops would gladly have temporized, for they knew how widely spread and deeply rooted the objections to these vestments were; but the queen would not allow them. She made use of the power that the royal supremacy gave her over the bishops to force them to put the Act of Uniformity into operation, and this led to Puritanism becoming a protest in the end against a royal supremacy and an Episcopal constitution, and a demand for such an exercise of the popular voice in the government of the church as Presbyterianism or Congregationalism alone can give. During the years 1565 and 1566 a great many ministers were deprived of their livings because they would not conform to the established usages.

---

[1] The *cope* is the mediæval *cappa* or greatcoat. Mediæval cathedrals were cold places, and clergymen sensibly wore their overcoats when officiating there. What had been first worn for comfort was afterwards worn from custom, and gradually a meaning was invented, and the dress became symbolical. The *surplice* is the survival of the white toga or garment of ceremony (dress-coat) of the Roman Empire.

The queen deemed that her position as governor of the Church warranted her making continual inquiries into the way in which public worship was conducted in the parishes of England. She appointed royal commissioners to inspect and bring her information, and these commissioners of Elizabeth grew to be the Court of High Commission, which became such an instrument of ecclesiastical tyranny in the reigns of her successors. Through these commissioners Elizabeth was informed of nonconformity, and insisted on compliance with usage.

For the most part the people made common cause with the deprived ministers. Imprisonment and fines, as usual, only fanned the flames of nonconformity. It made its appearance within the universities. The students refused to wear the surplice or to attend the ministry of clergy who wore vestments. So many parishes were vacant that clergymen could not be had to fill them; and when compliant ministers were found, the parishioners not infrequently mobbed them. Some of the more zealous ministers seceded from the National Church.

The great Puritan leader was Thomas Cartwright. He was a Fellow of St John's College, Cambridge, was transferred to Trinity, and became Professor of Divinity. He was a pious, learned, and eloquent preacher. He was deprived of Fellowship and Chair for his opinions, and forced into exile. Two Puritans, Field and Wilcox, wrote a temperate tract – *An Admonition to Parliament* – on the discipline of the church, and the harsh measures taken against the Puritans. They were sent to Newgate, like common felons. Cartwright wrote a *Second Admonition* in defence of his friends, and had to flee the country a second time. The queen answered every appeal for toleration with fresh deprivations, until in one diocese alone, that of Norwich, it is said that there were no less than three hundred ministers suspended. Archbishop Parker died in 1575, worried to death by having to act as the executioner of the queen sorely against his will.

ENGLAND AND PROTESTANTISM BEYOND THE REALM

Some excuse may be found for the measures taken by Elizabeth against the Puritans in the earlier part of her reign. England was in a feeble, impoverished state, and the throne of Elizabeth was not secure. She had no sympathy with the Reformation in its deepest meaning, and she had no wish to see her people a nation of enthusiastic reformers.

England, she felt, needed rest and peace to recruit its exhausted energies. Had England grown enthusiastically Protestant, it could not have endured as it did the cruelties inflicted on the French and Dutch Protestants by France and Spain. It must have taken arms as the Protestant champion in Scotland, the Netherlands, and France. Elizabeth's cold-blooded policy saved her people for the greater future that lay before them. 'No war! my lords, no war!' was her constant exclamation when Cecil or some other minister wished her to place herself at the head of a Protestant league.

Elizabeth, also, notwithstanding her previous rebuffs, did not wish utterly to break with the Papists, or to show herself either to her own Roman Catholic subjects or to the continental nations as a strong and resolute queen. England needed rest, and the queen was determined to give her country peace.

This partly explains her cold-blooded policy towards the struggling Protestants out of England. Cecil, Elizabeth's greatest minister, wished his mistress to put herself at the head of a great Protestant league, and give effectual help to the Protestants in Scotland, the Netherlands, and France.

Elizabeth's jealousy of Mary Stuart forced her to give a good deal of assistance to the Protestant party in Scotland – such assistance as enabled them to make their very thoroughgoing form of Protestantism dominant. But in the Netherlands and in France Elizabeth gave, at first at least, no more assistance than sufficed to keep the Protestant party in existence, and this was tendered more for the purpose of exhausting France and Spain than of helping persecuted members of the same faith.

STRUGGLE AT HOME WITH ROMAN CATHOLICISM

The policy of the Roman court, and especially the avowed intentions and designs of the Jesuits, forced Elizabeth, after she had reigned nearly twelve years, to take a more decided stand on behalf of the Protestant faith, both in England and abroad. The Jesuits had urged over and over again, that no faith was to be kept with Protestant rulers; some of their emissaries had preached assassination as a lawful mode of ridding lands of Protestant rulers, and examples were not lacking to warn Elizabeth of her fate.

Her rival, Mary Stuart, driven from Scotland, was a dangerous prisoner in England. The death of Elizabeth would make her the hope of the Roman Catholic party, the nearest heir to the English throne.

In 1570, Regent Moray, the political head of the Reformation in Scotland, was foully murdered. In 1572 the Massacre of St Bartholomew was planned, and barbarously carried out. The same year the Duke of Alva, Philip II, and the Pope, conferred with Ridolfi, a Florentine who had long resided in England, about the possibility of a Roman Catholic insurrection in England, headed by the Duke of Norfolk. The plot was discovered, and Norfolk beheaded. All these warnings made Elizabeth see that her strength lay in trusting the Reformation, and they also made her people see how essential Elizabeth was for the Protestant triumph.

Perhaps evidence of the fact that the queen and her Protestant subjects drew nearer each other may be found in the appointment of Edmund Grindal, a clergyman of pronounced Puritan leanings, to the See of Canterbury, vacant by the death of Matthew Parker.

At all events, if Elizabeth was not less intolerant at home, she felt it to be her duty to send more help to Protestants abroad. The Huguenots were assisted with money. English adventurers, like Sir Francis Drake, were allowed to do all the harm they could to Spanish commerce. Elizabeth actually sent an army to assist the Netherlanders in their struggle against Spain.

These acts increased the eagerness of the Roman Catholic powers to cripple England. A seminary was established at Douai, and a college at Rome, to train English Roman Catholic priests, who were meant to return to their own land and stir up the English Romanists. And there were continual rumours of new plots to place Mary Stuart on the throne of England.

Elizabeth and her counsellors were at last roused to a sense of danger. Parliament passed Acts subjecting Romanist missionaries to penalties of high treason; and when Babington's conspiracy to murder Elizabeth and set Mary free was discovered, and Mary's cognizance of the whole plot had been proved, the execution of the Queen of Scots was at last resolved on. Elizabeth did not play a very heroic part in this tragedy; but she felt that she had at last (1586) broken with Rome, and Rome and the Roman Catholic powers felt also that the time for plots had come to an end, and that England must be subdued, or the Reformation be acknowledged as an accomplished fact.

THE SPANISH ARMADA

Rome and Spain at last saw what shrewd William Cecil had seen from the very first. 'The Emperor is aiming at the sovereignty of Europe, which he cannot attain without the suppression of the Reformed religion; and unless he crushes the English nation, he cannot crush the Reformation.' Charles V had seen this, but not clearly enough, when he was so anxious about the English alliance in the beginning of Mary's reign. Philip II had seen it when he offered to marry Elizabeth. Now the Pope saw it also, and, with Philip, bent all his energies to crush England.

The time seemed to be propitious. Philip II and the Holy League in France were apparently triumphant. England was without allies.

Pope Sixtus V excommunicated Elizabeth, and commissioned Philip II to execute the sentence. His Holiness also contributed large sums of money to aid in the work. The Spaniards gathered together a great fleet, which was to sweep down on England, while Alexander of Parma, the ablest general in Europe, was to cross from the Netherlands with the flower of the Spanish troops.

Elizabeth appealed to the patriotism of the whole nation, and it responded to her call. In spite of Mary's death, Scotland would not rise against England. France remained inactive, for the league was not so triumphant as had been supposed, and the Huguenots had not been crushed. All England armed. Two hundred ships were equipped. The nation in a stern enthusiasm waited for the attack.

The Armada came, a huge fleet of great unwieldy vessels, and bore down on England. The winds had damaged it ere it reached the English coast. The English ships hung round it, fighting in a series of naval skirmishes, which sadly harassed the already damaged fleet. Storms did the rest; and the navy which Spain had exhausted itself to equip was miserably cast away, few vessels ever reaching the ports whence they had sailed.

Then Protestant England sprang forward to take its place as the foremost European power. The Reformation could not be suppressed, for England could not be crushed.

It is hard to say how much the meaner side of Elizabeth had helped to this final consummation; her husbanding the resources of England; her careful repression of enthusiasm until at last it could safely be called out; her determination to make all England one outwardly by an Act of Uniformity enforced by severe penalties. If the means did not seem needful, at least the end was gained.

THE PROPHESYINGS

The appointment of a Puritan archbishop did not bring all the relief that was expected. Elizabeth was in the habit of making her bishops aware that the royal supremacy was a real thing. The rigorous suppression of nonconformity had led to a scarcity of ministers. Men not well qualified to preach were frequently inducted. Certain well-meaning pastors gathered together in clerical meetings to discuss questions in theology, and to train themselves in preaching. These meetings, not unlike the 'Exercise' in Scotland, and perhaps borrowed therefrom, were called *Prophesyings*. The queen did not like them. She did not see the need of preaching at all, and thought that clergymen should be content to read the *Homilies* to their congregations. Archbishop Grindal looked on these *Prophesyings* with favour, and when he was ordered by the queen to forbid them he refused to do it. The queen, in her wrath, threatened to depose him, and actually suspended him from all exercise of his episcopal functions. The suspension was continued almost until the close of his life.

CONVENTICLES; THE MARPRELATE PAMPHLETS

On the death of Grindal, Whitgift, the uncompromising opponent of Cartwright and of Puritanism was made Archbishop of Canterbury. The disastrous policy of the queen, carried out rigorously by him, had its natural result. The people, deprived of the services of the clergymen they respected, and forced to listen to others who had no claims upon them, refused to attend church. They gathered together in private houses and other places of resort, and held prayer meetings and other services of public worship. These conventicles were declared illegal, but they multiplied. Nonconformist sects arose.

Knox in Scotland, and Beza in Geneva, became alarmed at the state of the church in England. They knew how the Roman Catholic power threatened, and how English Protestantism required to be united. They had no sympathy with the policy of Elizabeth, and yet they thought that the Puritan horror at vestments was somewhat strained and exaggerated. They wrote to the leaders of the party begging them to conform; but the iron of persecution had entered too deeply into their souls. Forbidden to preach, they began to write, and sent pamphlet after pamphlet forth from the press among the people. The most remarkable was a series of pamphlets called the *Marprelate* pamphlets. These tracts fiercely attacked the episcopalian government in the Church of England, and exposed with relentless severity the various Popish ceremonies which it still retained. One of the writers, Nicolas Udal, was discovered, and was executed in 1593.

THE ENGLISH REFORMATION

The English Reformation was firmly established after the defeat of the Spanish Armada. England at last recognized that her place was to lead the Protestant powers of Europe; and in spite of the anomalous character of the English Reformed Church, the country did rise to its position.

Yet the English Reformation was of such a character that it cannot be easily compared with the same movement in other lands. In the earliest stage a capricious and absolutist monarch had on the one hand forced his realm to break away from the Papacy, and on the other had savagely repressed all attempts at a religious reformation either in doctrine or in worship.

Then a minority of the nation, no doubt containing the ablest and best men, but still a minority, coming to the head of affairs, pushed on a reformation of doctrine and worship. The movement, imposed from the outside during the reign of Edward VI, was scarcely responded to by the nation at large, which easily fell back into Papal allegiance when the government was changed.

Under Elizabeth the nation was at last really roused to take an interest in the religious Reformation which had been stirring other countries, but the shape which the national movement took was so controlled by the royal supremacy as to represent very ineffectually the aspirations of the church. It has become the fashion of late years among Anglican and Ritualist writers to represent history as if the Church itself had been guided by its own wisdom to assume the attitude which it did towards Romanism on the one hand, and decided Protestantism on the other; but these representations are not borne out by contemporary evidence. Anglicans set great store by the church's own right to direct and govern itself through its regularly appointed episcopal organization; and they are also anxious to prove that the position which they call catholic, and which others call anomalous, was assumed by the church itself, acting under the guidance of its orderly episcopal jurisdiction; but the facts of the case are against them. The anomalous position in which they boast was not given to the church by its bishops, but by the civil power acting through the royal supremacy.

It was the royal supremacy, which they dislike, that made it possible for the church to take such a shape as to give a show of historical basis for their theories.

It was the royal supremacy which altered the Protestant Prayer Book of Edward VI into one within whose formulas there was room for persons who would have preferred to remain Roman Catholics had not political considerations forced them over to the Protestant side.

It was the royal supremacy which insisted on retaining the vestments and rites against which the Puritans revolted, and which strove to retain images, crucifixes, holy water, and so on.

It was the royal supremacy and its court of High Commission – a court outside of the episcopal government of the church, and representing direct state control – which established the Act of Uniformity, and enforced conformity under the severe penalties of deprivation, fines, imprisonment, and even death.

The ecclesiastical leaders, the bishops and the higher clergy of England, were for the most part desirous to make the Church of England much more in harmony in doctrine and worship with the Reformed Churches on the Continent, which had taken Geneva as their model. The bishops prepared the *Thirty-nine Articles,* which Bishop Jewel, who was entrusted by his brethren with the last revision, declared were drawn up of set purpose to show that there was perfect uniformity in doctrine, and especially in the doctrine of the sacrament of the Lord's Supper, between Geneva and Canterbury.

The bishops, if left to themselves, would have wisely tolerated the Puritan objections to copes and surplices, and would have preferred the Second Prayer Book of Edward VI, long used in Presbyterian Scotland, to the one designed by Elizabeth to satisfy Roman Catholic scruples.

The bishops forced the queen to declare against images, crucifixes, holy water, the celibacy of the clergy – all which she would gladly have retained; and compelled her to accept the 29th Article, which asserts the Calvinist theory of the Lord's Supper.

If the bishops had had their way, there would have been room in the Church of England for the nonconformists of the present time – for their quarrel, to begin with, was not against episcopal rule, but against superstitious symbols and rites forced on them by the queen and her Commission; but there would scarcely have been place for the modern Anglican Ritualists.[1]

They owe the position, which must be legally and historically conceded to them, to two things – (1) to the royal supremacy, which was strong enough to put down and keep down the episcopal and national desire for a thorough reformation; and (2) to the fact that a large body of the clergy of England were so indifferent to changes that they managed to keep their livings under Edward, Mary, and Elizabeth – *i.e.*, under Puritan, Romanist, and Anglican rule.

The royal supremacy gave the Church of England the halting character of its Reformation, and enabled people living now to talk about the catholic, *i.e.* the mediæval, principles of the English Church.

Historians have pointed out how necessary it was for Elizabeth to act in the cautious manner she did, and in her high-handed fashion to prevent the church of her land from becoming thoroughly Reformed. There is some truth in their criticism. Still the policy was short-sighted, from hand to mouth, and very much on the principle of 'after me the deluge'. It was the royal supremacy of Elizabeth, enforced through the court of High Commission, which prepared the way for the Puritan revolt under Charles I, and for Black Bartholomew's Day under Charles II. Had the Church of England been left to its own spiritual instincts, unthwarted by state control, both those calamities might have been spared it.

---

[1] The Ritualists emphasized ceremonies in worship and were seen as favouring a return to the practices of the Middle Ages.

Part Four

THE PRINCIPLES OF THE REFORMATION

I

THE REFORMATION A
REVIVAL OF RELIGION

THE REFORMATION WAS A REVIVAL OF RELIGION AMIDST PECULIAR SOCIAL CONDITIONS

*T*he Reformation movement arose in one of the most remarkable periods of European history. The taking of Constantinople by the Ottoman Turks in the middle of the fifteenth century had dispersed the literary treasures and the scholars of that rich and learned city all over Europe. Men began studying diligently the old Latin authors; they learned the Greek language, and awoke to sympathy with the noble thoughts uttered by the old Greek poets and philosophers; they read the New Testament in the language in which it had been written; and Jewish rabbis found to their astonishment men in the rude Western World eager to be taught their ancient Hebrew tongue, and to study the Old Testament writings under their guidance. A whole world of new thoughts in poetry, philosophy, and sacred literature was seen opening before the men of the period in which the Reformation arose.

The discovery of America by Columbus not only revolutionized trade and commercial enterprise, but fired the imagination of Europe. When man had done so much, and discovered so much, what might not man do? The thoughts and speech of the time come from men who feel themselves on the eve of great events. It was a time of universal expectation.

The political condition of Western Europe had changed also. The fourteenth and fifteenth centuries were the birth-time of the nations of modern Europe. They had broken away one after another from the mediæval political system, and become independent, with national feelings and sympathies and aspirations, which made each nation feel that it had a career of its own.

The result of all this new life was that men felt that the world of social customs and political and religious restraint in which they had previously lived had become too small for them; they felt that they needed more room to breathe in. The world was larger; man's life had more manifold sides to it than their fathers had fancied. Old things were passing away, and all things were becoming new.

While mediævalism lasted, the church, the empire, and scholastic philosophy had ruled men's souls, bodies, and minds, and laid down the boundaries beyond which they were not to go. Those barriers had burst with the new life pressing out on them on all sides, and men felt that religion was wider than the Holy Catholic Church; that social life was too manifold to be confined within the limits of the Holy Roman Empire; that there were thoughts in man's heart which had been beyond the knowledge of the most learned of the schoolmen.

In earlier days a few daring but solitary thinkers had thought out for themselves these ideas and aspirations only to find themselves in the dangerous position of social isolation in which every thinker in advance of his age must stand. The invention of printing made these thoughts common property, and they began to act on men in masses, and to move the multitude.

Such was the world of social life amidst which the Reformation arose; but the movement itself cannot be explained simply by stating these social conditions.

It was a genuine revival of religion, a fulfilment of the promise of the outpouring of the Spirit of God upon his waiting church, and this religious movement springing up in these conditions took shape and force from its surroundings.

A REVIVAL OF RELIGION AND NEARNESS TO GOD

What most stirs the hearts of men who are in the midst of a great religious movement within the Christian Church is the desire to get near to God, to feel in personal fellowship with that God who has revealed himself in his pardoning grace in the life and work of the Lord Jesus Christ. Men who are really under the influence of a great religious awakening, and come within the sweep of a revival movement, must feel this yearning; and nothing can chafe them more than to find barriers thrown across their path at the very place where they had hoped to find access to his presence.

When the revival of religion began in the sixteenth century, and when it had gone on for some time, men under its influence felt such barriers in their way. The church which called itself the door of entrance into God's presence had barred the road with its priesthood, with its sacramental system, with its wearisome round of prescribed 'good works'.

The church which ought to have shown the way into God's presence seemed to surround the inner shrine of his sanctuary with a triple wall of defence which prevented entrance. When a man or woman felt sorrow for sin, the church told them to go, not to God, but to a man, often of immoral life, and confess their sins to him because he was a priest. When they wished to hear the comforting words of pardon spoken, it was not from God, but from man, that the assurance came. God's grace to help to holy living and dying was given, they were told, through a series of sacraments which fenced man's life round. He was born again in baptism; he came of age in the church in confirmation; his marriage was cleansed from the sin of lust in the sacrament of matrimony; penance brought back his spiritual life slain by deadly sin; the sacrament of the Lord's Supper fed him year by year, and deathbed grace was imparted in extreme unction. These were not the signs and promises of the free grace of God under whose wide canopy, as under that of heaven, man lives his spiritual life. They were the jealously guarded doors from out of which grudgingly, and commonly not without fees, the church and the priests dispensed the free grace of God.

And the Christian life could not be lived in free dedication of all one's talents to God. Holy living meant doing a set of small observances which the church demanded, eating less food, repeating more words of prayer, flogging one's back, and a whole round of wearisome ceremonies which, if they manifested love to God, did not do so according to St John's maxim, by benefiting one's neighbour.

At all points the church stood sentry over God's presence, declaring that man thirsting to get near his pardoning Redeemer could only get near by the wickets she guarded, and taking toll in sordid money in the shape of baptismal, confirmation, marriage, and other fees, or levying a wholesale tax in the shape of indulgence.

The great Reformation was a religious movement inspired by the irresistible desire to get near to God, and it fulfilled its aspiration by bursting these barriers asunder and sweeping them away.

HOW THE MEDIÆVAL CHURCH CAME TO BAR THE WAY TO GOD

The question naturally arises, How could the church so far forget its mission and the very end of its existence as to appear, as it did to the Reformers, to be doing the very opposite of what it was meant to do? The church is in the world to bring men to God, and keep them near him.

But Luther and his fellow-believers found it standing between them and God, and keeping them far from him. How could the church become the very opposite of what it was meant to be? How could the church of God become, as Knox graphically put it, 'a synagogue of Satan'? The answer, given fully, is too long to write here; but in brief something like this took place.

'Separation from the world' is one of the maxims of Christian life, foreshadowed in Old Testament precepts and embodied in New Testament rules of life. The church should live separate from the world, and leaders of religious thought in every age have set themselves to show how this could be done in a fashion that would work.

Gregory VII, better known by his private name of Hildebrand, living at the beginning of mediæval times, and the great organizer of the Mediæval Church, answered by declaring that there must be a visible separation such as men can see with the eyes; he laboured to convert the church into a kingdom of Christ, which could be as easily seen as any political kingdom; and this answer of his took shape in the policy of the Mediæval Church. In his days all political rule was gathered up into the hands of the Emperor of the Holy Roman Empire, and Gregory VII strove to make the kingdom of Christ as visible as the Empire, and its rival on earth. The idea was not a new one, it was borrowed from the great Augustine; but Gregory gave it practical shape. In his hands the church became a kingdom set over against the Roman Empire of the Middle Ages, its visible opponent. This could not be done without turning the church into a political monarchy, for two things cannot be compared and contrasted unless there be some fundamental resemblance between them.

The fatal defect in Gregory's idea of separation from the world was that he took one part of the world, the political empire which ruled, to be the whole of the world to be separated from, and actually made the church another part of the world set over against the political part.

The church was holy, it was spiritual, it was God's own kingdom; and all these phrases, used in Scripture to describe an inward spiritual relationship between the whole of God's people and their covenant God, were perversely applied to this political organization established in visible separation from the political empire of the Middle Ages. A man was called *holy* if he belonged to the one kingdom, and secular if he belonged to the other; a monk was a holy man, one of the emperor's guards was secular. A field was *holy* if a Pope or bishop or priest got the rents; it was secular if the landlord was not an ecclesiastic. The whole of the words and phrases which ought to have been kept to denote inward spiritual relations, were used to describe what was visible and external, and belonged to this visible kingdom which was called the Church.

The church was that within which men worshipped: it was the sphere of religion; and when men were taught of set purpose, or by the use and wont of language, that the church was simply a visible society, heart religion languished, and a religion consisting in performing a round of ceremonies took its place. This petrification of the church and of religion went on for long, growing more and more unbearable, and had been practically protested against in many a revival of religion. When the Reformation came it was felt to be intolerable, and men insisted that spiritual names should be kept for spiritual things, and not used to mislead pious souls.

MEDIÆVAL REVOLTS IN FAVOUR OF HEART RELIGION; *THE IMITATION OF CHRIST*

Although the Mediæval Church had tended to become more and more a political kingdom, and less and less a church, it is not to be supposed that there was no heart religion during the Middle Ages. The Church of England Prayer Book was mainly composed from old service books which had been written in times when the dominant idea of the church was political; and it is full of the deepest devotional feeling. Hymns which, in translations, are sung in all Protestant Churches in public worship were written by devout mediæval poets who consecrated their talents to the cause of Christ. This heart religion lived on inside the Mediæval Church, and was nourished by its services.

In most cases it never came in contact with the theories and doctrines which were unspiritual and coldly political. It lived on in its own life of real separation from the world after its own fashion, without seeking to express its ideas in definitions, or to question the limitation of the meaning of the evangelical phrases which the political guides of the church had given. Times came, however, when men were stirred to express their thoughts, and these expressions were not always in harmony with the definitions of ecclesiastical statesmen. Two revival periods may be taken as illustrations.

FRANCIS OF ASSISI

Francis of Assisi, moved by the sights of suffering in towns, where the poorest of the population, for the most part peasants who had fled from the country districts to escape the exactions of rent and forced service made by rapacious feudal lords, were crowded together in misery, resolved to give his life in preaching to the lapsed masses among the cities of Europe.

He was an enthusiast, but a noble one, and went to his work not in stolid business fashion, but under the influence of a great idea. His idea was the maxim of 'separation from the world', the same maxim which, wrongly used, had made the church political; but he put another meaning into it. Separation from the world, he thought, was not to be defined by spaces – the one space occupied by the church and the other by political society – but by personal conduct. Gregory VII had defined separation negatively; the Church is what the world is not, and where the world is not. Francis defined separation in a more telling and picturesque way. Separation from the world is being where Christ is, and doing what Christ did.

Francis seized an idea which Anselm of Canterbury had put in dry scholastic fashion, the thought of *imitation of Christ;* and he took this idea to help him to describe a real and personal separation from the world, very different from the political separation of Gregory VII. Anselm and Bernard of Clairvaux had both, the one in cold dogmatic way, the other in fervent revivalist preacher fashion, taken this thought of imitating Christ, and declared it to be the way in which sinners could appropriate the benefits won by Christ for men. Sinners can share in the Redeemer's work by imitating him. Francis took this thought, and joined it to the maxim of separation from the world, and said: 'See, here is the true separation. Christ was not of this world. His kingdom is not of this world. Separation from the world is found when men feel like Christ.'

But Francis lived in times when men could not see widely, and Christ's life and work, Christ's separation from the world, appeared to his vision in a picturesque but limited fashion. Our Lord was un-married; he was separate from the world of social married life. He was poor; he was separate from the world of wealth and property. He was obedient even to the death; he was separate from the world of self-will, and independent wayward life and action. He fastened on those outside aspects of Christ's life, he made the imitation of Christ, and the consequent separation from the world, consist in these outward modes of being like Christ; and to be Christlike meant, among his followers, to have taken the monastic vows of poverty, chastity, and obedience.

The revival movement he headed had vast results and speedy success; but like all movements which rest on outside imitations of a divine life, it soon exhausted itself, and pious men looked round for a better separation from the world which should go deeper, and for an imitation which should be truer.

The Mediæval Mystics

The Mystics took up the problem. They said, imitation of Christ and separation from the world after Christ's fashion must be deeper and more inward. It must be brought into connection with heart religion, for it is the soul and not its surroundings that can be brought near enough Christ to imitate him and follow him in his separation from the world. Man lives a double life, they said; a life within the circle of his own soul, and a life environed by society in the outside visible world. He meets God, not in the outside life which all men live, but in the solitude of his own heart. Separation from the world cannot mean any external course of conduct, any separation from parts of that visible life which all men must live, for separation from the world is communion with God, and that is found, not in the outward life, but within in the silence of soul fellowship. Let man renounce every affection, every desire, every action which might mar the soul's communing with its God, and seek in solitary self-surrender that Christ who is waiting to meet his people. They had the same thought of 'separation from the world' which Gregory had. They put meaning into it by the same idea of *imitatio Christi* which Francis loved to dwell on.

But they, living in evil times when wars and famine and pestilence abounded, felt, as few men before or since have done, the truth that the 'kingdom of God is within'. Renunciation became their watchword, and their renunciation was of an inward spiritual kind, and became a passive endurance of what God in his providence might send on them. They taught Luther what heart religion was, and that all religion must be heart religion, and they were undoubtedly nearer Christ than Gregory could be in his political church, or than Francis could be in his picturesque imitation of aspects of Christ's life in the world.

THE REFORMATION SENSE OF PARDON

All these movements were revivals of religion. They were all attempts to lay hold of and make real 'separation from the world', which is just nearness to God. The church went through this long struggle in preparation for the Reformation, rising on stepping-stones of dead selves to higher things. And Luther, in his own personal experience, went through all of them. Like Gregory VII, he recognized the omnipotence of the claims of conscience when, in spite of father and family, he left the study of law for theology. He was Francis when he thought that the monastic life and the imitation of Christ after monastic rule would bring him that peace of soul which is the fruit of living near Christ. He was John Tauler or Nicolas of Basle when he found that all true religion is heart religion. But with all this he was not satisfied. He was not as near God in Christ as he knew that he must be before he felt the blessed sense of pardon he longed to feel. And because he had put this question: How can I get the sense of pardon? how can I get over that insurmountable barrier of sin which rises between me and the holy God? and had made that the one question of his life throughout all the varying experience of his spiritual life, he was fitted to be spokesman for thousands of pious people who were feeling the revival of religion which was the Reformation.

All down the stream of pious mediæval life men and women had been yearning to get near God, but their yearning came out in different questions, and in each succeeding revival probed deeper. Gregory asked, How can I be separate from the world? Francis said, How can I be like Christ? The Mystics sighed, How can I have inward fellowship with God? Luther asked, How can I have the sense of pardon, and know that God has forgiven me my sin?

They are all feeling the same difficulty, they are all yearning for the same thing; only each generation of revival gets nearer the heart of the problem, till at last the pious people of the Reformation revival put the question of pardon, and therefore of sin, in the very forefront, and so got at the root of the matter. Let us get rid of sin, they said; let us get forgiveness, and we have separation from the world, imitation of Christ, and fellowship with God.

The Reformation revival of religion has this question of heart religion always before it, and always answers it in the same way. Men get pardon from God by going to God directly for it, trusting in his promise to pardon. God's free pardoning grace revealed in the Person and work of Christ, and man's trust in this promised grace, are the two poles between which the religious life of the Reformation always vibrates. God, for the sake of Jesus Christ, has promised to pardon his people's sin. The sinner trusts this promise. That is the simple religious aspect of the Reformation movement. All men who, having felt the need of pardon, and having perfect trust in the promise of pardon that God has given in Christ Jesus, go to him, and, casting aside all thought of themselves or of what they can do, simply rest on that promise and leave all to God, have the pardon and the sense of it.

ANTICIPATIONS OF THE REFORMATION REVIVAL OF RELIGION

If this be the true way of regarding the Reformation movement, it is manifest that it is not a solitary, isolated experience in the history of the church. For all pious Christians have felt in somewhat the same fashion, and have had somewhat the same inward experience. They have gone to God for pardon; have gone trusting in the work of Christ, and in God's promise revealed in that work. The prayers of all generations of Christian life bear witness to this, the hymns of Christian experience say the same thing, and what the Reformation revival did was once for all to put down in clear definition what all pious Christians had with more or less consciousness of the fact been feeling. Mediæval Christians had not felt how this spiritual experience of theirs, which was the central thread of their religious life, was contradicted in manifold ways by the creed and worship and theoretical organization of their church.

Nothing can be more surprising than the contrast between the doctrinal statements and ecclesiastical positions of many distinguished leaders of the Mediæval Church and the hymns they not only sang but wrote, and the prayers they used in their devotions. Their theology owed a great deal to the pagan philosophy of Aristotle, their worship had incorporated many pagan rites, their church government had modelled itself on the government of the Roman Empire rather than on the polity of the New Testament church. But pious Christians lived on in the midst of these uncongenial circumstances until the pagan elements which had entered into their church life grew so masterful that they were forced to protest against them.

Luther found pardon before he had broken with Rome, and might never have been compelled to revolt had not the paganism in the church insisted on selling God's pardon for money. This roused him and many others to look into matters, and they saw once for all that selling forgiveness of sin was not a horrible profanity accidentally grafted on the church they venerated, but was a real and logical deduction from principles which up till then they had not questioned. When, therefore, we look for the anticipations or antecedents of the Reformation, we ought to see them in that evangelical succession always present in the Mediæval Church, showing itself in pious living, in noble hymns, in confessions of sin and of trust in the promises of a covenant God.

Protestants do not need to claim kindred with men whose sole mark of a religious life is to disown the authority of the Pope, or to protest against the religious life of their time in favour of ideas borrowed from Muslim or pagan writers. They have a nobler ancestry in all those pious men and women who, even in the darkest ages of the church, went direct to God and trusted themselves, for this life and for the life to come, to his pardoning and renewing grace revealed in Christ.

2

HOW THE REFORMATION CAME INTO CONTACT WITH POLITICS

THE OLD ECCLESIASTICAL SYSTEM DEEPLY ROOTED IN THE SOCIAL LIFE OF THE TIMES

*T*he Reformation began simply in an attempt to worship God in simpler fashion, according to the dictates of conscience and the prompting of the inward spiritual life; but it could not stop there: it meant in the end a revolution in the conditions of society, and a great change in the political condition of Europe.

The Mediæval Church was very wealthy, and possessed a great deal of landed property, and when the parish, or district, or country became Protestant, questions arose as to what was to be done with this property. Were the priests to keep it, or was the Protestant pastor to get it, or were the civil authorities to take it for uses of state? The church had the right to levy tithes – the great tithe, or tenth of the corn or wine crop; and the lesser tithe, or every tenth lamb, calf, pig, or egg. Priests and monks got fees for baptizing, marrying, confirming, burying. When families became Protestant, and did not require the services of the clergymen of the Mediæval Church, because they would not engage in superstitious rites, what was to become of these tithes and dues?

Questions of money, which involved an appeal to law courts, and not infrequently led to a change of laws about property and ownership, were involved in the simple demand to be allowed to worship God as conscience demanded.

The Mediæval Church had its system of celibacy. All clergy were forbidden to marry, and besides the parish priests and curates, there were monks, nuns, and friars who were celibate and lived under vows of virginity sanctioned by the state. If any of these men and women became Protestants, were they to be allowed to break their vows and leave their monasteries? And if they had taken money with them to the monastery, could they take it back again? If all the inmates of a monastery embraced the Protestant faith, could they keep the monastery and its endowments? All these legal questions were raised by the Reformation.

There were others much more serious. The Mediæval Church, according to the customs of the age, took charge of and judged a whole class of disputed questions, which in modern Europe are decided by the law courts of the country. The relations of husband and wife, parents and children, wills and succession, belonged to the jurisdiction of church courts, and did not come before the ordinary law courts of the realm. The church declared what was a legal marriage and what was not; what were the prohibited decrees; who were legitimate children, and so forth. Whenever such questions arise, they involve questions of property, for only legitimate children can inherit their parents' property. Marriage was only lawful if within the degrees permitted, if performed in the face of the church by an ordained priest. For marriage was a sacrament according to the ideas of the Mediæval Church. Thus, no Protestant could be legally married, for legal marriage came from participation in a sacrament which could not be administered to rebels against church authority. And the law of the church was the law of the land; for before the Reformation the church was left to decide in all these cases.

Unless the laws were altered, no children of those Protestants who were married by Protestant pastors could inherit property, for the law of the Mediæval Church declared that there had been no marriage between the parents. Thus questions of personal honour and the honour of wife and children were involved, as well as questions of property.

Cases might be multiplied indefinitely; those cited may be taken as illustrations of the way in which the simple desire to worship God according to conscience altered all the conditions of social life. The old ecclesiastical system went down to the very foundation of daily life, and took everything within its grasp. When the Reformation attacked it, it seemed to attack everything: laws of property, of marriage, of succession.

THE REFORMATION OVERTHREW THE MEDIÆVAL IDEA OF POLITICAL SOCIETY

According to mediæval notions, Christendom was one, one church and one political state. The whole ecclesiastical power was summed up in the person of the Pope, who was the world-priest; and the whole of the civil power was gathered together under one head, the Emperor, who was the world-king. The one was priest of priests, or bishop of bishops, and the other king of kings. A man was in the church if he was under the jurisdiction of the Pope; he was within civil society if he was under the rule of the empire.

Three powerful Frankish chiefs, one after another, in the end of the eighth century, had cleared a space in Western Europe within which the Christian religion could extend itself in peace. With their strong arms they had kept back the hordes of Frisian and Saxon savages who tried to overwhelm Europe with a new Wandering of the Nations, and they had driven the Muslims back over the Pyrenees. In gratitude the Pope had conferred on Charles the Great [Charlemagne], the last of the three, the title of Emperor of the Romans, and had gathered round him the prestige of the Roman name and what heritage of Roman law, arts, and sciences remained.

The empire thus founded was dual. It had civil and spiritual heads, Caesar and the Pope; and all European jurisprudence rested on the double theory of representation involved; for the Emperor was reckoned God's vicar in civil or earthly matters, while the Pope ruled for God in spiritual things.

According to mediæval notions, when a man refused to obey the Pope in spiritual matters he rebelled against the whole order of society, for that was based on the idea that the Pope and the Emperor were the supreme rulers. Protestantism broke up the unity of Christendom at a

time when unity seemed to mean political existence and the upholding
of society on a firm moral basis.

REVOLTS AGAINST MEDIÆVALISM BEFORE THE REFORMATION

Mediæval ideas had suffered somewhat before the Reformation came.
The birth of modern nations, with separate interests continually
conflicting, and with feelings of independent unity, went against the
mediæval idea of one Christendom. This national independence meant
revolt against the Emperor, and it was followed in less distinct fashion
by national revolts against the Pope. The English statute of *Praemunire,*
which forbade appeals to Rome, meant that there was within the realm
of England itself a jurisdiction from which there was no appeal; and
that was a revolt against the mediæval idea of the united Christendom,
in which all appeals would be carried to the foot of the Emperor's
throne or of the Pope's chair.

Independent nations meant independent churches, and the revolt of
Henry VIII did not go much further than Edward III or Philip the
Fair had gone. The Gallican theory of later date, by which the Roman
Catholic Church in France was regarded as national and more or less
independent, was a revolt against the same mediæval idea of central-
ization of church power in Rome.

The Reformation intensified this revolt. It made it mean more where
it had taken place; it helped on the tendency to decentralization; and it
made it permanent. After the Reformation arose, nations had one more
cause of quarrel, for difference of creed came in to embitter their
relations.

The mediæval mystics, with their theories of heart religion, had set
small store by the ideas of political and ecclesiastical unity which
prevailed in their time in Europe, but they had not attacked them. Their
conviction that religion consists in solitary heart communion made
them supremely indifferent to all external combinations and associations. Among the Reformers, Luther alone seemed to share in their
quietism or passive indifference to political or ecclesiastical cooperation.
But the Reformation was not a mere individualist movement: it taught
men to combine, only it made the centre of association and the
combining force quite different from mediæval notions of what they
should be. It fostered national life; men, because they had fought

together side by side, lived in the same land, shared the same traditions, undergone the same misfortunes, grew to form a national unity from the inside, as it were. National churches, if Protestant, obeyed the new law of growth from within.

The Reformation, which broke away so thoroughly from Rome, and yet which did not destroy society, made all men see that there might be social life and religious fellowship without pressure from the outside, without order and association being impressed from without by the idea of a world-wide empire and church. The mediæval idea of a united Europe meant that all the various nations were constrained to obey one central power, the Emperor; the Reformation idea is a brotherhood of peoples.

DANTE'S *DE MONARCHIA*, AND THE *DEFENSOR PACIS* OF MARSILIUS OF PADUA

Two remarkable books appeared in the century before the Reformation, one of which belonged to the past that was departing, and the other to the future which was at hand.

Dante, sorrowing over the endless quarrels of Italian states and European nations, wrote his *De Monarchia* to show his contemporaries how they could live in peace. His proposal was to restore in all its strength the old mediæval empire, which, even at its best, had scarcely been more than a dream, doing its work by the power it had of compelling the imagination. The reign of universal peace would come, he thought, if the mighty empire of the Caesars or of Charles the Great could be revived, when a strong Emperor, sitting at the centre of the civilized world, heard and judged appeals sent in from all parts of the earth for final decision, and put down with a strong hand those who rose in quarrel against their brethren. The book is the epitaph of mediævalism.

Marsilius of Padua, about the same time, wrote his book, the *Defensor Pacis*, which explained how real peace and national security begin from within. With Marsilius the State is the people, and out of the people – their wishes, their aspirations, their fears, and their intentions – social life is evolved. The government is by the people for the people. So it is in the church. All rule is ministerial; its power is derived from those for whom it is exercised.

While Dante sought a compelling power from the outside, Marsilius predicted that the force which would control nations would be a self-restraining one which had its spring within the nation itself. The Reformation helped to make his predictions come true, and his theories to become descriptions of actual political and social life.

This was the political revolution the Reformation worked. It changed the centre of national life from an external controlling force to an inward spring of action. It did for the political life of Europe what Kepler did for astronomy and Kant for metaphysics: it changed the centre from the outside to within.

3

THE CATHOLICITY OF THE REFORMERS

THE REFORMERS DID NOT MEAN TO CREATE A NEW CHURCH

None of the Reformers – neither Luther, nor Zwingli, nor Calvin – thought that in seeking to worship God in the simpler fashion which Scripture directed, and which their inward spiritual experience approved of, they were deserting the church. They were forsaking the Pope, and refusing to have spiritual communion with him; but they remained, they thought, in the church into which they had been born, by which they had been baptized, and in whose communion they had worshipped since childhood.

They did not think that reformation meant leaving the church of their ancestors. They had no wish to make a new church, still less to create a new religion. The religion they professed was the religion of the Old Testament and of the New, the religion of the saints of God from the day of Pentecost downwards. The church to which they belonged after their severance from Rome was the church of the Apostles, and of the Martyrs, and of the Church Fathers. It was the church in which God had been adored, and Christ trusted, and the presence of the Holy Spirit felt from the times of Christ's Apostles down to their own day.

Reformation kept them within, they thought; it did not send them out of the church of their fathers. How could they make this fact, which they set great store by, evident to all who looked to see it?

THEY VINDICATED THEIR POSITION BY AN APPEAL TO THE LEGAL CONSTITUTION OF THE MEDIÆVAL EMPIRE

The Reformers had broken away from the Pope, and they held no further communion with him or with the Roman Curia. In their days, however, to be in the church was to be in communion with the Pope and with Rome. To be outside the pale of the Pope's pastoral care meant, in those days of wholesale excommunications and interdicts, to be outside of church privileges.

If the Pope refused to have communion with any man, or city, or province, by launching an interdict against him, or by issuing sentence of excommunication, all the services of the church ceased. There could be no baptisms, no marriages, no death-bed consolations while the excommunication hung over the devoted place. The churches stood closed, and all services of public worship were at an end until the excommunication was removed. In the common thought and speech of the time, to be out of communion with the Pope was to be outside the church. It was difficult to show men the contrary in a clear way without any theological distinctions about it.

Luther's ready mind seized on a way by which he could show people that the church was wider than the circle of those in communion with the Pope. The Holy Roman Empire of the Middle Ages was more than a kingdom, it was also in one aspect a church. Its Emperor was made a deacon. It was spoken of as Christendom. Above all, its citizens owed their position within its protecting limits to the fact that they accepted the Nicene Creed in the Latin form approved by Pope Damasus. The Middle Ages presented, therefore, two pictures of the church of Christ – communion with the Pope, and citizenship within the limits of the Roman Empire.

Luther ostentatiously maintained his right of citizenship within the Empire. He over and over again declared his adherence to the Nicene Creed in the form prescribed. He was an orthodox Christian according to the test set by the Emperor. He was in Christendom, and a member of the great Christian community, although he was not in communion with the Pope. Luther took advantage of the ecclesiastical character of the empire of the Middle Ages; he took care to declare, in the most patent way possible, that he was a member of the empire, and was therefore, according to ancient ecclesiastical reckoning, a Christian, and a member of the Christian Church, although not in communion with Rome. He made it plain to his contemporaries that the church was wider, even according to mediæval ideas, than communion with Rome. He himself was out of communion with Rome, and yet he was a member of Christendom, and therefore within the church.

THE CATHOLICITY OF THE REFORMATION ACCORDING TO LUTHER AND CALVIN

The mediæval Empire had the Nicene Creed for its test of citizenship, and therefore was supposed to be coextensive with the Christian Church. Luther, in order to show that after he had broken with Rome he nevertheless had not deserted the Catholic Church of Christ, took the Apostles' Creed, the Nicene Creed, and the Athanasian Creed, and published them as his Confession of Faith.

He says in his preface, 'I have caused these three Creeds or Confessions to be published together in German, Confessions which have hitherto been held throughout the whole church; and by these publications I testify once for all that I adhere to the true church of Christ, which up till now has maintained these Confessions, but not to that false, pretentious church, which is the worst enemy of the true church, and which has surreptitiously introduced much idolatry alongside of these beautiful Confessions.'

Luther, too, in his first controversial treatise against the errors of the Roman Church, followed out the idea of the preface just quoted. He calls the book *On the Babylonish Captivity of the Church of God*. He tried to show that the church had been led away captive by the Pope and the Curia, just as the Israelites had been when they were carried off to Babylon. The church, freed from the Roman yoke, had all the privileges which the church of God ever had, and besides had also freedom from bondage.

The Reformation, according to Luther, brought the church back out of bondage worse than Babylonian, and the leaders of the Reformation were men like Zerubbabel or Ezra or Nehemiah. They were not founding a new church, they were leading the old church of the Apostles back out of bondage into freedom.

Calvin also held this idea very strongly, although he does not put it so picturesquely. In the preface to his *Institutes* he tells us that he wrote the book to answer those who called the doctrines of the Reformers new, doubtful, and contrary to the Fathers. He answers these questions by showing the catholicity of the theology of the Reformation. He proves that all the Reformers hold and maintain the great catholic doctrines which the church has ever held, and that when they break away from the teaching of the church of Rome, or any doctrine, they part company at the very point where pagan ideas and superstitious practices have been unwarrantably introduced.

THEIR POSITION VINDICATED BY THE APOSTLES' CREED

The leaders of the Reformation, at the head of a great religious revival, did not imagine that they were heading a new movement, still less that they were founding a new religion. They had a spiritual ancestry, they thought, and considered themselves the true heirs and successors of the church of the Apostles, of the Martyrs, of the Fathers, and of the Middle Ages also. It was the Roman church, not theirs, that was new. They belonged to the old church reformed, and were the true heirs of centuries of saintly life that had gone before.

They were charged by their opponents, however, with being schismatics and heretics, with deserting the Catholic Church of Christ, and with striving to create a new church and to found a new religion. They were told that the church of Rome was the only Christian community, and the one holy Catholic and Apostolic Church.

How did they make answer? Their answer lay ready for them in the admissions of the Roman Catholic Church itself. The Church of Rome claims to accept and believe the Apostles' Creed, and that Creed gives a definition of what is meant by the church, which is quite at variance with the Romanist claims.

The Apostles' Creed teaches men to say, 'I believe in the Holy Catholic Church, the communion of saints', not 'I believe in the Holy Catholic Church in communion with Rome.' There is no word in those early creeds to say that catholicity is to be defined by communion with Rome; on the contrary, catholicity is said to mean *saintly fellowship*.

The leading Reformers dwell upon this. The Creed says that the Holy Catholic Church rests on saintly fellowship, and that saintly fellowship rests on forgiveness of sins.

True catholicity springs from holy fellowship, which is possible because of common forgiveness of sin through the redeeming work of the Lord Jesus Christ.

4

THE DOCTRINAL PRINCIPLES
OF THE REFORMATION

THE FORMAL AND MATERIAL PRINCIPLES OF THE REFORMATION

A favourite method of describing the theological or doctrinal principles which gave distinctive shape to the Reformation revival of religion is to say that they may all be brought under two heads, one of which has been called the *formal*, and the other the *material* principle of Reformation theology.[1]

The German church historian, Dr Isaak Dorner, has stated this mode of looking at the Reformation movement with very great clearness and force in his *History of Protestant Theology*. According to Dorner, the

---

[1] These terms are intended to distinguish the Reformation's source of authority, Scripture, from its central doctrinal topic, justification. The first is the *formal* principle of the Reformation, the second its *material* principle. See Terry L. Johnson, *The Case for Traditional Protestantism: The Solas of the Reformation* (Edinburgh: Banner of Truth, 2004), pp. 75–76.

doctrine of the Word of God is the *formal* principle, and the doctrine of justification by faith is the *material* principle of Reformation theology.

The use of these technical terms is apt, however, to obscure the real meaning of the movement, both in religious life and in theology. The leading impulse in the movement was simply that which must inspire every revival of religion, viz., the earnest desire to get near to God, the yearning to come face to face with God, who has revealed himself for salvation in the Lord Jesus Christ. What have been called the *formal* and *material* principles of the Reformation are alike connected with this impulse. The right of entrance into God's very presence, the Reformers believed, had been conferred by him on all his people; but the right of entrance is what is meant by priesthood, and a key principle of the Reformation is *the priesthood of all believers* – the right of every believing man and woman, whether lay or cleric, to go to God directly, with confession seeking pardon, with ignorance seeking enlightenment, with solitary loneliness seeking fellowship, with frailty and weakness seeking strength for daily holy living.

Direct Access to God Is Central to the Reformation

When Luther and Zwingli rebelled against the Roman Catholic abuses which disfigured the Mediæval Church, the most scandalous of these abuses were indulgences on the one hand, and wholesale excommunication on the other. In the one, in indulgences, the Mediæval Church practically said that sinners need not go to God for pardon, because the church could give that pardon on easier terms. The pardon which God gave for the sake of Christ's work, the church gave on the payment of a few ducats. It deliberately stood between sinners and God, and lured sinners away from God by blasphemously pretending that it could sell pardons at a cheap rate. Man did not need to go to God with sorrow and repentance of heart, and faith in God's promises. The church met the sinner who had money more than half-way.

At other times the church absolutely refused pardon. If a town or a diocese or a country had, through its rulers, offended the Pope or his court at Rome, it was put under an interdict, which meant that no sins could be pardoned while the interdict lasted. The church stood between the new-born child and baptism, between the dying Christian and death-bed grace, between young men and women and lawful wedlock blessed by God, between the people and daily worship. The God of grace could not be seen or approached because the magistrates or the bishops or the king and his counsellors had offended the Pope. The church had been able to bar the way, because it had said that the only path of access to God was through the priests; and when the priests were forbidden to act as priests, and officiate at the rites of religion, God could not be approached at all. The Pope by a stroke of the pen could prevent a whole nation from approaching God, because he could prohibit priests performing the usual religious services; and, according to mediæval theory, these services performed by priests were the only ways of getting near to God.

The Reformers, on the other hand, said: Man may get near to God in prayer, in pardon, in fellowship and enlightenment, whenever he faithfully seeks to approach him; it is impossible that the way to God can be barred in such a fashion. Luther said that he had no objection even to indulgences if they were to be looked at as one way of saying that God is always gracious. But he refused to believe in them or in any other rite of the Mediæval Church if it was used to declare that men could get pardon without drawing near to God in contrition, or that they could be entirely excluded from God's presence at the dictates of their fellow-men.

This thought – that God's presence is free to the faithful seeker, that God will not refuse to hear the prayer of any penitent, that God makes his promises speak directly to the hearts of all his people – lay at the basis of the whole of Reformation theology. It was made possible through the doctrines of Scripture and of justification by faith.

This Access Is Made Possible (1) through the Reformation Doctrine of Scripture

All the Reformers believed that in the Bible they had God speaking to them in the same way as he had spoken in the church in earlier days by his prophets and apostles. They taught that the people, having the Bible in their hands, translated into a language which they knew, out of the original Greek and Hebrew, could hear God speaking to them directly, could go to him for instruction and warning and consolation. In Old Testament times God had spoken to his people sometimes by dream or waking vision, but mostly by ambassadors taught by himself, who were called prophets. In New Testament times God spoke in the midst of his people by his Son, and his Spirit spoke also through Christ's apostles. All these revelations, committed to writing in the Scriptures of the Old and New Testaments, were so preserved that in the Bible God speaks to his people from them just as he spoke to his people by the voice of his holy men of old. The Reformers taught that in the Bible all believers can hear God speaking to them directly, and that he can be listened to by every one in whose hands the Bible is. The Reformation doctrine of the Word of God makes possible one side of the fulfilment of that yearning for entrance into the very presence of God which is a principle, not merely of the Reformation, but of every true revival of religion.

THIS ACCESS IS MADE POSSIBLE (2) THROUGH THE REFORMATION DOCTRINE OF JUSTIFICATION BY FAITH

The doctrine of justification by faith asserts that the yearning for access to God is no vain longing, but a thing that can have real and actual fulfilment. According to mediæval theology, the sinner could not go to God directly for pardon. He had to go to a priest, and the priest could stand between him and God, and refuse God's pardon if the Pope or his superior in the church commanded him. No matter how sincere the sinner's sorrow, no matter how strong his trust, the priest stood between him and his pardoning God, and he could neither tell God his sins nor hear from God the sentence of forgiveness unless the priest spoke it. The doctrine of justification by faith means that God himself speaks the pardon, that he pardons for the sake of what Christ has done for the sinner, and that man can hear this pardon spoken if by faith he trusts in the mercy, the salvation, and the promise of God.

THE REFORMATION DOCTRINE OF SCRIPTURE CONTRASTED WITH THE MEDIÆVAL

The Reformation doctrine of Scripture is very often stated in a fashion which does not bring it into direct connection with the over-mastering impulse of the Reformation movement. The Reformers, it is said, set the Bible, an infallible book, over against the word of an infallible church. In mediæval times men appealed to the church in the last resort, and accepted the decisions of Popes and Councils as the last decisive utterance on all matters of controversy about doctrine and morals; at the Reformation the Reformers put the Bible where the church, *i.e.* where decisions of Councils and Popes, had been, and made the last and final appeal to the decision of the Bible. This mode of stating the difference between the Reformers and their opponents has found most concise expression in the saying of William Chillingworth (1602–44), a famous English divine, that 'the Bible and the Bible only is the religion of Protestants'.

All this is true, and yet it is not the whole truth, and therefore is to some extent misleading. For Roman Catholics and Protestants do not think of the Bible in precisely the same way; and the difference in the use of the word brings out a truth which is sometimes forgotten. When Roman Catholics speak of the Bible they mean one thing, when Protestants speak of the Bible they mean another thing, and in this difference in the use of the word there lies a very important part of the Reformation doctrine of Scripture.

The Mediæval Church did not as a rule warn its people against reading the Bible for edification. On the contrary, it was a maxim in mediæval theology that the whole doctrinal system of the church was founded on the Word of God. Thomas Aquinas, the greatest authority among mediæval theologians, says expressly in the beginning of his great work, *The Sum of Theology*, that the whole round of Christian doctrine rests on the Scripture, which is the Word of God. Translations of the Scriptures into the languages of the peoples of Europe were made continually during the Middle Ages: it is quite a mistake to suppose that the first translations of the Bible were made during Reformation times; and as a rule the people were encouraged to read and know Scripture.[1] In the earlier stages of the Reformation controversy Roman Catholic disputants appealed as freely to the Bible as Luther and his friends did. It was reserved for the post-Reformation Catholic Church to debar the laity from reading the Word of God.

THE MEDIÆVAL DOCTRINE OF SCRIPTURE

Yet mediæval theologians used the Bible in another way than Protestants did, and in the Protestant controversy the difference of meaning soon

---

[1] However, the pre-Reformation translations were made from the Latin Vulgate and did not represent a return to the inspired Hebrew and Greek texts.

emerged. Mediæval theology never looked on the Bible as a means of grace; they regarded it as a book full of information, divine information, about doctrine and morals. They thought that it was a storehouse of doctrinal truths and moral precepts, and nothing more.

Protestants believe that the Bible is a storehouse of infallible truths, but they believe that it is something more. It is a means of grace. They believe that men can get from the simple reading of the Bible not only information but fellowship with God, not merely knowledge about God but communion with him. It gives not merely new truths about divine things; it actually quickens to the divine life. It is to the Protestant all that it was to the mediæval theologian, and it is something more. It is as effectual a stimulus of faith and holy living as the sacraments, or prayer, or worship can be. By the diligent use of the Bible, according to Protestant divines, men can not only know about God; they can actually share in that blessed experience of communion between God and his people which the Bible records.

THE FOURFOLD SENSE OF SCRIPTURE

There is one great difficulty attending the mediæval idea of the Bible – that it is a storehouse of information about doctrines and morals and nothing more – this, namely, that such a description does not seem applicable to a great part of the Bible. The Scriptures contain long genealogies, chapters with little other than a description of temple furniture, descriptions of simple human life, or of national history. In these portions of the Bible, comprising no small portion of it, there does not seem to be much doctrinal information or many rules for holy living, and yet these make up the whole Bible according to the mediæval definition.

The mediæval theologian had, therefore, either to cut out what seemed to be irrelevant matter, or to invent some means of changing tables of genealogy into doctrines or moral rules. He chose the latter alternative, and said that every passage in the Bible had more meanings than one.

The Bible, he said, had a fourfold sense. There was, first of all, the *historical* sense of the passage read, the plain prose meaning which grammar and the ordinary rules of interpretation gave. Then there were three other senses: the *allegorical,* the *moral,* and the *anagogic* [mystical].

These various senses gave meanings different from the historical, and mediæval expositors drew elaborate doctrines from the genealogies of Abraham and David, and rules of conduct from the description of the high priest's robes or from the narrative of the journey of our Lord from Capernaum to Nain.

It is sometimes difficult to know what is the precise meaning of certain passages of the Bible, even when the reader thinks only of the plain historical signification; the labour becomes fourfold if each passage has four senses. Any passage of the Bible can be made to mean almost whatever the reader chooses if the use of mystical senses is brought to bear upon it.

THE MEDIÆVAL DEFINITION OF SAVING FAITH

While mediæval theologians made it almost hopeless to know precisely what the Bible did say by their doctrine of the fourfold sense, another theory of theirs made it all-important that the believer should have precise and certain information of what the Bible actually did say. They held that faith was not trust in a person, but the assent to correct information; the faith which saves was, they said, assent to the propositions about God, the universe, and the soul of man contained in the Bible. On the one hand, their doctrine of the fourfold sense made it almost impossible for any individual to ascertain what Scripture did teach; on the other, their definition of saving faith made it all-important for this life and the next that every one should have clear and correct views about what the Bible taught. Thus the Mediæval Church was forced to say that, over and above the Bible, there was an authoritative mode of interpreting the Bible, and this led them to their doctrine of infallible decisions of Councils and Popes about what the Bible taught.

It is needless to say that if the Bible by itself be of doubtful interpretation, and if it be also essential to salvation that the believer have the true and correct interpretation to which he can assent, what gives the infallible interpretation will have more practical value than what is interpreted. And this is what actually happened. The decisions of Councils and Popes, the traditional and authoritative interpretation of the Bible by the church, became of much more practical value than the Bible itself. Men going simply to the Bible might go wrong, and it was death to go wrong; men trusting in the church's interpretation of the Bible could not, they thought, go wrong.

All this, however, made it impossible that the Bible could be a means of simple communion between God and man. Between the Bible and the believer the mediæval theologian placed Councils and Popes and the opinions of theologians; in a word, the church. The church barred the way to God through his Word by placing itself and its authoritative interpretation between the believer and the Bible.

The Reformers, yearning for fellowship with God, and knowing by their own spiritual experience that they had it by the simple reading of the Word of God, felt bound to clear away this barrier, and they did so. But the barrier could not be cleared away by simply saying that the Bible, and not the traditions of the church, was the infallible guide. For the Bible as the Roman Catholics understood it, the Bible which taught only doctrinal and moral precepts, whose every passage had four senses, was simply bewildering and not infallible. The Reformers had to give another meaning to the Bible before they could say that it was infallible and the supreme judge in controversies.

THE REFORMERS AND THE BIBLE

They gave the Bible the meaning they had themselves found in it. God had spoken to them in and through it. The personal God, who had made them and who had redeemed them, spoke to them in the Bible and made them know his power and his willingness to save. The speech was sometimes obscure, but they read on and got other passages which were plainer, and they made the easier explain the more difficult. Plain men, perhaps could not understand it all, nor fit all the statements into a connected system of theology; but they all, plain men and theologians alike, could hear their Father's voice and learn their Redeemer's purpose and have faith in their Lord's promises.

It was a good thing to put text to text and build up a system of Protestant theology which made things plainer; but the one essential thing was to hear and obey the personal God, speaking to them as he had spoken all down through the ages to his people, telling them his salvation and the promise of it, now in direct words, now in pictures through the history of his dealings with a chosen people or a favoured man. No detail of life, national or individual, was useless; for it helped to fill out the picture of fellowship between God and his people which would be fulfilled in their own blessed experience of fellowship with a covenant God, if they had the same faith which these Old Testament and New Testament saints had.

With these thoughts burning in their hearts, the Bible could not be to them what it was to the mediæval theologians. There could not be the fourfold sense. The Bible was God speaking to them, their Father speaking to his children, speaking as a man speaks to his fellows; and the plain historical sense was the only one there. It was more than a storehouse of doctrines and moral rules. Over and above, it was a record of the blessed experience which God's saints had had in fellowship with their covenant Lord since the first revelation of the promise. Faith was more than a cold assent *(frigida opinio)* to truths of doctrine and morals: it was personal trust in, and rest on, the personal Saviour who spoke to them in and through the Bible.

So they made haste to translate the Bible into all languages, and place a Bible in every man's hands, and said that a poor man with the Bible, *i.e.* with God speaking to him, knew more about the way of salvation than Councils and Popes without it.

Their doctrine, the fruit of their own inward spiritual experience, declared that yearning after communion with God was fulfilled in the reading and preaching of the Word of God. Through the Bible men came into the very presence of God, and heard him speak comfort to their souls.

THE REFORMATION DOCTRINE OF JUSTIFICATION CONTRASTED WITH THE MEDIÆVAL

The second great principle of Reformation theology is by universal consent the doctrine of justification by faith alone. This may also be brought into direct connection with the principle of the priesthood of all believers, or the right of access into the presence of their covenant God promised them in his Word.

The same difficulty occurs in contrasting the Reformation and mediæval doctrines of justification which appeared in contrasting the two doctrines of Scripture. It is commonly said that the Reformers taught a justification by faith alone, and their opponents taught a justification by works; but while this is perfectly true, it should be remembered that the word justification is used in two distinct senses by the two disputing parties.

With mediæval theologians, *justify* means to make righteous; with the Reformers, it means to pronounce righteous. With the one it is a work taking time; with the other it is an instantaneous act – an act of God's free grace, whereby he pardons all our sins and accepts us as righteous in his sight. With the one it is a work of cleansing from sin and making holy; with the other it is an act of judgment, or, as theologians say, a *forensic* act. The Reformers found mediæval theologians using the word justification in the way mentioned, and they deliberately took the word and gave it another meaning. They justified their action by saying that their use of the term is the New Testament use, where the word always means an act, a sentence, a judgment, and never a work.

The first contrast is therefore not between the mediæval justification and the Reformation doctrine, but between the Reformation doctrine of justification by faith and what corresponds to it in the Mediæval Church. Justification in Reformation theology means the act of pardoning and accepting as righteous; the mediæval counterpart to this is the doctrine of priestly absolution, for that is the act of pardon in mediæval theology.

PRIESTLY ABSOLUTION AND JUSTIFICATION BY FAITH ALONE

According to mediæval theology, God's pardon for sin had always to be pronounced by a priest. When the penitent had confessed and shown sorrow, by word and deed, the priest was entitled to pronounce the sentence of absolution or pardon, and this word of pardon was believed to be God's, because the priesthood was the organ through which, and through which alone, God spoke pardon.

Luther and the other Reformers saw the priest who was supposed to stand in God's stead and speak for God doing things which were ungodly, and conscience told them that in these cases the priest's pardon could not be God's. Luther saw a man with an indulgence ticket go to a priest and get pardon without showing any sorrow either in word or deed, and without, to all appearance, feeling any sorrow in his heart. He saw priests pretending to be the mouthpiece of God, and pronouncing pardon when pardon could not be spoken by a just and holy God.

Luther and his friends had seen or heard of cases in which God's pardon had been withheld at a time when a merciful God would have spoken pardon. A succession of Popes had smitten the city of Strasbourg with an interdict because it had taken a side in German politics with which the Papal court did not agree, and during all that time no word of pardon could be spoken to the contrite and repentant sinner. Priests pardoned when God would not, and refused to pardon when God would have pardoned.

Luther, seeing this, and knowing in his own heart how pardon had come to him by simple trust in God's promises, declared that the sinner can go to God directly in contrite sorrow and trusting in God's promises, and obtain pardon from God. He said that unless God's pardon is first obtained, the priest's pardon is worthless, and that when God's pardon has been obtained the priest's pardon is needless. He put pardon obtained from God by going to him in the place of pardon obtained by going to the priest and hearing him pronounce absolution. The Protestant doctrine of justification teaches the way of access to God for pardon, and declares that no priest dare bar the way between the repentant sinner and his God. It swept away the mediæval doctrine that divine pardon is only obtained through priestly absolution, and that the repentant sinner goes not to God's footstool, but to the priest's confessional.

JUSTIFICATION BY FAITH AND JUSTIFICATION BY WORKS

According to mediæval theology, before pardon could be ordinarily obtained through priestly absolution, confession of sins, contrition, and penance had to go before. In confession the sinner must name to the priest every sin committed since his last time of confession, and the catalogue of sins done must be gone over in detail. Every sin must be named before it can be forgiven. The confession must be mechanically complete. After confession comes contrition or sorrow, and this sorrow, according to mediæval doctrine, must be shown in certain stereotyped ways whose use the church has sanctioned. Then, and not till then, is absolution or pardon possible.

The Mediæval Church put two things between the sinner and God's pardon spoken by the priest: a mechanically complete confession in which every sin to be pardoned had been named, and a contrition exhibited in certain stereotyped ways, such as saying so many prayers, abstaining from food, etc., and the absolution was made to depend on the mechanical completeness of confession and of contrition. The Reformers felt that sin was too awful a thing for forgiveness to depend on a complete confession, and on an externally manifested contrition. God forgave for Christ's sake, not because of perfect confession or complete contrition. They declared, therefore, that while the sinner ought to confess his sins, and show honest endeavour after new obedience, the pardon depends on the sovereign grace of God revealed in Christ.

They found it necessary again to sweep away barriers erected between God and man by the Mediæval Church – the barriers of a mechanical confession and contrition or penance. Heartfelt sorrow was the great matter, for this meant confession and contrition and trust; and God pardoned for Christ's sake, seeing evidence of these.

Justification by faith, therefore, means that the sorrowing sinner can go to God at once, trusting in the finished work of Christ, and get pardon without the intervention of priest or mechanical routine of ceremony. God pardons because of what Christ has done, not because of what we may be able to do; and since pardon is won by Christ's work, and not by our own exertions, it may be and is given at the beginning of the Christian life, and need not be painfully waited for till the end, as a doctrine of justification by works would imply.

The doctrine of justification by faith, the second pillar of Reformation theology, answers the Reformation yearning to get near to God. It means that the sinner who repents, and believes in God's promises, can go to him at once for pardon, and find that pardon without priestly or mechanical intervention.

CONCLUSION

The Reformation, which was a great revival of religion, animated by the yearning to get near to God, with sorrow, confession, and trust, thus sent believers to have fellowship with him through the Bible, and to obtain pardon and acceptance at his footstool, and swept away the barriers between the free sovereign grace of God and the sinner which the mediæval political church had erected. The new spiritual experience which the Reformers and their fellows had, fed by the Word of

God, and taught by his Spirit, blossomed on all sides into a Reformation theology, where a doctrine of predestination took the place of
the theory of communion with God through the Pope and his bishops,
where the theory of the sacraments was purified by a doctrine of the
Holy Spirit, where the Scriptures were the final test in controversies,
and where pardon was spoken by God and not by man; and in every
area there can be traced, as a central theme, the spiritual priesthood
conferred by God on every believer.

CHRONOLOGICAL
SUMMARY

Contemporary Events	Lutheran Church	Reformed Church
1493–1519 – Jan 12, Maximilian I, Emperor. At his death the Elector Frederick the Wise of Saxony (1480–1525), viceroy. 1499–1535 – Elector Joachim I (Nestor) of Brandenburg. 1500–1539 – Duke George of Saxony. 1509–1547 – Henry VIII of England. 1515–1547 – Francis I of France.	1517 – Oct. 31, MARTIN LUTHER [b. 1483, Nov. 10, at Eisleben; 1497, at Latin School at Magdeburg; 1499, at Eisenach (Frau Cotta, d. 1511); 1501, at Erfurt; 1505, Master of Arts; 17 July, entered the Augustinian Cloister at Erfurt; 1508, Professor at Wittenberg; 1510, at Rome; 1512, Oct. 19, Dr of Theology] nailed 95 theses against the abuse of indulgences on the door of the Castle Church at Wittenberg. Counter theses of John Tetzel, composed by Conrad Wimpina.	ULRICH ZWINGLI: b. 1484, Jan. 1, at Wildhaus, in county of Toggenburg; scholar of Henry Wölflin (Lupulus) at Berne; of Thomas Wyttenbach at Basle; 1499, student of Joachim Vadianus at Vienna; 1506, M.A.; 1516–18, preacher at St Mary's, Einsiedeln. (Diebold of Geroldseck and Abbot Conrad of Rechenberg.)
1518–1567 – Philip the Magnanimous of Hesse (b. 1504).	1518 – Silvester Mazzolini of Prierio: *Dialogus in praesumptuosas M.L. conclusiones de potestate Papae;* Luther's *Resp. ad Silv. Prier.* April 26, Luther at Heidelberg Disputation. Aug., Cited to appear at Rome. Aug. 25, Melancthon at Wittenberg. Oct. 13–15, Luther at Augsburg before Card. Thomas Vio de Gaeta; appeals *a papa male informato ad melius informandum.* Nov.: Luther, *On the Sacrament of Penance.*	1518 – Zwingli against the indulgence preached by Bernardine Sampson (guardian of the Franciscan Cloister at Milan). Dec.: Zwingli pastor in the Minster at Zurich.
1519 – June, Charles V (since 1516 King of Spain) – 1556, Aug. 27, Emperor of Germany (d. 1558). 1519–56 – Sulaiman I Sultan. 1519–21 – Fernando Cortez discovers and conquers Mexico.	1519 – Jan.: Luther's interview with Charles of Miltitz, papal chamberlain at Altenburg; Truce. June 27–July 16, Disputation at Leipzig: (1) between Eck and Carlstadt, on the Doctrine of Free Will; and (2) between Eck and Luther, *De primatu Papae.* The controversy is no longer one about a point in scholastic theology; it involves the whole round of ecclesiastical principles. Break with the Roman Christendom. The doctrine of the priesthood of all believers. Christian freedom and the right of private judgment.	1519 – Jan. 1, Zwingli delivers his first sermon in Zurich; sermons on St Matthew's Gospel, Acts, and the Pauline Epistles: Reformation sermons, pointing out a clear distinction between a biblical and Romanist Christianity; Humanist study of Scripture (Pauline Epistles).

Revolutionary Movements	Roman Catholic Church	Protestant Theology
	1513, Mar. 11–1521, Dec. 1. – Leo X.	
	1517 – The Lateran Council grant to the Pope the tithes of all Church property. Indulgence (the fifth between 1500 and 1517) for the building of St Peter's and for the Pope's private needs. Three Indulgence Commissions granted for Germany, one farmed by Elector Archbishop of Mainz (consec. 1514), the Dominican John Tetzel, (d. 1519) his Commissioner.	PHILIP MELANCHTHON (b. 1497, Feb. 16, at Bretten; 1509-1512, at Heidelberg; 1512-1514, at Tübingen; 1514, M.A.; Prof. of Hebrew and Greek at Wittenberg; Aug. 29, Introductory Lecture, *De corrigendis adolescentiae studiis;* 1519, Sept. 19, Bachelor of Theology; d. 1560, April 19). *Loci communes rerum Theologicarum, seu hypotyposes Theologicae,* 1521; 3 editions in 1521; edition of 1525 modifies
	Thomas Vio de Gaeta (Card. Cajetan): 'The Catholic Church is the bond-slave of the Pope'; asserts Papal infallibility in the widest sense.	absolute predestination; edition of 1535, reconstructs his theology; edition of 1543, Synergism.
		ZWINGLI: *Commentarius de vera et falsa religione,* 1525; *Fidei ratio ad carolum imperatorem,* 1530, July 3; *Sermonis de providentia Dei Anamnema,* 1530; *Christianae Fidei expositio,* 1531.
	1519 – The Cortes of Aragon ask three Briefs (never sent) from Leo X to restrain the Inquisition. Similarly fruitless applications made by the Estates of Aragon, Castille, and Catalonia to Charles V in 1516.	(a) *Lutheran Theologians* George Spalatin: b. 1484 at Spalt, in the bishopric of Eichstädt; 1514, Court Chaplain to Frederick the Wise; 1525, Superintendent at Altenburg; d. 1545.
	Romanist Theologians in the first period of the Reformation	Justas Jonas: b. 1493, at Nordhausen; 1521, Provost and Prof. at Wittenberg; 1541-1546, at Halle; 1551, Superintendent at Eisfeld; d. 1555.
The Mystics The New Prophecy, Spiritualism, Millennarianism, a Congregation of the perfectly holy, opposition to the baptism of infants. First stage to 1535.	John Eck, Prof. of Theology at Ingolstadt since 1510; b. 1486, in the Swabian village of Eck; d. 1543. Jerome Emser, Court preacher to Duke George of Saxony; d. 1527.	Nicholas of Amsdorf: b. 1483; since 1502 at Wittenberg; 1524, at Magdeburg; 1528, at Goslar; 1542-1546, Bishop of Naumburg; after 1550, at Eisenach; d. 1565.

Contemporary Events	Lutheran Church	Reformed Church
	Luther's sermons on the Sacraments of Repentance and Baptism, and on Excommunication. Demand for the celebration of the Lord's Supper under both elements.	
1520 – Magellan sails round the world.	1520 – April: Ulrich v. Hutten (b. 1488, April 21; d.1523, Aug. 29); Dialogue: *Vadiscus or the Roman Trinity;* June 15, Bull of Excommunication against 41 propositions of Luther; 60 days for recantation; June 23, Luther 'To the Christian Nobles of the German Nation', 'Of the Bettering of the Christian Estate'; Oct.: *De Captivitate Eccles. Babylonic.; De libertate Christiana* (Of the Freedom of a Christian Man); Dec. 10, Papal Bull burnt.	
1521-1526 – First war between Charles V and Francis I. 1525 – Battle of Pavia. 1526 – Peace of Madrid.	1521 – April 17, 18, Luther at the Diet of Worms; April 26, leaves Worms; at the Wartburg, May 4-Mar. 3, 1552. [In Dec. begins translation of the NT; Tracts: *On Penance, Against Private Masses, Against Clerical and Cloister Vows, The German Postille.*] May 26, Edict of Worms falsely antedated May 8. May 28, Imperial decree against Luther. June: Carlstadt against celibacy. Oct.: The Mass abolished at Wittenberg by the Augustinian monks (Gabriel Didymus). Dec.: Carlstadt's innovations. Dec. 25, Lord's Supper in both kinds. Dec. 27, The Prophets in Wittenberg.	IN FRANCE, spread and preaching of Reformed doctrines through William Briçonnet, Bishop of Meaux from 1521. With him Le Fèvre and Farel. 1521 – Cornelius Hoën, Dutch jurist, writes *De Eucharistia* (The Lord's Supper purely symbolical); the doctrine brought to Wittenberg and Zurich by John Rhodius, President of the House of the Brethren at Utrecht.
	1522 – Feb.: Riots in Wittenberg against images and pictures. Mar. 7, Luther back in Wittenberg. Mar. 9-16, Sermons against fanaticism.	1522 – April 16. Zwingli: *Von Erkiesen und Fryheit der Spysen;* Aug.: *Apologeticus Archeteles,* to the Bishop of Constance. The Zwinglian theology gradually becomes more powerful in the Netherlands.

Revolutionary Movements	Roman Catholic Church	Protestant Theology
	John Cochlaeus (Dobeneck), Dean at Frankfurt am Main, Canonicus in Mainz and Breslau; d. 1552; *Commentaria de actis et scriptis M. Lutheri* (1517–46); 1549, *Historiae Hussitarum.*	John Bugenhagen: b. 1485; from 1521 in Wittenberg; 1523, pastor; 1536, General Superintendent there.
		Casper Cruciger: 1528–48, when he died Prof. at Wittenberg.
	John Faber, 1518, Vicar-General at Constance (Costnitz); 1529, Provost at Ofen; 1530, Bishop of Vienna; d. 1561; 1523, *Malleus haereticorum.*	Fred. Myconius, Franciscan at Annaberg, then pastor in Weimar; 1524, Court preacher at Gotha; d. 1546.
		Paul Speratus: 1521, at Vienna, then at Iglau; 1523, at Wittenberg (1524, 'Salvation has come to us.'); 1524, in Königsberg; 1529–51, when he died Bishop of Pomerania in Marienwerder.
		John Brenz, b. 1499: 1520, Romanist preacher at Heidelberg; 1522-1546, Lutheran preacher at Hall in Swabia; from 1553, Provost at Stuttgart; d. 1570, Sept. 11.
1521 – The (Zwickau) Prophets in Wittenberg, Nicholas Storch, Marcus Thomae, Marcus Stübner, Martin Cellarius.

Andrew Bodenstein of Carlstadt: 1504, Prof. in Wittenberg; 1520, at Copenhagen; 1522, riots about images and vestments; 1523-1524, in Orlamünde; then excommunicated in South Germany, East Friesland, Switzerland; d. Basle, 1541. | 1521 – Henry VIII of England: *Assertatio vii. Sacramentorum contra Lutherum* (Defender of the Faith).
April 15, Decree of the Sorbonne condemning Luther's doctrines.
May 8, Edict of Charles V (founded on Edict of Worms) against the spread of Reformation doctrines in the Netherlands. [1522, the Augustinian cloister at Antwerp closed for heresy.]

1522-1523 – Sept. 14, Pope Hadrian VI (tutor to Charles V, Bishop of Utrecht), learned in the Old Learning; aspiration after a reform of the clergy through the hierarchy.
In Spain, from 1520, circulation of Lutheran writings in Spanish translations made at Antwerp.

1523 – Juan de Avila, 'the Apostle of Andalusia', suffered persecution for Lutheran doctrine. | (b) *Zwinglian Theologians*
John Oecolampadius, b. 1488; 1515, pastor at Basle; 1519, in Augsburg; 1522, Prof. and preacher at Basle; d. 1531, Nov. 24.
Leo Judaeus: 1523, Curate in St Peter's at Zurich; b. 1482; d. 1542.
Oswald Myconius (Geisshüsler): b. 1488 at Lucerne; 1532 – d. 1552, Oct. 14, Antistes at Basle.
Conrad Pellican (Kürsner): b. 1478; 1493, Franciscan; from 1502, Lecturer in Franciscan cloister in Basle; 1527, at Zurich as Prof. of Hebrew; d. 1556.

(c) *Intermediate Theologians*
Urbanus Rhegius: b. 1490 at Argau on the Bodensee; 1512, Prof. at Ingolstadt; 1519, priest at Constance; 1520–22, preacher in Augsburg; from 1530, Reformer in Brunswick, in the service of Duke Ernest; d. at Celle, 1541, May 23. |

Contemporary Events	Lutheran Church	Reformed Church
	July: *Contra Henricum regem Angliae.* Sept.: Translation of NT finished (whole Bible in 1534). Dec.: Diet at Nürnberg; The Hundred Grievances of the German Estates, in answer to Hadrian VI's Brief of Nov. 25.	
	1522–3 – The Reformation conquers in Pomerania, Livonia, Silesia, Prussia, Mecklenburg; in East Friesland from 1519; 1523, in Frankfurt am Main, in Hall in Swabia; 1524, Ulm, Strasburg, Bremen, Nürnberg.	
1523–33 – Frederick I of Denmark. 1523–60 – Gustavus Vasa of Sweden.	1523 – July 1, Heinrich Voes and Johann Esch (Augustinians) burnt at Brussels; the first martyrs. Gustavus Vasa establishes the Reformation in Sweden (Olaf and Lorenz Petersen, Lorenz Andersen). May 7, Sickingen slain; revolt of nobles called by the princes. Luther: Of the Order of Public Worship; Dec.: *Formula Missae* (Lord's Supper *sub utraque*).	1523 – Jan. 29, Disputation in Zurich between Zwingli and John Faber, the Bishop's Vicar-General; Zwingli's 67 theses. Oct. 26, Disputation at Zurich about image-worship and the Mass. Nov. 17, Instruction of Zurich Council to pastors and preachers.
	1524 – The first German Hymn-Book. June–May 1525, PEASANTS' WAR; peasants slaughtered at Frankenhausen. [Twelve Articles of John Henglin.]	1524 – Thorough reform of church at Zurich; pictures taken down; Friars' convents closed. Victory of the reformation in Berne (Berchtholdt Haller, Nic. Manuel), Appenzell, Solothurn; Romanist League of the Forest Cantons at Lucerne.
1525 – Albert of Brandenburg (d. 1568); head of the German knights; Duke of Prussia under Polish lordship. 1525–32 – Elector John the Constant of Saxony (brother of Frederick the Wise).	1525 – Jan: Luther: *Against the Heavenly Prophets.* May: Exhorts princes and peasants to keep the peace, with comments on the twelve articles. Then: *Against the robber-murdering Peasants.* June 13, Marries Catherine von Bora. Conservative tendency of Lutheran Reformation; separation of reformatory elements. Dec.: Luther, *De Servo Arbitrio* (strictest supralapsarian predestination) against Erasmus, *Diatribe de libero arbitrio*, Sept. 1524.	1525 – The Mass abolished in Zurich; public worship very simple in German language; Lord's Supper *sub utraque*. Zwingli's Commentary and first part of Zurich translation of Bible. (First complete edition 1531.) Zwingli's distinctive confessional statement of his doctrine of the Lord's Supper. [Carlstadt publishes his theory of the Lord's Supper in South Germany; Δεικτικῶς:This My Body, Is the Body, etc.]

Revolutionary Movements	Roman Catholic Church	Protestant Theology
		Ambrose Blaurer: b. 1492, at Constance; 1534–8, Reformer of Würtemburg; to 1548 at Constance; d. at Winterthun, 1564. (1534, *Stuttgart Concord.*)
		Martin Bucer: b. 1491, at Schlettstadt; 1505, Dominican; from 1524, pastor in Strasburg; 1549, under Edward VI in England, and Prof. at Cambridge; d. 1551, Feb. 28.
		Wolfgang Fabricius Capito: b. 1478; 1515, in Basle; 1520, in Mainz: 1523 to d. 1541, Dec., Provost of St Thomas, Strasbourg.
1523 – Conrad Grebel, Felix Manz, and Stumpf in Zurich, against Zwingli. 1524 – Disturbances in Stockholm; Melchior Hoffmann.	1523–34 – Sept. 25, Pope Clement VII (Julius Medici, natural son of Julian de Medici).	(d) *Zwinglian Confessions* 1523 – Jan. 29, Zwingli's 67 Articles. Nov. 17, Instructions to the Council of Zurich. 1530 – July 3, *Fidei Ratio ad Carolum V.* (Zwingli, assented to by Oecolampadius and other Swiss Reformers).
	1524 – Cardinal Campeggio, Pope's Legate at the Diet of Nürnberg. League of South German Roman Catholic States at Regensburg (Ferdinand of Austria, the Dukes of Bavaria, and the South-German bishops). Terms: a certain measure of ecclesiastical reform, and alliance with the civil power; but no further spread of the new doctrines.	1530 – *Confessio Tetrapolitana* (Strasburg, Constance, Lindau, Memmingen); Bucer, Capito, Hedio; during the sitting of the Diet of Augsburg. 1534 – *Confessio Basiliensis* (Myconius) accepted by Mühlhausen in 1537, and called *Conf. Mühlhausiana.* 1536 – *Confessio Helvetica Prior* (Basil II) drawn up at Basle (Jan. to March) by delegates from the Evangelical Cantons, and by their theologians, Bullinger, Myconius, Grynaeus, Leo Judaeus, etc.
1525 – Thomas Münzer at Mühlhausen; executed May 1525. Tract: *Wider das geistlose sanftlebende Fleisch zu Wittenberg*, 1522. Jan. Rise of the Anabaptists; Jürg Blaurock, a monk from Chur. Severe persecution of the Anabaptists (Manz drowned at Zurich, 1527; Balth. Hubmaier burnt at Vienna, 1528; Hetzer beheaded at Constance, 1529.	1524 – Peter Caraffa, Bishop of Theate [Pope Paul IV], instituted the Order of the Theatini to stay the spread of the Reformation.	(e) *Lutheran Confessions* 1529 – Luther's *Larger and Shorter Catechism* in German: appeared simultaneously.

Contemporary Events	Lutheran Church	Reformed Church
1526 – Aug 29: Louis, king of Hungary and Bohemia, falls fighting at Mohacs against the Turks. His successor, Ferdinand of Austria (Oct., chosen king of Bohemia), has to make good his claims to Hungary against the Turks.	1526 – May 4: League at Torgau between Philip of Hesse and John the Constant, joined in June at Magdeburg by other evangelical princes. June and July, DIET AT SPEYER. *'In matters of religion each State shall live, govern, and behave itself, as it shall answer to God and his Imperial Majesty.'* Oct. 20, Synod at Homberg; Hessian Church Order by Francis Lambert (b. 1487, at Avignon; Franciscan; fled 1525 to Germany; 1527, Prof. In Marburg; d. 1530): unconditional independence of the Christian community, and strictest church discipline. Luther – German Mass; Order of Public Worship. Frederick I of Denmark adheres to the Lutheran doctrine (John Tausen in Jütland from 1524).	Zwingli to Matth. Alber at Reutlingen, 1524, Nov. 16, *Manducatio spiritualis;* then in his Commentary. *Against* Zwingli; Bugenhagen. *For* Zwingli; Oecolampadius. The *Syngramma Suevicum,* 1525 (at Hall), by Brenz, Schnepf, Griebler, etc., later Calvin. Luther against Zwingli – (1) In his Preface to Agricola's translation of the *Syngramma Suevicum;* (2) In 1527, 'That the Word', etc. Zwingli's ecclesiastical and political church principles; his political reformation of Switzerland; political league of the Roman Catholic Forest Cantons to preserve their supremacy. 1526 – The Roman Catholic Cantons attacking the Evangelical. May; Disputation at Baden (Eck and Oecalampadius).
1527-1529 – The second war between Charles V and Francis I; Peace of Cambrai, Aug. 1529. 1527 – Henry VIII of England seeks divorce from Catherine of Aragon (Charles V's aunt; 1529, Wolsey in disgrace; Thomas More, Chancellor.	1527 – Melanchthon's Visitation Book; Gustavus Vasa proposes the reformation to the Diet of Westerås. Frederick I of Denmark, at the Diet of Odensee, gives the Reformed religion the same privileges as the Roman Catholic. 1528 – Otto von Pack's statement of a Roman Catholic League formed at Breslau, 1527; the Reformation spreads in Norway.	1528 – The Reformation victorious in St Gallen (Joachim Vadianus, John Kassler).
1529 – Sept.-Oct. 14, Sulaiman lays siege to Vienna.	1529 – Feb. 26, Diet at Speyer; April 12, the decision of the Roman Catholic majority of Electors and Princes, 'Whoever has enforced the Edict of Worms is to do so still; the others are to allow no further innovations; no one to be prevented from celebrating Mass'; April 19, agreed to by the cities.	1529 – Reformation conquers in Basle (Oecomlampadius, Captio, Hedio). League of five Forest Cantons with the House of Hapsburg. June 24, Peace of Kappel; the Forest Cantons abandon the Hapsburg League and recognize liberty of conscience.

Revolutionary Movements	Roman Catholic Church	Protestant Theology
Melchior Hoffmann: b. at Hall, in Swabia; 1523, in Livonia; 1527, in Holstein; 1529, at Strasburg; thence to Friesland, where he joined the Baptists; then in the Netherlands; 1533, in Strasburg; d. 1540. (Ordinanz Gottes): a strict millenarian of the more spiritual kind; spreads millenarian views among the Baptists.	1526 – May 29: League at Cognac against Charles V (the Pope, Francis I, Venice, and Milan).	1530 – *Confessio Augustana;* or *Augsburg Confession.* Framed out of – (1) the 15 Marburg Articles; (2) the 17 Schwabach Articles drawn up by Luther; (3) Torgau Articles, compiled by Luther, Melanchthon, Justus Jonas, Bugenhagen, and presented to the Elector at Torgau in March 1530. The work of Melanchthon assisted by the Evangelical theologians assembled at Augsburg, and revised by Luther.
		Statement of Evangelical Doctrine, 'In qua cerni potest, nihil inesse, quod discrepit a Scripturis vel ab ecclesia catholica vel ab ecclesia Romana, quatenus ex scriptoribus nota est ... Sed dissensus est de quibusdam abusibus, qui sine certa auctoritate in ecclesiam irrepserunt.' Philip of Hesse signed with protest against Article X on the Lord's Supper.
Caspar Schwenkfeld: b. 1490, at Ossing, near Liegnitz; in the service of the Duke of Liegnitz; 1525, believed that he had found an explanation of the words of the insititution: 'Quod ipse panis fractus est corpori esurenti, nempe cibus, hoc est corpus meum, cibus videlicet esurientium animarum'; hence his doctrine of Christ, the Inner Word (*De cursu Verbi Dei, origen fidei et ratione justificationis,* 1527): of the Person of Christ (not made man, but begotten by the Divine nature): his flesh, Divine; 1528, driven from Silesia; in Strasburg, Augsburg, Speyer, Ulm, persecuted from 1539 by Lutheran theologians; in many controversies; d. 1561, at Ulm; followers in Silesia; since 1730 in Pennsylvania.	1527 – Process of the Sorbonne against Jacques le Fêvre (d. 1537, on a journey to Strasburg, under the protection of Margaret of Navarre). 1527 – May 6, Charles of Bourbon storms Rome; the Pope shut up in St Angelo till June 6; Charles V, master of most of the States of the Church, proposes to limit the temporal power of the Pope; the Pope appeals to England and France; a French army equipped by English money marches to his assistance. 1528 – June 29: Peace between Emperor and Pope at Barcelona; the Pope gets back the States of the Church and Florence; Heresy to be exterminated.	Impossible to fix the exact text of the German or the Latin editions; Melanchthon's first printed edition, Wittenberg, 1530, in 4to. The *Variata* (Variations especially in Article X) since 1540. *The Apology for the Augsburg Confession* – The *prima delineatio apologiae* by Melanchthon in Sept. 1530, at Augsburg; fully prepared, Nov. 1530-April 1531; first edition, April 1531; German edition by Justus Jonas, Oct. 1531. The Schmalkald Articles, by Luther, for the Protestant Convention at Schmalkald, 1557, with reference to the proposed General Council at Mantua [Strictly Lutheran].

Contemporary Events	Lutheran Church	Reformed Church
	PROTEST: April 25, Appeal taken to the Emperor and Council by Saxony, Hesse, Brandenburg, Anhalt, Lüneburg, and fourteen cities.	
	Separation between the Lutheran and South German Protestants; Luther objects to armed resistance; Zwingli plans to abolish the Papacy and the mediæval and papal empire; Philip of Hesse tries to bring about union.	
	Oct. 1–4, Religious conferences at Marburg (Luther, Melanchthon, Zwingli, Oecolampadius, Justus Jonas, Osiander, Brenz, etc.); on Oct. 4, union on fourteen articles, divisions on fifteenth – Sacrament of Supper. *Zwingli:* 'There are none on earth's round I would more gladly be at one with than the men of Wittenberg.' *Luther:* 'You have another Spirit than we.' Zwingli's hand refused.	
	Oct. 16, Luther at the Convent of Schwabach; Nov. 30, at Sschmalkald; Saxony breaks away from South Germany.	
	1530 – DIET AT AUGSBURG: June 15, entry of Emperor; fruitless negotiations with the Evangelical princes to induce them to join the Corpus-Christi procession. June 20, Diet opened; June 25, Aug. Confess. read and given in (Aug. 3, Confutation read); July 11, *Confess. Tetrapolitana* read (Confutation, Oct. 17), and Zwingli's *Fidei Ratio;* Aug. 16-29, Negotiations with Melanchthon, in which he proves too pliable. Nov. 19, Decree of Diet. Protestants to get till April 15, 1531, then suppression by force.	The Roman Catholic Cantons do not observe the terms of peace.
1531 – Ferdinand of Austria, king of the Romans, Bavaria and Saxony oppose.	1531 – Schmalkald League of Protestants – at the head, Hesse and Saxony.	1531 – May 15, at Aarau the Forest Cantons are refused provisions, Zwingli objecting.
1532 – Aug. – 1547, John Frederick the Magnanimous, Elector of Saxony; d. 1554. Henry VIII divorced by Parliament from Catherine of Aragon. Nov.: Marries Anne Boleyn.	1532 Diet of Nürnberg: Toleration till a General Council. Dessau receives the Reformation.	Oct. 11, Battle of Kappel; *Zwingli slain;* Second Peace of Kappel. Henry Bullinger, Zwingli's successor.
1534 – Restoration of Duke Ulrich of Würtemberg by Philip of Hesse.	1534 – Lutheran Reformation conquers in Würtemburg.	

Revolutionary Movements	Roman Catholic Church	Protestant Theology
		Controversies in the Lutheran Church
		1548–55 – *Adiaphoristic:* Flacius, Wigand, Amsdorf, against Leipzig Interim.
		1549-1566 – *Osiander:* Andrew Osiander (at Nürenburg, 1522-1548; at Königsberg, 1549-d. 1552); 1550, *De Justificatione;* 1551, *De Unico Mediatore Jesu Christo;* 'Justification is a participation in the righteousness of Christ', *cujus natura divina homini quasi infuditur.* In connection therewith his doctrine of the Divine image in man.
	1530 – Reformed congregations in *Spain.* In Seville; Rodrigo de Valero, Joh. Egidius, Ponce de la Fuente. In Valladolid, 1555, Augustin Cazalla. Francis Enzinas translates the NT; 1556, new translation by Juan Perez. All stamped out by Philip II and the Inquisition.	In Opposition: Francis Stancarus from Mantua (1551–2 in Königsberg, then in the Siebenbürgen, and in Poland; d. 1574); 1562, *De Trinitate et Mediatore,* 'Christ's righteousness our righteousness only as regards his human nature.'
	Italy – The German Reformation awakens religious life and Augustinian theology; Contarini, Reginald Pole, Joh. de Merone (Archbishop of	1551–62 – *Majorist:* George Major (d. 1574, Prof. at Wittenberg); *bona opera necessaria esse ad salutem.* Against him, Amsdorf; *bona opera perniciosa esse ad salutem.*
1533 – *The Kingdom of Christ* in Münster. Bernhard Rothmann, Evangelical Superintendent in Münster, joins the Anabaptists; Henry Roll and the Wassenberg preachers from Jülich. Summer: Melchiorites in Münster. Nov.: Jan Matthiesen.	Modena), *Peter Paul Vergerius* (went over to the Reformation in 1548; d. 1565). Reformation at Ferrara (Renée married, 1527, to Hercules II); at Venice; at Naples (Juan Valdez, d. 1540; and Bernardino Ochino); at Lucca (Peter Martyr).	1556–60 – *Synergist:* Pfeffinger, 1555, *Propos. de libero arbitrio* (In Melanchthon's synergistic sense); against him Amsdorf (1558, *Confutatio*); and Flacius. 1560 – Disputation at Weimar between Flacius and Strigel. Flacius: Original Sin is of the substance of man. The Lutheran doctrine overcomes.
1534 – Lent: riot, destruction of images and cloisters. Easter Eve: Matthiesen overthrown; John of Leyden at the head of the Anabaptists (theocracy with community of goods and wives).	1534-1549 – Paul III Pope (Farnese); Vergerius his Legate in Germany.	Heshusius: *de servo arbitrio.*

Contemporary Events	Lutheran Church	Reformed Church
1535 – Joachim II, Elector of Brandenburg.		*Reformation in French Switzerland under Calvin*
1536-8 – Third war between Charles V and Francis I.	1536 – Wittenberg Concord; Melanchthon and Bucer; *Lord's Supper* in Lutheran sense only; eating of the unworthy, 'of the unbelieving', avoided; *Baptism; Absolution;* came to nothing; difficulties concealed, not explained. Reformation victorious in Denmark.	*William Farel* (b. 1489, in Dauphiné; from 1526, Reformer in Berne; 1530, in Neufchatel; d. 1565, in Geneva); and *Peter Viret* (b. 1511, at Orbe; 1531–59, at Lausanne; from 1561, at Nimes and Lyons; d. 1571); from 1534, Reformation preachers in Geneva.
	1537 – Convention at Schmalkald; the Schmalkald Articles.	1536 –JOHN CALVIN at Geneva; b. 1509, July 10, at Noyon; studied at Orleans and Paris;
1538 – Ten years' truce at Nice.	1538 – Roman Catholic League at Nürnberg.	1531, joined Reformation in Paris; at Basle; 1536, *Institutio Christianae Religionis*; then in
	1539 – Reformation victorious in Ducal Saxony and in Electoral Brandenburg.	Ferrara; strict ecclesiastical discipline; Easter, 1538, banished from Geneva, goes to
	1540 – June; Conference at Hagenau. Nov. 25-Jan. 14, at Worms (Granvella, Melanchthon, Bucer, Capito, Brenz, Calvin, Eck, Cochlaeus). Feb. Regensburg Interim.	Strasburg; recalled 1541; d. 1564, May 27.

Calvin's Ecclesiastical polity in Geneva. – Worship: prayer and preaching. Organization: Pres- |
| 1541-53 – Duke Maurice of Saxony; made Elector, 1547.

1541 – Diet of Regensburg; Sulaiman conquers the Hungarians. | 1541 – April 27-May 22, Conference at Regensburg (Contarini, Melanchthon, Bucer, Eck), Transubstantiation the diffculty. | byterian. 1542. – Jan.: *Ordonnances ecclésiastiques de L'église de Genève.* Pastors, doctors, elders, deacons. Church discipline. |
| 1542-44 – Fourth war of Charles V with Francis I; Peace of Crespi.

1542 – Diet of Speyer; union against the Turk. | 1542 – Nicholas v. Amsdorf, Bishop of Naumburg.

1543 – Reformation in the Archbishopric of Köln; Herman von Wied, the archbishop, advised by Bucer and Melanchthon; excommunicated 1546; abdicates, 1547; d. 1552. | *Reformation in France,* 1559–98 Earlier: *Francis I,* Humanist, careless in religion, treated the Reformation as a politician; his sister Margaret, Queen of Navarre (d. 1549), protected the Reformers; severe persecution of French Protestants in spite of alliance with German |
| 1544 – Diet at Speyer; recognition of the Protestants; peace all round till a General Council. | | Protestant princes, and an invitation to Melanchthon to settle in France, 1535.

Henry II: Anthony of Navarre, |
1545 – Reformatio Wittenbergensis.		and his wife Joan d'Albret, at the head of the Protestants in
1546 – Second Religious Conference at Regensburg; Feb. 18, Luther dies at Eisleben; the Protestants do not appear at the Diet.		France.
1546-47 – The Schmalkald War; June 19, league between Maurice and the Emperor; July 20, decree against John Frederick and Philip; Oct. 27, Maurice made Elector; April 24, Battle of Mühlberg, John Frederick, prisoner; Philip surrenders at Halle; Emperor breaks faith.		1559 – May 25–29, First Reformed Synod at Paris, assembled by a Parisian pastor, Anthony Chandieu; Conf. Gallica.

Revolutionary Movements	Roman Catholic Church	Protestant Theology

1535 – Eve of St John: Münster taken.

1536 – Jan. 22, John of Leyden, Knipperdolling, and Krechting executed.

1534 – David Joris: b. 1501, at Delft; joins the Anabaptists; reforms them; has influence in the Netherlands and East Friesland; 1542, his *Wunderbuch;* 1544, in Basle; a Mystical -spiritualistic speculation with a rationalist tendency.

The Mennonites
Menno Simonis: b. 1496 at Witmarsum; 1524, priest; 1536, resigned his office, disgusted with the persecution of the Münster Annabaptists; baptized by an apostle of Jan Matthiesen; reformed and organized the Anabaptist communities in Holland and Friesland; d. at Oldesloe; expelled the enthusiastic fanatical elements, and increased the tendency towards Donatism. His followers, Mennonites, tolerated in 1572 by William of Orange in the Netherlands; also found in Emden, Hamburg, Danzig, Elbing, in the Palatinate, and in Moravia; moderated the original Anabaptist spirit; rejected all dogmatic; forbade oaths and war; appealed to the letter of Scripture.

1536 – Paul III summons the long-promised Council to meet at Mantua; 1537, adjourned; called to meet at Vicenza; again adjourned.

1542 – Antonio Paleario (burnt 1570); *Del beneficio di Gesu Christo crocifisso verso i Christiani.*

1540 – Sept. 27, SOCIETAS JESU constituted by Paul III; *Don Inigo (Ignatius) of Loyola,* b. 1491, at the Castle Loyola in the Basque Provinces; wounded (1521) at Pamplona; legends of the Saints; studies at Barcelona; from 1528 in Paris. In 1534, with six companions (Francis Xavier, Jac. Lainez, Pet. Lefevre, etc.), he took the three monastic vows and a fourth of absolute obedience to the Pope. Loyola d. 1556; Lainez d. 1564. 'To advance the interests of the Roman Catholic Hierarchy against Protestantism within and without the Romish Church.'
Xavier's mission work in East Asia.
Society's morals; casuistry.
Its dogmatic; superstition systematized.

1542 – Cardinal Caraffa advises the reconstruction of the Inquisition to crush Protestantism in Italy.

1545 – *Council of Trent* opened: First period, Mar. 11, 1547, at Trent; April 21, 1547-Sept. 13, 1549, at Bologna. Second period, May 1, 1551-April 28, 1552, at Trent. Third period, Jan. 13, 1562-Dec. 4, 1563 (25 Sessions). Romanist doctrinal teaching concluded and petrified.

1527–40, and renewed 1556 – *Antinomian;* John Agricola b. 1492 at Eisleben; d. 1566, Court preacher at Berlin; 1527, against Melanchthon; and 1537 against Luther. Contrition is taught not by the Law but by the Gospel. Recants 1540. From 1556 controversy about 'Tertius usus legis'.

1567 – *Crypto-Calvinist:* Melanchthon's admissions to Calvinists in doctrines of Lord's Supper, Christology, and Predestination.

From these controversies a need for concord in the Lutheran Church; hence various forms of concord, out of all which came the *Formula Concordiae.*

(1) Swabian Concord of Jac. Andreae (from 1562 Prof. at Tübingen, d. 1590) in 1574; 1575, Swabian Concord of Martin Cheminitz; 1576, Maulbronn Formula of Lucas Osiander.
(2) Torgau Convention with the *Torgau Book.*

Thence 1577, *Formula Concordiae.*

The Principal Lutheran Theologians
Martin Cheminitz: 1554-d. 1586, Superintendent in Brunswick; *Examen Concilii Trid.* 1565–73, *Loci theologici.*

Matthew Flacius: b. 1520 at Albona in Illyria; 1545, at Wittenberg; 1549 at Magdeburg; 1557–61 at Jena; d. at Frankfurt am Main, 1575, March 11.

Contemporary Events	Lutheran Church	Reformed Church
1547–59 – Henry II of France; spouse, Catherine of Medici, d. 1589.	1548 – May 15, Augsburg Interim retains Roman Catholic hierarchy, ceremonies, feasts and fasts; marriage of clergy and Lord's Supper permitted.	1561 – Sept.: Religious conference at Poissy; Theodore Beza.
1547-53 – Edward VI of England: b. 1537.	Leipzig Interim (Maurice of Saxony and Melanchthon).	1562 – Jan.: Protestants gain right to worship outside the towns; Francis Guise massacres Protestant congregation at Vassy.
	1551 – Vehement desire of the Emperor that the Protestants should submit to the Council of Trent; Secret League of Maurice of Saxony with Henry II of France.	1562–3 – Huguenot War. Anthony of Navarre d.; Francis Guise shot before Orleans.
	Oct. Würtemburg ambassadors, and Jan. 1552, Saxon ambassadors at Trent.	1567–9 and 1569–70 – Huguenot Wars.
1553-1558 – (Bloody) Mary of England.	1552 – Mar. 20, Maurice breaks loose; May 19, seizes Ehrenberg Castle and Ehrenberg Pass, the keys of the Tyrol; the Council breaks up; July: Treaty of Passau; John Frederick and Philip free.	1572 – Aug. 24, Paris massacre on eve of St Bartholomew; Coligny and 50,000 Huguenots murdered.
1554 – July 9, Maurice slain in battle near Sievershausen, against Albert Margrave of Brandeburg.		1574-1576 – Huguenot War; Holy League of the Guises.
1555–98 – Philip II of Spain.	1555 – Sept. 25: *Religious Peace of Augsburg;* the Lutheran Church (*Augs. Confes.*) has the same legal rights as the Roman Catholic: *Cujus regio ejus religio;* the *Reservatum ecclesiasticum;* the Reformed Church not recognized.	1588 – Henry and Louis Guise slain.
1556–64 – Ferdinand I, Emperor.		1589 – Henry III murdered by a League fanatic, J. Clement, Aug. 1.
1558–1603 – Elizabeth I of England.		1593 – *Henry IV becomes a Roman Catholic.*
1559–60 – Francis II of France (married Mary of Scotland).	1558 – Disputes between old Lutherans (*Gnesiolutherani*) and Melanchthon's followers.	
1560–74 – Charles IX of France.		1598 – EDICT OF NANTES: liberty of conscience; right of public worship; full civil privileges; cities of refuge for the Huguenots.
1560–78 – Mary, Queen of Scots; executed 1587.	1560 – Death of Melanchthon, April 19.	
1564–76 – Maximilian II, Emperor.	1586-91 – Crypto-Calvinist troubles in Electoral Saxony; suppression of Calvinsim; execution of Krells, 1601.	1620–28 – Huguenot Revolts.
1574–89 – Henry III of France.		1629 – La Rochelle taken. Edict of Nîmes. *Ecclesiastical* rights guaranteed to the Huguenots.
1576–1612 – Rudolph II, Emperor.	The Lutheran Church loses to : the Roman Catholic Church	
1588–1648 – Christian IV, king of Denmark.	1558 – Bavaria.	
	1578 – The Austrian Duchy (Rudolp II).	
1589–1610 – Henry IV of France; became Roman Catholic, 1593; murdered by Ravaillac, 1610, May 14.	1584 – The Bishoprics of Würzburg, Bamberg, Salzburg, Carinthia (Ferdinand II).	
	1607 – Donauwerth.	

Anglican Church	Roman Catholic Church	Protestant Theology
England, 1547–1600, under Henry VIII: John Frith, William Tyndale.	1564 – *Professio Fidei Tridentinae:* 1566, *Catechismus Romanus* (Leonardo Marini, Egidio Foscarari, Muzio Calini).	*Catalogus Testium Veritatis,* 1556: *Ecclesi. Hist. per aliquot . . . studiosos et pios viros in urbe Magdeburgica* (The Magdeburg Centuries), 13 vols., 1560–74; *Clavis Script. Sac.,* 1567; *Glossa Compendaria in N.T.,* 1570, etc.
1534 – Act of Parliament about Royal supremacy; the King 'the only supreme head on earth of the Church of England'; at the head of the evangelical party, Thomas Cranmer [1533, Archbishop of Canterbury] and Thomas Cromwell; Translation of the Bible, 1538.	1548 – Philip Neri founds the Oratory. 1550–64 – Julius III (del Monte). 1551 – Foundation of Jesuit Collegium Romanum. 1552 – Foundation of Collegium Germanicum.	*John Gerhard:* b. 1582, at Quedlinburg; 1606, Superintendent at Heldburg; 1615, General Superintendent at Coburg; 1616–d. 1637, Prof. at Jena. *Loci theologici,* 1610-1625; *Medit. Sac.,* etc.
1539 – July 28, Transubstantiation; refusal of cup to the Laity; celibacy of the clergy; Masses for the dead; auricular confession. The Reformation of Henry VIII the act of the King, and meant only, revolt from the Mediæval system, with the King in the place of the Pope. Isolation of the Church of England; no relation to the Papacy; no relation to the Reformed Churches.	1555–59 – Paul IV (Caraffa) protests against the Peace of Augsburg; Inquisition. 1559–65 – Pius IV (Medici) rules under the influence of nephew Cardinal Charles Borromeo, Archbishop of Milan, d. 1584. 1564 – *Index librorum prohibitorum.* 1566-1572 – Pius V, a zealous Dominican. 1567 – Bull of Excommunication against 79 Augustinian propositions of Michael Baius (d. 1589), Chancellor of University of Louvain.	*Leonhard Hotter:* 1596–d. 1616, Prof. at Wittenberg; *Compendium Loc. Theol.,* 1610; *Loci Commun. Theolog.,* 1619. *The confessional writings of the Reformed Church universally recognized.* *Catechismus Ecclesiae Genevensis;* 1541, French; 1545, Latin; Calvin. *Consensio in re sacramentaria ministrorum Tigur.; Eccles. et Joh. Calvini.*
1547 – Under Lord Protector Somerset: Peter Martyr Vermigli (b. 1500, at Florence; 1542, in Strasburg; d. 1562, in Zurich) and Bernard Ochino (b. 1487) brought to Oxford; Martin Bucer and Paul Fagius, to Cambridge. *The Book of Homilies.*	1568 – *Breviarium.* 1570 – *Missale Romanum.* 1572–85 – Gregory XIII: congratulatory letter to Charles IX about Massacre of St Bartholomew; *Te Deum* at Rome in honour of event.	The *Heidelberg Catechism:* 1563, written at the suggestion of Frederick III of the Palatinate by Zachary Ursinus (from 1561 Prof. at Heidelberg; d. 1583) and Casper Olevianus (Prof. at Heidelberg; d. 1587).
1548 – *The Book of Common Prayer,* revised, 1552. 1552 – *The 42 Articles.*	1582 – Reform of Calendar. 1582–1610 – Jesuit missions in China.	*Confessio Helvetica Posterior:* 1566, sent by Bullinger to Frederick III of Palatinate.
[1554 – Cardinal Reginald Pole, Papal Legate; 1555-1558, Bloody persecutions under Mary; 1556, May 21, Cranmer burnt at Oxford.]	1585-1590 – Sixtus V; Vatican Library. 1588 – Baronius's *Eccl. Annales.* 1590 – Infallible edition of the Vulgate. 1592–1605 – Clement VII. 1592 – New edition of Vulgate (declared the edition of Sixtus V).	*The Decrees of the Synod of Dort:* 1619, recognized in the Netherlands, Switzerland, the Palatinate, and in 1620 in France; not universally recognized.

Contemporary Events	Lutheran Church	Anglican Church
	The Lutheran Church loses to the Reformed Church:	*Reformation Restored Under Elizabeth*
	1560 – The Palatinate; 1563, Heidelberg Catechism (Reformed under Frederick III; Lutheran under Louis VI, 1576–83; Reformed under Frederick IV, 1583–1610).	1559 – June: Acts of Uniformity, Matthew Parker, Archbishop of Canterbury. *Book of Common Prayer* revised and restored.
	1569 – Bremen.	
	1596 – Anhalt (John George, 1587–1603); repeal of Consist. Syst. and Lutheran Catechism; 1597–1628, Calvinist Articles.	1562 – Jan. 23, *The 39 Articles:* Calvinist doctrine of Predestination; doctrine of Lord's Supper, Calvinist.
	1605 – Hesse-Kassel reformed under Landgrave Maurice (1592–1627).	1567 – Puritans extruded from the Church. [Puritanism; Reformation from within through the church community; in England strict acceptance of the spiritual priesthood of all believers, and consequent objection to clerical vestments, cope, and surplice.]
	1613 – Dec. 25, Brandenburg reformed under Elector John Sigismund; 1614, *Confessio Marchica*.	
		1570 – Thomas Cartwright expelled from Cambridge.
	Anti-Trinitarians	1582 – Robert Browne, Chaplain to the Duke of Norfolk: no union between Church and State; each congregation an *independent* church. From 1589 in England.
	Michael Servetus from Aragon; 1530, in Basale; 1531 *De Trinitatis erroribus;* 1534 in Lyons; 1537, in Paris; 1540, in Vienna; 1553, *Christianismi resitutio;* burnt at Geneva, 1553.	
	Valentinus Gentilis, from Calabria; beheaded at Berne, 1536.	
	Laelius Socinus: b. 1525, at Siena; 1546, in Venice; 1547, travels in Switzerland, Germany, and Poland; d. 1562 in Zurich.	
	Faustus Socinus: b. 1539, at Siena; 1559, in Lyons; 1562, in Zurich; at Florence, then Basle, 1574-1578; in Poland, 1579-98; d. 1604. – *De Jesu Christo servatore; De Statu primi hominis ante lapsum,* 1578.	
	1605 – Racovian Catechism.	

Reformed Church		Protestant Theology
Scotland	*The Netherlands*	JOHN CALVIN: *Institutio Religionis Christianae*, 1535–36. Three editions, each an enlargement, 1535, 1539 (-43-45). 1559; *Commentaries* on O.T. and N.T. from 1539; *De Aeterna Dei Predestinatione*, 1552; *Defensio orthodoxae fidei de S. Trinitate*, 1554; against Servetus.
1558 – Lords of the Congregation; Pure Gospel; King Edward's Prayer Book.	1559 – Margaret of Parma Stadtholder; Granvella, Bp of Arras.	
1560 – Meeting of Estates at Edinburgh; *Scotch Confession;* First Book of Discipline; Presbyterian Government by General Assemblies, Synods, and Kirk-Sessions; Superintendents.	Erection of 14 new bishoprics; Inquisition. 1562 – *Confessio Belgica;* Guido de Brès, Adrian de Savaria, H. Modetus, G. Wingen; revised by Francis Junius, 1571.	
John Knox: b. 1505, at Haddington; from 1546 preacher in St Andrews; 1547-49, in the galleys; 1553-1559, at Frankfurt and Geneva; 1559-1572, in Edinburgh.	1566 – Compromise in favour of Protestants. Riots about images and relics. 1568–73 – Duke of Alva. Council of Blood; persecution of Protestants; 18,000 slain; Egmont and Horn in 1568.	*Henry Bullinger,* Zwingli's successor in Zurich, b. 1504, at Bremgarten, d. 1578, Sept. 17; Commentaries on the whole N.T., 1554; *Compendium relig. Christianae; Histoire des Persecutions de l'Eglise.*
1572 – Convention of Leith; Bishops, but without Episcopal functions; Tulchans.	1572 – Capture of Brill by the Sea-Beggars; William of Orange.	*Theodore Beza:* b. 1519; 1549, in Lausanne; 1558, Professor and pastor in Geneva; d. 1605. N.T. translation with annotations, 1565; *Histoire Eccles. des réformateurs au royaume de France,* 1580.
1576 – Government by visitors appointed by the Assembly.	1576 – Nov. 8, Treaty of Ghent.	
1578 – Second Book of Discipline.	1579 – Jan. 23, Utrecht Union of Northern Provinces; July 26, Declaration of Independence.	*Rudolf Hospinian,* pastor in Zurich; d. 1629; *De origine et progres. controv. Sacramentariae,* etc.
1580 – Government by Presbyteries.	1584 – July 10, William of Orange murdered; Maurice of Orange succeeds.	*J. H. Hottinger,* Professor in Heidelberg and Zurich; d. 1684; *Thesaurus Ecclesiasticus.*
	Foundation of Universities – Leiden, 1575; Franecker, 1584; Gröningen, 1612; Utecht, 1638; Harderwijk, 1648.	*J. Dallaeus,* Prof. at Saumur, d. at Paris, 1670; *Traité de l'emploi des S. Pères,* 1632.

INDEX

Also available from the Banner of Truth Trust:

THE REFORMATION IN ENGLAND

J. H. MERLE D'AUBIGNÉ

The immense popularity of d'Aubigné's *History* in his own day was largely due to the fact that it was written by an expert in the field, not for fellow-experts but for the ordinary Christian public. He judged that public interest could best be stirred . . . by continual stress on the personal factor in history, the emotions of the human soul, the mental strains and stresses occasioned by the impact of ancient and yet newborn truth upon minds long in bondage to Roman Catholicism, and the tortures experienced by the human spirit when the moment came for decisive action. It was this aspect of the Reformation which d'Aubigné's pen portrayed with a skill hitherto lacking in Church historians. Undue concentration on the merely legislative and political aspects of religious history leaves the human soul unmoved, whereas the graphic portrayal of souls agonized by the awful tensions that can and do result from an experience of new birth in an intensely hostile ecclesiastical, not to say domestic, environment – this it was, as described by a writer able to weep with those who wept, which stirred the soul of Victorian England, and made d'Aubigné's work a potent factor in holding thousands to Protestantism and Biblical truth at a time when Rome was making a fresh effort to repair the ravages of centuries . . .

History, to live, must pulsate with the life of the historian. He must himself be stirred by the events on which he chooses to dilate. And it is here that d'Aubigné achieves his greatest success. He is no mere spectator from afar, dissecting, as it were, the dry bones of men of the bygone years. He lives in the age he depicts. He shares the agonies of sixteenth-century martyrs. His heart throbs and aches as he walks with confessors of the faith on the highroad of the Tudor age . . .

S. M. HOUGHTON

Vol. 1: From the Introduction of Christianity to Britain to 1530,
476 pp., large pbk.
Vol. 2: From 1530 to 1547, 528 pp., large pbk.

ISBN 0 85151 488 X

THE REFORMATION
IN SCOTLAND

JOHN KNOX

John Knox was incapable of writing history in a detached fashion. These pages breathe the sense of excitement and expectancy possible only to an eyewitness and participant in the unfolding drama of the Reformation in sixteenth-century Scotland.

Despite the rigours of the time and the harshness of the persecution he witnessed and endured, Knox's fervent desire was to strengthen his fellow-believers, and his *History* offers immense encouragement to Christians in difficult circumstances today. He wrote:

'Stand with Christ Jesus in this day of his battle, which shall be short and the victory everlasting! For the Lord himself shall come in our defence with his mighty power; He shall give us the victory when the battle is most strong; and He shall turn our tears into everlasting joy.'

'We would urge both young and old to obtain this volume to become firmly established in the virile Protestantism for which Knox stood.'

FREE PRESBYTERIAN MAGAZINE

ISBN 0 85151 358 1, 392 pp., pbk.

For free illustrated catalogue please write to
THE BANNER OF TRUTH TRUST

| 3 Murrayfield Road, Edinburgh EH12 6EL UK | | P O Box 621, Carlisle, Pennsylvania 17013, USA |

www.banneroftruth.co.uk